AUTOMOBILE SHEET METAL REPAIR

SECOND EDITION. *Revised, Enlarged and Improved*

AUTOMOBILE SHEET METAL REPAIR

by ROBERT L. SARGENT

CHILTON BOOK COMPANY *Radnor, Pennsylvania*

All Rights Reserved
Published in Radnor, Pa., by Chilton Book Company
and simultaneously in Don Mills, Ontario, Canada,
by Thomas Nelson & Sons, Ltd.
ISBN   0-8019-5460-6
Library of Congress Catalog Card Number 69-18330
Designed by Harry Brodsky
Manufactured in the United States of America

Preface

In preparing material for the second edition of this book, I find myself even more convinced of the need for it than when I started the first edition. I first became convinced of this need from my contacts with vocational high school teachers, automobile service people, and representatives of the automobile insurance companies. I find my convictions strengthened from further contacts with these people.

Since the first edition was introduced, I have had many contacts with vocational high school teachers who are using it in their body shop classes. Nothing gleaned from any of these contacts has weakened my original opinion that *the emphasis should be on the fundamentals.* The primary element of all skills is knowledge. The man who understands the technical reasons why a job should be done in a certain manner is well on his way to learning to do it. Skill is the inevitable result of coupling knowledge and normal manual dexterity with diligent practice. The essential technical knowledge is here; almost any student enrolling in a sheet metal repair class will possess normal manual dexterity; whether or not he will practice diligently, he alone will determine.

The problems of the body shop teachers have been kept in mind in preparing this material. These men vary widely in their backgrounds. Some have come to teaching directly from the body shop; others are auto mechanics or industrial arts teachers who, by choice or necessity, find themselves teaching sheet metal repair in body shop classes. It seems likely that the teacher without body shop experience needs the help of a text such as this. It is my hope that this book will aid the teacher, regardless of background, to present the fundamentals to his students effectively.

There is no intention to leave out the individual who is interested in self-help. Although this book is beamed primarily to the vocational high school classroom situation, it can be used advantageously by the individual, even though he will have to study harder to master the subject without the assistance of a teacher.

ROBERT L. SARGENT

v

Acknowledgments

Specific and grateful acknowledgment is made to the following organizations which supplied copyrighted illustrations and information used in this book:

Air Reduction Sales Co.—Figs. 112-116
Albertson & Co., Inc.—Fig. 80
Allen Electric & Equipment Co.—Fig. 135
Blackhawk Mfg. Co.—Figs. 191, 193, 196-198, 217, 220, 222
Blair Equipment Co.—Figs. 57, 88, 195, 199, 205-216
Fairmount Tool & Forging, Inc.—Figs. 38-43, 49-50, 54-55, 58
General Food Machinery & Chemical Corp.—John Bean Div.—Figs. 221, 223
General Motors Corp.—Chevrolet Motor Div.—Fig. 224
General Motors Corp.—Fisher Body Div.—Fig. 9
Kansas Jack, Inc.—Fig. 218
Marquette Mfg. Co.—Figs. 138-139
H. K. Porter, Inc.—Figs. 46-47, 51-53, 56, 59-60, 192, 194

A book such as this cannot be written without the co-operation of many business firms and people. The author wishes to extend his sincere thanks to the following firms for their co-operation in furnishing information and material on request: Blackhawk Manufacturing Co.; John Bean Division of General Food Machinery Corp.; Air Reduction Sales Co.; Blair Equipment Co.; Fairmount Tool & Forging, Inc.; H. K. Porter, Inc.; Marquette Manufacturing Co., Inc., Division of Marquette Corp.; Allen Electric and Equipment Co.; Albertson & Co., Inc.; and Lincoln Electric Co.

Within General Motors Corporation, the co-operation of the following Subsidiaries and Divisions is acknowledged and appreciated: General Motors Institute, Motors Insurance Corporation, Chevrolet Motor Division, and Fisher Body Division.

The sincere thanks of the author are extended to the following persons who have been helpful in many ways: Messrs. E. D. Hougen, M. B. Nelson, Herman O. Swanson, E. E. Smith, C. A. Brown (deceased), Uriel Hoskins, Harry Ferguson, John C. Pursell, Keith Willoughby, G. S. Barguist, Morris J. Thomas, Neil Lucey, Willard J. Duddles, Morley Wiederhold, and R. J. Kakuska.

The name of Glen Madere, now retired from his position as Director of the T. H. Harris Trade School, Opalusas, La., has been left to the last so that special mention could be made of his advice, moral support, and opinions on the manuscript which were very valuable in the preparation of the material in the first edition. Although he has not been involved in any way with the material in the second edition, the author still remembers with gratitude the conversations with him and his suggestions which led to the decision to write this book. The original contact was in 1949, when he attended the Teacher Training Program at General Motors Institute. There have been several additional contacts since that time which have been enjoyable and rewarding.

ROBERT L. SARGENT

Suggestions for the Use of This Book

These suggestions are directed to the teacher of a class of students beginning the study of automobile sheet metal repair. However, the individual studying this book alone, either as a beginner or for the purpose of skill improvement, will do well to follow the general pattern suggested.

The material in this book has been organized in logical sequence, starting with sheet metal and ending with a suggested practice routine for the beginner. It is not intended to be studied through progressively, as would be the case with many texts. The beginner has a natural interest in getting the feel of the tools. If he has the potential to develop skill, he will see the need for technical information as he progresses. For this reason, it is suggested that he should be assigned to practice exercises, as outlined in Chapter 9, at the start of his training period. He should be given study assignments in Chapters 1, 2, and 3 at the same time.

The first phase of the student's training should be to absorb the information in the first three chapters. As he does this, he should also be developing enough skill to control his tools, particularly the hammer and dolly block, the body file, pick hammer, and the disc sander. At this point he is ready to be assigned to simple repair work on automobiles owned by other people. He also should begin to study the material in Chapters 4 and 7.

The study of welding, Chapter 5, and filling, Chapter 6, may be started at any time. If the supply of torch equipment is limited, the students should be rotated on these operations. This will permit each student to develop these skills as he learns the basic metal working operations. Where welding is taught as a separate subject, the student should be required to do some welding on actual repair work as well as on straight practice operations.

It is much more difficult to establish where the second phase of the beginner's development ends and the third begins because this is a gradual transition rather than an abrupt change. However, he is beginning to enter the third phase when he can analyze damage conditions and relate them to a suitable repair procedure. Many students will be developing this ability very early in their training, sometimes long before they have developed the manual skill to perform the repair operations.

The student who has reached the point where he can figure out proper repair procedures should be assigned to study them in Chapters 8 and 9. They by no means cover all possible repair procedures, but are complete enough to offer a pattern to follow in the approach to most common damage. Group discussion of these procedures can be used to lead into a group agreement on the procedure to be followed on a job to be done by the class.

The teacher also is warned about one of the common problems of many beginners. They often will know exactly what they should do but are not able to control their hands so that they accomplish what they are attempting. Such students should be watched closely to see whether it is a lack of self-discipline or an actual inability to work with their hands.

The rate of progress of individual students will vary considerably. Experience has shown that some will start slowly and others will make rapid progress at the beginning. However, early rapid progress is not necessarily an indication that a student will develop higher skill than another who started much more slowly.

No study plan has been suggested for those whose interest in this book is secondary. A partial list of such users includes service managers, insurance adjusters settling automobile physical damage claims, and people in the service departments of the automobile manufacturers. They will have their own reasons for referring to this book. If they wish to become well informed about the metal man's work, they will do well to follow the general pattern outlined for the student.

ROBERT L. SARGENT

Contents

AUTOMOBILE SHEET METAL REPAIR

1

Steel and Automobile Sheet Metal Parts

The purpose of this chapter is to provide general information about steel and some specific information about automobile sheet metal, and to explain the basic shapes and reinforcements which are common to all panels. The discussion is limited and nontechnical. No attempt has been made to go beyond the minimum knowledge the metal man should have about the material with which he works.

Sections on the general subject of steel include the following: a discussion of the nature of steel; an explanation of the grain structure of steel; an explanation of the plasticity of steel; an explanation of the tendency of soft steel to harden as it goes through plastic deformation; and a discussion of the elastic properties of the various grades of steel.

On the specific subject of sheet metal the following is included: a discussion of the properties that are required of sheet metal to be suitable for automobile use; a brief explanation of the rolling process by which steel is made into sheets; and a brief explanation of the stamping process by which sheets are made into automobile parts.

Knowledge of the basic shapes and reinforcements provides a means by which panels and structural members can be classified, regardless of make and model. This is done by drawing attention to the various areas of the complete panel and showing how they can be considered as some combination of basic shapes. Reinforcing parts are covered in a similar manner.

Such knowledge is essential to the successful metal man because he must know enough about the sheet metal with which he works to understand *why* it is affected as it is by collision impact. This is his first step toward understanding how to go about using his tools and equipment to apply force to correct the damage. The study begins with the basic material, steel, because the metal man's work is affected by conditions set up by the steel rolling mill and the stamping operations.

1

STEEL

An exact definition of steel is difficult because it is made in many grades for use in almost countless products. The fact that it can be produced with special properties to meet almost any need has made it the world's most important industrial alloy. The different grades of steel are produced by varying the combination of basic materials, or *elements,* used in its manufacture. Some of these elements are common to all grades of steel; others are used only to impart special properties to it.

A broad definition of steel often is used in which it is described as a commercial form of iron containing carbon as an essential alloying element. The amount of carbon in steel is very small in comparison to the amount of iron; it is rarely ever more than 1.7% and in most cases it is much less. It is the amount of carbon that determines the hardness and the strength of a particular grade. Mild or soft steel has the least carbon, less than 0.25%; this type also is called low carbon steel. Medium steel has from 0.25 to 0.60% carbon. High carbon steel has over 0.60% carbon.

There are also other elements common to all grades of steel, though found in only very small amounts. These are manganese, silicon, phosphorus, and sulfur. Still others are added to produce special properties such as toughness, corrosion resistance, high strength, wear resistance, etc.

The sheet metal parts of the automobile are made of low carbon steel. Metal to make such parts must be relatively soft so that the flat sheet can be stamped into shape. Harder, higher carbon steels have greater strength but are not flexible enough to withstand the amount of forming necessary to make body parts without breaking, so they never are used. Even though mild steel is used, the required strength can be provided by designing the part so that it has the necessary reinforcements. Extra metal thickness, welded-on reinforcements, and shape are some of the ways in which this can be done.

Many parts in the engine, transmission, and chassis require extra hard steels. In most cases, the operating conditions of such parts are such that special alloys are required to provide the needed strength and wearing properties. Parts such as these are never repaired in the same manner as are the sheet metal parts of the automobile. For that reason they will not be considered further.

GRANULAR STRUCTURE OF STEEL

The properties of any piece of steel, hardness, weldability, strength, etc., are the result of the particular combination of elements which make it up. These elements are not combined in a smooth, uniform mixture, however, such as is glass. Steel and other metals are made up of tiny grains.

The individual grains of steel are large enough to be seen with the aid of a microscope if the sample has been prepared properly. In preparation, the surface is polished and etched with acid to bring out the shape of the individual grains. The grains will form a pattern called the grain structure.

The grain structure of a particular grade of steel will very according to the way it has been heat treated and worked. However, the changes follow a definite pattern so that a microscopic test of the grain structure can be used to determine important information for the metallurgist and the engineer.

The condition of the grain structure of any piece of steel determines the amount that it can be bent or formed. To change the shape of the piece, it is necessary to change the shape and position of every grain in the affected area. In mild steel, which bends easily, the individual grains can withstand a considerable amount of deformation and movement. In harder steels, this amount is much less. In all steels, there is a definite limit of such action, and when it is reached the piece breaks.

A simple demonstration of the action of the grains in a piece of sheet metal can be made by bending it back and forth several times rapidly. There will be a noticeable increase in temperature because of internal friction.

SHEET METAL

It is the purpose of this section to provide all the basic information about automotive sheet metal needed by the metal man in his work. More detailed discussion of the most important properties is contained in following sections. There are many sources of information for the student who wishes to delve deeper into the subject—public libraries, textbooks, and literature released by the steel manufacturers.

The term *sheet metal* is used instead of *sheet steel* because of common usage. Other metals in sheet form are used in the manufacture of automobiles, but in relatively small quantities as compared to the use of sheet steel. Also, no other metal is used in structural parts, such as the body and chassis. Thus, unless some other metal, such as brass, copper or aluminum, is mentioned *sheet metal* means *sheet steel*.

The properties of sheet metal that make it suitable for automotive use are due to the combination of elements in its composition and the way it was processed in the steel mill. All such metal is very low in carbon, making it very soft. It must be soft and plastic enough so that it can be shaped by dies to make the various parts. And, because there are more problems involved in making some panels than in others, there are different grades of automotive sheet metal. The chief problem is that of shape. More complicated shapes require the metal to be worked much more severely than would be necessary for simple ones. For example: to make a panel with a sharp reverse curve in it will require metal which

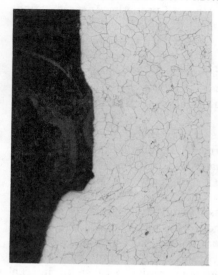

Fig. 1 Grain structure of steel. Magnified 150 times after polishing and etching with acid.

Fig. 2 *(Below)* Typical stretcher strain pattern.

can be much more severely worked than that needed for a panel which has a smooth, shallow crown. Metal must be available to make both the simple and the complicated panels.

This difference in the grades of automotive steel is not particularly noticeable to the metal man when he repairs the various panels. He never works on the flat, unworked sheet which goes into the die to be formed. The metal that has been pressed into shape has been subjected to severe cold working and has been made much harder. The extra-soft metal required for the complicated shape is made much harder after it has been shaped.

There is a very definite surface difference in the metal used for the inner and the outer panels. Many of the inner panels show patterns of wavy lines on the surface called *stretcher strains,* Fig. 2. These patterns are duplicated exactly on both sides of the metal. It is the result of yielding under tension when the panel is stamped. These lines may have almost any pattern; some may look like fern or grass leaves, others like the branches of a tree. Sometimes they have the appearance of worms pressed into the surface.

Metal used for outside panels has been processed in the steel mill so that it will not form stretcher strains; otherwise excessive labor would be necessary to file or sand the surface of the panel smooth. Inner panels which cannot be seen are not harmed by the presence of stretcher strains, so the metal to make them need not be processed to prevent them from forming. There is no difference in the way such metal will work when it is being straightened, so stretcher strains are not a problem to the metal man.

WORKING PROPERTIES OF SHEET METAL

There are certain properties or characteristics of sheet metal that determine and limit the manner in which it may be worked. These properties will vary for different grades of steel. Automotive sheet metal requires primary properties that will permit it to be formed into the shape of the various panels, and be fabricated by welding. It also must have a surface with which paint can form a lasting bond. Strength and surface texture are related and important to the primary properties.

Most of the properties of sheet metal are manufacturing requirements. However, these same properties permit and limit the work that may be done by the metal man in repairing collision damage, and for that reason they should be studied. Those that directly affect his work are: (1) plasticity, (2) work hardening, and (3) elasticity.

Each of these properties will be dealt with separately in the following pages. However, it must be remembered that they are all closely related in that they are different aspects of the effect of force applied to sheet metal. The key point in this relationship is the *yield point.* The yield point may be defined in terms of the amount of force that a piece of metal can resist without bending or otherwise deforming. The yield point has been reached when enough force has been applied to cause deformation.

Plasticity. Plasticity is the property of sheet metal that permits it to change shape when sufficient force is applied to it. Plasticity permits the flat sheet to be reshaped into any of the body or chassis parts with one stroke of the press. In doing this, the sheet metal is subjected to tremendous forces. Without plasticity, it would break or split open. Sheet metal having a high degree of plasticity is required to make some of the complicated shapes found on the surfaces of present-day automobiles.

Changing the shape of a sheet of metal may be called *plastic deformation*. The amount of plastic deformation that a piece of sheet metal can undergo without breaking is related to its hardness. Harder grades of steel cannot withstand as much plastic deformation as the softer grades can. However, softness and plasticity are not necessarily the same. It would be possible to have soft steel that did not have a high degree of plasticity.

The opposite of plasticity is rigidity. The best example of metal with no plasticity is cast iron. It is used for engine blocks because it will not bend or deform in any way. A cast-iron part designed so that it has the strength to withstand the forces that will be applied to it will maintain its shape permanently. Instead of bending, it will break under a severe overload.

Plastic deformation takes place under both tension and compression. The property that permits deformation under tension is *ductility*. The property that permits deformation under compressive force is *malleability*. (Malleability in this case should not be confused with malleable iron castings.) The result of deformation under tension is *stretching*. The result of deformation under pressure is *upsetting*.

Plasticity is important to the metal man because both stretching and upsetting take place in various areas of most of the damaged panels that he works with. This is explained in much more detail in the section dealing with the effect of force on sheet metal (pages 34 to 44).

Work Hardening. The common term used to describe the plastic deformation of steel without the use of heat is *cold working,* or sometimes the more simple term *working*. These terms are used in all discussions that follow. Any area of metal that has been bent, stretched, upset, or changed in shape in any way at any temperature below red heat has been cold worked.

The amount of cold working possible for a certain piece of steel has a limit. When it is worked past this limit, it breaks. As cold working progresses toward this limit, the metal becomes progressively harder.

This causes a corresponding increase in stiffness and strength. This increased hardness is called *work hardening*.

A very simple experiment can be performed to demonstrate the effect of work hardening. A piece of soft utility wire may be used—it has essentially the same properties as automotive sheet metal and is small enough so that it can be stretched by hand. To do this experiment, tie one end of the wire to a rigid support and the other end to something that will serve as a handle to pull on. Best results will be obtained if the wire used is several feet in length, because the increase in length will be more apparent. Measure the over-all length and stretch the wire until it breaks. The total increase in length should be close to 25%.

A noticeable increase in stiffness can be felt by bending a section of the stretched wire between the fingers and comparing it to the stiffness of another section of the same wire that has not been stretched. This increase in stiffness is due to the strain on the individual grains. For the wire to grow smaller and longer, it is necessary for the individual grains to grow longer and smaller in diameter. It is this distortion of the shape and position of the individual grain that causes the metal to work harden.

When comparing the stiffness of the stretched wire to the unstretched wire, the full increase is not apparent because the stretching reduced the diameter of that piece. If an unstretched wire of the smaller diameter were available for the comparison, the difference would be more evident.

This experiment can be carried out under more scientific conditions by supporting the wire overhead and attaching weight, in increasing amounts, to the lower end. If this is done, it will be found that when enough weight is added to reach the yield point, the wire will stretch a short distance and stop. It then will be necessary to add still more weight to cause further stretching. This can be repeated several times, each time with additional weight, until the limit is reached and the wire breaks. This need for additional weight is proof of additional strength resulting from the stretching. Each time the wire is stretched, the yield point is raised slightly.

This experiment can be carried further by using a strip of automotive sheet metal and the proper equipment. A hydraulic body jack and sheet metal clamps, such as are shown in use in the repair section of this book, are satisfactory for the purpose. If the proper gauges are available to record the force used, it will be found that a strip of mild steel will more than double in strength if it is stretched to the breaking point. This is illustrated in Figs. 3 to 7.

Fig. 3 shows a strip of metal 1 inch wide and 0.037 inch thick set up in clamps. A length of salvage steel tape has been clamped to it at one end, and crayon marks, 8 inches apart, have been aligned with the 1- and 9-

Fig. 3 *(Top)* Tensile test of body sheet metal strip. The gauge registers 0. Arrows indicate crayon marks on the strip, 8 inches apart and aligned with numerals 1 and 9 on the tape.

Fig. 4 *(Bottom)* Strip stretched ⅛ inch. The gauge registers slightly over 1,000 pounds load on the jack.

inch marks on the tape. Note that the gauge hand is slightly below the 0 mark on the gauge. In Fig. 4, the jack has been extended enough to stretch the strip ⅛ inch, as indicated by the crayon mark on the right side which is one-eighth past the 9-inch mark. Note that the gauge hand now reads slightly over 1,000 pounds.

In Fig. 5, the jack has been extended enough to stretch the strip 1¾ inches, as indicated by the crayon mark now at the 10¾-inch mark. Note that the gauge pressure has built up to about 2,100 pounds, approximately double the force needed to stretch the strip the first eighth. It was expected that the strip would break soon after this picture was taken, but after the jack has been extended another ¾ inch, the picture in Fig. 6 was taken. This shows a reading of approximately 2,500 pounds on the gauge, which was the maximum. Fig. 7 shows the strip stretched another ⅜ inch, and the gauge reading has dropped back to 2,000 pounds. Note that the

Fig. 5 *(Top)* Strip stretched 1¾ inches. The gauge registers 2,100 pounds—more than twice the original yield point.

Fig. 6 *(Bottom)* Strip stretched 2½ inches. The gauge registers 2,500 pounds, the maximum pressure reached.

Fig. 7 Strip beginning to break at arrow.

strip has begun to fail by narrowing sharply close to the clamp on the left end. The actual breaking is not shown, but only a little more stretching was needed; the gauge pressure dropped rapidly as the piece was stretched from the point shown in Fig. 7.

Both amount of stretching and the increase in yield strength obtained with the strip in these illustrations are more than can be expected normally. Failure at twice the first yield point, in this case about 2,000 pounds, would be more probable. In fact, another strip cut from the same piece of sheet stock did yield at the lower figure. The significance of this test is that unworked sheet metal elongated more than 25% and in doing so increased in strength more than 100%. (Actual figures for the strip shown are 34% increase in length and 150% increase in strength; however, they are probably higher than can be expected with most available sheet metal.)

Fig. 8 shows another example of work hardening. This strip of metal was bent double by pressing on the ends, and straightened by resting the bent area against a solid surface and pushing the ends apart. When bent double, this piece was in the shape of the piece shown on the left in Fig. 12. The work hardening caused by the first bend stiffened the metal in the bent area. The additional stiffness resisted the straightening action, causing two new bends to form on each side of the first one.

The importance of understanding how metal stiffens, making it stronger, in areas which are bent or otherwise worked cannot be overemphasized in the study of sheet metal repair. It is the basis of practically all damage. Some work hardness will be found in any undamaged automobile body panel. It is the result of the cold working that was done in the die which formed the panel in manufacturing. The bending caused by a collision adds still more work hardening in the areas affected. More, sometimes much more, will be added by the cold working used by the metal man as he straightens the damaged area. If excessive work hardening is caused by working the metal improperly, the job will be made more difficult.

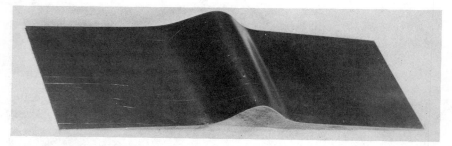

Fig. 8 Typical buckle formed by bending and straightening a piece of sheet metal.

Elasticity. Automotive sheet metal has a limited amount of *elasticity*. Elasticity may be defined as the ability of an object to regain its original shape after a deflecting force has been removed. Reducing this to a more simple statement as it applies to automotive sheet metal, elasticity may be considered as the tendency to spring back after force has been applied to it and released.

Sheet metal made of a soft grade of steel has less elasticity than if it were made of harder steel. The need for a high degree of plasticity makes it necessary to use relatively soft steel in making automotive sheet metal. However, the tendency of the steel to harden and become stronger as it is worked causes a progressive increase in the amount of elasticity.

The amount of elasticity is determined by the *elastic limit*. Going back to the simple definition of elasticity above, the elastic limit is the point at which enough force has been applied to overcome some of the tendency to spring back. This is the yield point. However, even though yielding relieves some of the elastic strain, there is always enough of it left to cause a partial spring back. This may be proved by bending any piece of metal as the piece shown in Fig. 8 was bent. There will be partial spring back when it is released.

This partial spring back tendency makes it necessary for the metal man to learn to recognize the elastic strains in the damaged panels on which he works. This will enable him to plan his work to take advantage of any tendency to spring back which is present. Spring back will be found in any area which is still relatively smooth even though it has been carried out of position by buckles formed in adjoining areas. Many such areas will spring back to shape if they are released by relieving the distortions in the buckled areas that hold them out of place.

MAKING SHEET METAL PARTS

The sheet metal panels of the automobile are made by dies which form and trim the metal to shape. The dies are mounted in huge presses which are the operating or power unit.

Different types of dies are required to perform all the operations involved in making any of the larger panels of the automobile. The panel has to be formed, or *drawn,* into shape; this is done in the *draw die*. After being drawn, it has to be trimmed, flanged, and pierced. These operations may be performed by separate dies or in some cases they may be combined; the complexity of each individual panel would be the determining factor.

Knowledge of the action of the draw die is helpful in understanding the effect that force can have on automobile sheet metal. The plastic properties of sheet metal that permit it to be permanently deformed in the draw die also permit it to be permanently deformed by the force of a collision and, also, by the force the repairman uses in correcting the collision damage.

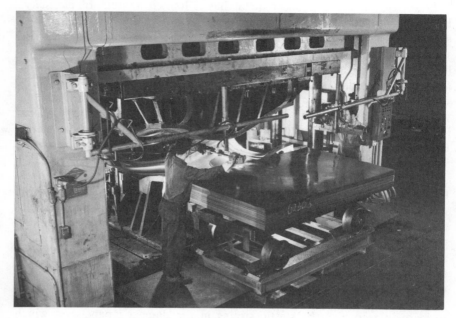

Fig. 9 Typical draw die mounted in a draw press.

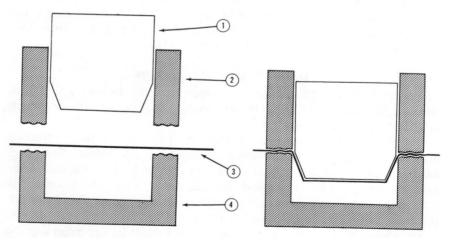

Fig. 10 *(Left)* Cross sectional sketch of a simple draw die in operation: *1*, male die; *2*, movable clamp ring; *3*, sheet metal blank; *4*, stationary clamp ring.

Fig. 11 *(Right)* Cross sectional sketch of male die at the bottom of a stroke.

Operation of the draw die includes two separate actions: clamping the sheet metal blank around the outer edges, and pushing the male die against the center area of the sheet metal blank to form it. These actions are illustrated by the sketches in Figs. 10 and 11. These sketches represent a cross sectional view of a die stamping circular metal pans. The basic principle of stamping such a pan or a hood or roof panel is essentially the same. Fig. 10 represents the die in the open position, with a sheet metal blank in place ready to be pressed.

The press which operates this type of die has two separate actions: the first raises and lowers the movable clamp ring; the second raises and lowers the male die. These actions are timed so that the clamp ring pressure is maintained throughout the entire downward stroke of the male die. Thus, the male die tends to draw the edges of the blank inward through the clamp ring as it shapes the panel.

The pressure on the clamp ring must be adjusted properly; if it is too tight, the metal will break instead of drawing inward around the die; if it is too loose, the metal will wrinkle as it draws inward. However, when this pressure is right, sufficient metal will be drawn through the clamp ring to permit a smooth, unbroken panel to be formed.

In stamping a part which has a complicated shape, the draw die exerts a tremendous tension on the sheet metal even though some of it is relieved by the movement through the clamp ring. This tension is enough to cause a slight spring back after the die pressure is released.

The press action is completed when the clamp ring and male die return to the positions shown in Fig. 10. The drawn panel is then removed, a new blank put in place, and the operation repeated.

The action of the draw die produces a piece of sheet metal that has the over-all dimensions and shape of the finished part, but instead of being properly trimmed and flanged, it is surrounded by the excess metal that has been held between the clamp rings. To remove this excess, the piece then is put into a trim die, which is simply a shear built to the proper shape for the particular part. The excess metal trimmed off in the trim die is useless for other purposes because of the beads pressed into it and the working it has undergone in being pulled through the beaded surfaces of the clamp rings. In any large pressroom operation, this scrap is baled and shipped back to the steel mill.

Up to the point of trimming, the operations in making the round pan and a body panel would be approximately the same. The difference would be in the shape of the dies and the fact that the die with the more complicated shape would have more complicated operating problems. For example, the clamp ring and male die for the round pan would be circular; the clamp rings for a hood panel would follow its outer edges, and the male die would have the exact shape of the inside of the hood. In some cases, trimming the edge of the automobile panel is all that is needed; in others it is necessary to form special flanges.

The action of a flanging die is to fold the edges of the panel to shape. The wide variety of types, or shapes, of flanges used on the different panels of the automobile make it necessary that such dies be designed to perform a specific operation. Such dies are never interchangeable from one operation to another. Some of them are very simple, others are quite complicated. However, detailed information on this type of die is beyond the scope of this book and will not be considered further.

The important fact for the metal man to gain from the preceding discussion of die operation is that any die stamped panel is left under a state of tension. As pointed out, there is some spring back as the die pressure is released. However, the tendency to spring back is not relieved completely by this action. There are remaining locked-up forces, properly called *residual stresses,* in the panel which continue to pull against the shape. Being less than the strength of the metal in which they are found, these stresses have no effect unless the panel is weakened in a spot or area. The presence of such stresses may be demonstrated easily by cutting through a flat section of any stamped panel. The edges of the metal adjoining the cut will pull out of shape. A straight edge laid across the cut will show that the edges have dropped below the original contour.

The amount of residual stresses remaining in the panel is governed by the amount of stretching that was required in drawing it. Panels that have been subjected to minor forces may be expected to have fewer stresses than those which have been subjected to much greater forces. Also, the condition will not be uniform over the entire surface of any particular panel.

Since the natural condition of the residual stresses in a panel is a slight state of tension, the metal man should remember that when a damaged panel is repaired properly, it is restored to a state of tension. This matter will be considered in much greater detail in later sections on metal finishing and shrinking with heat.

Effect of Heat on Sheet Metal

Heat, from one source or another, is involved in many of the repair operations performed on the sheet metal panels of an automobile. The most common source of heat is the oxyacetylene welding torch. Another source is friction, resulting from power-driven abrasives such as the disc sander.

There are three separate effects of heat to be considered: (1) scaling, (2) changes in grain structure, and (3) expansion and contraction.

These effects occur at the same time, but for study purposes it is easier to consider them separately.

Scale and Heat Colors. A light film of scale, which is iron oxide, will begin to form on steel when it is heated to 430° F. If the surface is clean and bright, it will be visible as a pale, yellow coloring. If the temperature is increased further, the color will deepen progressively through straw, brown, purple, light blue, and dark blue, which is reached at approximately 600° F.

Further heating will cause the dark blue to fade into a gray or greenish shade until the first reddish glow appears at approximately 900° F. Above this temperature, the red colors usually are described as blood red, dark cherry, medium cherry, cherry or full red, and bright red, which is reached at approximately 1,550° F. Above this, the red color increases in brightness through salmon, orange, lemon, light yellow, and white, which is reached at approximately 2,200° F. At approximately 2,600° F., steel melts.

The colors below the red heat range will not be affected by light conditions because they are simply a film which coats the surface. They can be used as an indication of the approximate temperature of the surface, essential in many of the straightening and shrinking operations the metal man uses.

The colors in the red range are affected to some extent by light conditions because they are a form of light. Metal which appears to be at bright red heat in dim light will not appear as bright in sunlight. This can be a confusing factor, because shop lighting conditions can vary widely at different hours of the day. This is not a critical problem, but it is well for the metal man to make allowance for light conditions when doing work where temperature is important, particularly in shrinking operations.

Metal heated to the higher temperature range will accumulate a heavy film of scale on the red hot area unless it is protected from the air. When the metal is heated with the oxyacetylene torch flame, the scale will be much heavier on the underside than on the side to which the flame was applied. This is because the burned gases in the flame exclude the air and prevent oxidation. The scale on the protected side does not begin to form until the flame has been removed, but the underside is subjected to the attack of oxygen in the air as soon as the proper temperature is reached.

Although the formation of scale is an actual burning of the metal, it is impractical to attempt to prevent its formation in the normal use of heat on sheet metal. Most spots are only heated once, so the effect is not of great importance. It is desirable to avoid heating the same area of metal to high temperature repeatedly. Each re-heating will cause some loss by oxidation, so that after enough re-heatings, the effect would be to weaken the piece by burning it away. Such conditions rarely occur in the normal repair operations, however.

Effect of Heat on Grain Structure. A progressive change in grain structure takes place when steel is heated from room temperatures up to the melting point. The structures that result have a direct effect on hardness. Hardness and strength are so closely related that they are almost the same thing; therefore, the structure also affects strength.

The effect of heat on mild steel, such as automotive sheet metal, is more limited than it is on higher carbon steels. The carbon content of mild steel is too low for the metal to harden to any appreciable extent by heat treating; the effect of heat on it is almost completely limited to softening or *annealing*. Higher carbon steels either may be annealed or hardened by following the proper procedure.

Work hardening of automotive sheet metal as a result of cold working was explained earlier. It can be completely relieved by heating to slightly above the bright red heat range. When the metal is turning to a salmon color, it has reached 1,600° F. Metallurgists call this point the critical temperature, because the grain structure undergoes a complete rearrangement. The new grains have none of the effects of working which hardened the old grain structure because they have been entirely re-formed. Cooling from this temperature to normal by exposure to air will leave automotive sheet metal in a very soft or annealed condition.

Fig. 12 Effect of heat on bending. The piece on the right was heated to a bright salmon red; the piece on the left was not heated. Both were bent by pushing the ends together.

Fig. 13 Effect of cold working. This is the same piece shown on the right in Fig. 12 after straightening, working the annealed area with hammer-on-dolly, and rebending.

The effect of annealing is illustrated in Fig. 12. These two pieces of metal were cut from the same sheet and were bent in the same manner, by pressing on the ends. The only difference is that the piece on the right had a band of metal annealed across the width before it was bent. This was done by passing the flame of a welding torch across it just fast enough to bring the metal to a salmon red heat just slightly above bright red. Note that all the bending of the metal has taken place within the area affected by the heat, and that it has bent in a much shorter radius than the unheated piece on the left. The shorter radius bend is due to the loss of strength caused by the annealing.

The pieces of metal shown in Fig. 12 were cut from flat stock that had not been worked in any way other than the cold rolling they were given in the steel mill. The same metal would show an even greater effect if it first had been through a stamping operation which would have cold worked it further. Similar pieces cut from a salvage panel would show greater resistance to bending than the unheated one. The heated piece would bend the same whether it had been further worked or not, because the work hardening would be lost.

Fig. 13 shows the same piece of annealed metal after it had been straightened and further cold worked by hammer-on-dolly blows over the annealed area. The entire area was covered with closely spaced, hard hammer blows to ensure uniform and severe cold working. Bending was done by pressing on the ends. Note that the previously soft area has become so stiff that it has bent less than the unheated piece in Fig. 12. It is now the stiffest area in the strip.

Part of this work hardening was the result of the bending and straightening; the rest of it was the result of the hammer-on-dolly work. More work on this area with the hammer-on-dolly would make it even harder. However, there is a limit to the hardening that can be obtained by cold working mild steel. Further working past that point would cause breaking.

The discussion so far has been limited to the effect on the metal of heating up to the critical temperature followed by slow cooling. Fast cooling, by immersing the heated metal in water, will tend to harden any steel. However, the hardening effect on automotive sheet metal is very slight, too little to have any practical significance. On higher carbon steels, such as would be used in a punch or chisel, the hardening effect is of great importance; such tools would be useless unless they were properly hardened by heating and quenching.

The hardening effect gained by *quenching*—immersing hot steel in water —results because the rapid loss of heat traps the metal in its finest, hardest grain structure. The hardness that can be obtained is directly related to the amount of carbon in the steel; however, the increase in hardness tends to level off when the carbon content exceeds 0.6%. Most ordinary hand tools are made of steel having less carbon than this.

Another characteristic of higher carbon steel is that it reaches the critical point at lower temperatures than mild steel. Steel used in a chisel will reach the critical point at about 1,450° F. At this temperature, it will be between cherry and bright red when viewed in bright light. Steel of the quality used in chisels will be too hard and brittle when quenched from bright red to normal temperatures. This is corrected by reheating to a much lower temperature and quenching again. This last operation is called *drawing* or tempering. The reheating would be up into the color range, usually light or dark blue. The old-time blacksmith's method of tempering tools such as chisels was to heat an inch or more of the end up to bright red; he then quenched part of the red-hot metal by dipping the end in water, keeping the tool moving up and down to avoid a sharp break line between hot and cold metal; when the end cooled enough to stop boiling off water, he scratched the scale off quickly so that he could see the color change as heat flowed back into the end; when the shade he wanted reached the tip, he plunged the complete tool into the water. This same procedure can be used by the metal man to reclaim many dull and soft tools. Heat from the welding torch and a pail of water are all that is needed.

The effect of heating above the critical point, into the orange or white heat range, is to set up a coarse and weak grain structure. Such a structure always is formed in the metal next to a weld. Most so-called weld failures occur in this area, rather than in the weld proper. Unless this condition is removed by reheating or cold working, it is the weakest area in a welded panel. More detailed information on the proper treatment of this area is found in the chapter on welding.

A mistake very commonly made by metal men is to overheat a section of metal that is to be straightened. Many sharp kinks are found that will straighten best if heat is applied, but best results will be obtained if heating stops at the critical point. Where overheating has occurred, it can be relieved by allowing the area to cool and then reheating to the critical point.

Free Expansion and Contraction. Expansion is the increase in size that occurs in nearly everything when the temperature is raised. Contraction is the decrease in size that occurs when temperature drops. Some materials expand and contract more than others. Automotive sheet metal expands and contracts more than many other materials, particularly nonmetallic substances.

The amount of expansion and contraction of anything is expressed in *linear* measurement—length, width, and thickness are the linear dimensions which are used to measure size or volume. As expansion occurs, each of these dimensions increases at the same rate. The rate at which 1 inch of linear dimension increases or decreases when the temperature is increased or decreased 1° F. is called the coefficient of expansion.

The coefficient of expansion of automotive sheet metal in the temperature range from normal to 1,500° F. is six-millionths of an inch per degree. Above that range it is less, decreasing to practically nothing at the melting point. This may seem to be an amount so small that it has no significance. However, it is a matter of simple mathematics to determine that 1 inch of metal heated 1,500° F. will expand 0.009 inch; 10 inches of metal heated 150° F. will expand the same. This becomes a matter of great importance, particularly when something acts to restrict the movement caused by expansion.

It should be kept in mind that the expansion is taking place in all directions. Reference was made to 1 inch of steel. This inch could be measured in length, width, or thickness. Expansion would be equal in all three if the application of heat were uniform. Of course, 1 inch thickness is never found in sheet metal construction, but the expansion in thickness would be proportional for the fractional part of an inch that it measures.

RESTRICTED EXPANSION

When sheet metal expands, it pushes outward in all directions. When a condition exists which tends to restrict this outward push, tremendous forces can be generated. The exact amount of such force will be governed by the amount of restriction offered, the amount of heat, and the strength of the metal expanding. If sufficient heat is applied to a small area, the result will be serious heat distortion, as shown in Fig. 14.

In the case of a spot heat application to sheet metal—which includes nearly every repair operation where the metal man uses heat—the restriction to expansion is offered by the surrounding metal which is either unheated or at a much lower temperature. The restriction is only to the expansion of surface area. There is no similar restriction offered to the expansion of thickness.

The limit of outward push is established by the force required to cause the particular area to bend or buckle. Once buckling has started, further expansion will not increase the outward push because it will be taken up in the buckle. This situation is further complicated by the fact that as the temperature rises, the resistance to buckling is lowered proportionately. Thus, as the metal expands, it begins to push up into a higher and higher bulge.

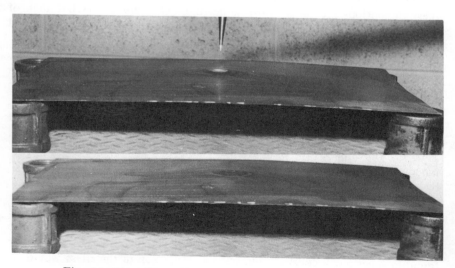

Fig. 14 *(Top)* Heat distortion due to spot heat application.

Fig. 15 *(Bottom)* The same piece of metal as shown in Fig. 14 after cooling.

The same piece of metal shown in Figs. 14 and 15 was scribed with parallel lines before the heat was applied so the heat distortion could be seen better. Note that, in Fig. 14, the buckle is slightly higher than in Fig. 15, which shows the piece of metal after cooling. This buckle remains because the expansion of the heated area has caused a bend strong enough to resist the tension set up by cooling. This tension tends to pull the buckle out but it is never as effective as the pressure of expansion. This is due to the time lag between the development of highest pressure and tension. Rapid cooling in this very short time restores the strength in the distorted area so that much greater resistance is offered when tension develops.

The heat experiment shown here was performed on a piece of unworked metal. A similar experiment on a flat body panel would create a similar but probably smaller condition because the outer edges would not be free to flex with the expansion of the hot spot. After cooling, such a spot on a body panel may cause hollow buckles to form on opposite sides of the heated area. If such buckles do form, they will be in the direction of the greatest curvature of the panel.

A much different-appearing distortion would be caused by heating an area of metal reinforced by its shape so that it tends to resist swelling. An example would be in heating a section of a panel with a bead pressed into it. The bead is too stiff to swell; instead, most of its expansion would be taken up as upset into the heated spot. When such an area cools, it will draw sharp buckles into the adjoining metal. In such cases, the upset in the stiffer area will serve as a drawstring on the adjoining metal surface.

An explanation frequently offered for heat distortion is that it is the result of relieving existing strains in the metal. Experiments similar to the one shown in Figs. 14 and 15 have not proved this to be true. This was done by taking several pieces of metal of the same size, three of which were annealed by heating and long cooling in a heat treat furnace, and performing an experiment similar to the one shown in Figs. 14 and 15. No appreciable difference could be seen in the amount of heat distortion on the annealed pieces and the unannealed pieces. As the result of this experiment, it is felt that the primary cause of heat distortion is the restriction offered by the adjoining, cooler metal.

The three illustrations in Fig. 16 indicate the importance of very slight changes in the length of flat, or very nearly flat, panel surfaces. In the upper photograph, a flat strip of sheet metal is shown lying on a flat surface and fitting exactly between square blocks on each end. In the center picture, the strip has been lifted out, a 0.005-inch feeler gauge placed against the edge of one block, and the strip fitted back into place. Note that the thickness of the feeler gauge added to the length of the strip has caused it to bulge upward nearly ¼ inch.

In the lower picture, the strip has been fitted back into place without

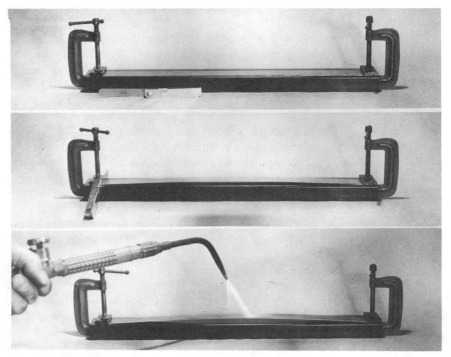

Fig. 16 *(Top)* Demonstration of the effect of a slight increase of length of a section of flat metal. *(Center)* A 0.005-inch feeler has been added to the length of the flat strip. *(Bottom)* The strip has been heated but kept below the color range.

the feeler gauge, but it has been expanded by passing a torch flame along its length. Note that it has bulged upward about twice as high as it did when the 0.005-inch feeler gauge was in place. This amount of bulging has been obtained without heating the strip enough to cause it to discolor.

The significance of these three illustrations is in what they reveal concerning the need for precise length restoration if flat metal is to remain flat after it has been heated. The feeler gauge in the center photograph shows that only a few thousandths of an inch will create a bad wave. The torch application in the lower photograph shows that only slight heating will cause much more difference in length.

The same amount of expansion would be obtained by heating a much smaller area to a much higher temperature. This was done in heating the metal sheet shown in Figs. 14 and 15. Of course, the effect would not be the same on a narrow strip as on a wide piece of metal because the strip, being free to move, does not offer the restriction to expansion which the larger piece does. Thus, the strip would not tend to distort nearly as much when heated as the surface of a panel would under the same conditions.

The metal man must understand the effect of heat distortion. Heat concentrated on a small spot causes the metal to push outward against the adjoining, cooler metal. This resistance will cause the heated spot to bulge and shorten because it is under a compressive strain. Then, when the surface cools, the heated spot remains shorter so that it tends to have a gathering effect on the adjoining metal surface. In relatively flat panels, this effect may be enough to cause buckles to extend on either side of the heated spot for several inches.

A very common mistake is to think of metal affected in the manner just described as being stretched. Stretching is dealt with in greater detail in later sections, but a similar condition may be demonstrated by folding a pleat in the edge of a piece of paper. The shortening effect of the pleat will cause the adjoining paper to bulge. The fact that only a few thousandths of an inch will cause an appreciable bulge in a flat surface indicates how important it is to be able to differentiate between heat distortion and stretching.

BASIC SHAPES AND REINFORCEMENTS

Many factors govern the shape and construction of the various sheet metal panels of the automobile. Some of these are basic in that they are established by the function of the part. For example: a door is a necessity because the passengers have to get into and out of the car and need the protection of a closed door while the car is in motion. Similarly, a fender is a necessity because of the need for protection from wheel spatter for the rest of the car.

Other factors governing the shape and construction of the sheet metal parts are dictated by style. For example: there are almost unlimited shapes in which a door or fender can be made and still be functional. The gradual change from the harsh, functional shapes of the early automobiles to the streamlined creations of the present day is the result of style trends.

As a result of the effect of style, the trend over the years has been to larger panels and window openings and far more complicated curves on the exterior surface. Style also has been an important factor in the trend toward larger cars with more spacious and luxurious interiors.

The dictates of function guided by style, which in turn is guided primarily by competition, have resulted in automobiles with the same or similar construction. Simple logic would indicate that if the construction is the same, the repair problems will be too. This is generally true, except that as styles change the construction changes accordingly. This creates a situation where there may be a considerable difference in the same panel of different year models of the same automobile. This difference might be greater than that between corresponding panels of same year automobiles built by various manufacturers.

It would be an almost impossible task to attempt to make a study of all the repair problems that might arise in the panels of all makes and year models. A more practical approach is to base the study on the basic shapes and methods of reinforcement found in the construction of all automobile sheet metal parts.

A very important advantage to placing the emphasis on basic shapes and reinforcements in studying sheet metal repair problems is that this knowledge also applies to future models. Even though the panels of future models may be changed drastically, they will be a combination of the basic shapes and reinforcements.

BASIC SHAPES

The effect of a damaging force on a panel is governed by the shape, size, and reinforcements of that panel. There are many different areas on the surface of an automobile that have the same or similar shapes. Even though such panels vary in both size and the kind of reinforcements that support their outer edges, they may be expected to form the same damage patterns when subjected to similar damaging forces.

The similarity of shapes is more readily understood when the various areas of the panel are considered separately. The over-all shape of the panel is a combination of the various areas representative of the basic shapes. The shape of a particular part, such as a door or hood panel, may vary for different year models of the same automobile, but it still is a combination of the basic shapes.

By classifying panels according to basic shapes, it is possible to establish basic damage patterns and related repair procedures. These can be applied to any sheet metal panel, whether it is on past, current, or future models.

Another factor that makes it desirable to classify panels according to shape is that it is rare for the damage to extend to the entire area of a panel. The repair problems will be confined only to a portion of the larger panels. The metal man need only concern himself with that portion of the panel that is damaged. He will find a direct relationship between the basic shape involved and the damage pattern that results.

There are different damage patterns for a basic shape, because damaging forces may be applied in so many different ways. However, two different panels of the same basic shape will be damaged in a similar pattern if the damaging forces are the same. Damage patterns are discussed in the following chapter.

Classifying panels by basic shapes is complicated by the fact that they do not follow exact geometric patterns, such as flat, spherical, or cylindrical surfaces. Furthermore, surface contours vary greatly in different areas of the same panel.

An easy way to describe shape is to consider the curvature of the length and width of an area separately. The shape of any particular area may be described accurately by placing two curved lines, at right angles to each other, over the area. In establishing these lines, length would be taken as lengthwise of the automobile. Width would be taken either vertically, as on the side of the automobile, or crosswise, as on the top or bottom. Front and rear end panels having their length in the crosswise direction to the automobile would be considered whichever way their over-all shape would suggest.

The combined effect of the shape of length and width will be considered as the *crown* of the area of the panel being discussed. There are four basic classifications used to describe the crown of any panel. They are: (1) low crown, (2) high crown, (3) combined high and low crown, and (4) reverse crown. Examples are shown in Figs. 17 and 18.

Fig. 17 Example of high crown panels. The cowl side is relatively flat, but most of the rest of the surface of this automobile is high crowned. The fender blends into a reverse crown at the headlight.

Fig. 18 Example of low crown panels. The door and quarter panel are relatively flat but blend into sharp reverse crowns at the upper and lower edges.

Low Crown. Panels in the low-crown classification have very little curvature; many of them can be found that are straight in the lengthwise direction. The impression gained from a glance at a small area is that it is a flat surface. For all practical purposes, the repairman must treat such panels as though they were flat.

Many low-crowned areas can be found on any of the postwar model automobiles. Best examples are: door lower panels, quarter panel lowers, fender skirts, hood tops, and the center area of roof panels. Of this list, the roof panel has the least appearance of being flat because in almost every case it has more curvature both lengthwise and crosswise than most other low-crown panels. However, it is also the largest panel on the automobile, which causes it to react to a force, either damaging or repairing, as if it were flat. This is because the load-bearing strength of such long, slight curves is very low.

It is difficult to define exactly the amount of curvature that a panel can have and still be considered low crowned. It is easier to define in terms of springiness or elasticity. The surface of an undamaged low-crowned panel will spring or flex out of shape when hand pressure is applied to it and snap back when the pressure is released.

In some cases, the entire area of a panel will be in the low-crown classification; in others only a portion will be low crowned—the rest of the area may blend into any combination of the other basic crowns.

High Crown. Surfaces in the high-crown classification have enough curvature to give the impression of a rounding shape in both directions. The curvature in both directions may not be the same, but in both cases it is enough to be obvious.

True high crowns were very common in the automobiles built in the prewar period, but the trend in design moved away from them in later years. Some remaining examples are: the rounded section on the front of many hoods; the rounded section on the corners of roof panels; and the rear end of many quarter panels. Almost without exception, the high-crown surface is only a small portion of the total area of the panel.

As with the low crown, it is difficult to define exactly the amount of curvature that is necessary for a surface to be classified as high crown. Defined in terms of stiffness, it cannot be flexed out of shape by hand pressure; when enough force is applied to a high crown to push it out of shape, it will not spring back when the pressure is released.

Metal in high-crown areas has been worked more severely than low-crown metal in forming and for that reason it is slightly stronger due to additional work hardening.

Combined High and Low Crown. The rounding edges of many of the low-crown areas are actually low crowned in one direction and high crowned in another. Many such panels, like doors and front fenders, are very nearly flat lengthwise but curve away very sharply in the crosswise, or width, direction along the edges. Many such surfaces can be compared to a portion of the outside of a cylinder.

Combined low- and high-crown surfaces have the strength characteristics of the high-crown rather than the low-crown surface. Although relatively flat in the one direction, the relatively short radius of the curvature in the other provides strong bracing to resist force.

The combined high and low, or *combination,* crown has been more widely used on the automobiles built in the postwar years. The trend in design is such that this type crown may be expected to continue in wide use.

Reverse Crown. In contrast to the other crowns, one curve of the reverse crown is hollow when viewed from the outside. This may be considered as an inside curve, because the center point of the curve is on the side from which it is viewed.

In most cases, the inside curve has a relatively short radius as compared to the radius of the outside curve. It is quite common to find considerable variation in the radius of the inside curve of a reverse crown which runs the length of a panel. The outside curve will usually have a relatively long

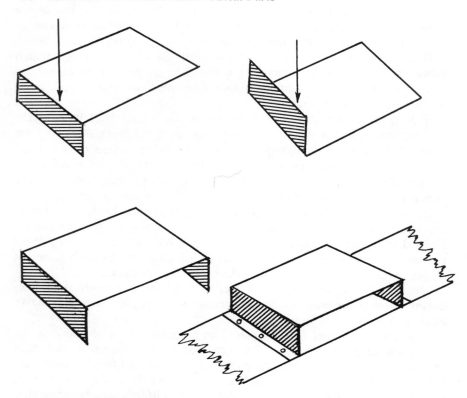

Fig. 19 *(Top, left)* Flange turned away from the load, indicated by the arrow.

Fig. 20 *(Top, right)* Flange turned toward the load, indicated by the arrow.

Fig. 21 *(Bottom, left)* Channel formed by adding a second flange.

Fig. 22 *(Bottom, right)* Box construction.

radius. However, variations of either of these conditions will be found.

The reverse crown presents a particular problem to the metal man because of its strength. A simple bend in one of them is not possible, because the two curves are braced against each other. A collapse of the metal surface is necessary for a bend to occur. As a result, damage in a reverse crown is usually severe as compared to damage in either a low or high crown. However, when damage does occur, often it is localized in one or more small areas. The reverse crown being stiffer, the damage tends to spread less than it will in the other crowns.

REINFORCING METHODS

The strength of the crowned surfaces of the panels of an automobile body is not enough to provide the rigidity that is necessary to hold alignment of parts and carry the loads that are normally required. Additional strength must be provided. The desirability of keeping weight down to the minimum rules out the use of heavy reinforcing members. An important part of the progress in body design has been the development of lightweight reinforcements made of formed sheet metal.

Reinforcements are of two basic types: those formed in the surface of an inner or outer panel; and those welded to a panel. The reinforcements formed in a panel are the flanges, beads, and offsets used primarily for stiffness. Examples are such sections as the flange on the lower edge of a fender skirt and the ribs or beads on door inner panels and floor pans; reinforcements of this type are essentially stiffeners intended to prevent vibration or flexing. Welded-on reinforcements are usually channel or box section pieces which serve as structural members. Examples are roof rails, windshield headers, and the crossbars used under the floor pan; there are many others.

Body engineers design light structural members of thin sheet metal by taking advantage of the stiffening effect of an angular bend. A strip of sheet metal has relatively little strength to resist bending when force is applied to it at right angles to the surface. The same strip can support far greater loads when it is turned so that the load is applied to the edge instead of to the flat surface. A flange turned on the edge of a flat sheet is, in effect, an attached strip. The far greater resistance to bending of the edgewise strip is added to the relatively low strength of the flat sheet.

The reinforcing effect is greatest when the flange is turned away from the load. It is very little when the flange is turned toward the load. These two conditions are illustrated by the sketches in Figs. 19 and 20. In Fig. 19 the outer edge of the flange is under tension and cannot yield except by breaking or stretching. The inner edge of this flange is under a compressive force that would tend to buckle it if it were free; being attached to the flat sheet, buckling is prevented. In Fig. 20, the opposite is true. The attached edge of the flange is under a tension force and the outer edge is under a compressive force. Being unsupported, the outer edge is free to buckle as the flat sheet bends.

In Figs. 19 and 20, only one edge is supported. By adding another flange on the opposite side, as shown in Fig. 21, the strip can be made into a channel. The channel is stronger than the single flanged strip, but it has the same basic weakness if the flanges are turned toward the load.

Maximum strength can be obtained by adding the fourth side to the three-sided channel, making what is commonly termed a box construction. Fig. 22 is representative of a very commonly used form of box construc-

Fig. 23 Cutaway section of a typical roof rail and roof, showing box construction.

Fig. 24 Cutaway section of a typical rocker panel, showing box construction.

tion. It is essentially a channel with narrow flanges turned on the outer edges of the wide flanges. These narrow flanges serve as a means of welding to a broad section of sheet metal. The crossbars on the underside of floor pans are excellent examples of this type of box construction.

Box construction is not limited to the square shape shown in Fig. 22. The possible variations of the shape of such parts, usually called members, is almost limitless. Regardless of shape, however, box construction offers more strength than can be obtained by any other method used to provide reinforcement in automobile bodies.

A cutaway section of a typical roof and roof rail is shown in Fig. 23. This is true box construction as is the rocker panel shown in Fig. 24.

QUESTIONS ON STEEL

1. Why must steel which will bend easily be used in the manufacture of automobile sheet metal parts?
2. What is the essential difference between steel which will bend easily and steel which is relatively stiff?
3. Why is it that the steel in an automobile body cannot be made extremely hard?
4. What is changed when steel is made harder by cold mechanical working?
5. a. What is the effect of heat on the strength of metal that has been subjected to cold working?
   b. What temperature, indicated by color, must be reached for this effect to occur?
   c. Is this effect reached suddenly at this temperature or does it begin at a much lower temperature and increase as the temperature increases?
6. What occurs when a piece of metal has been cold worked past its limit?
7. At what temperature does a color begin to show on the surface of a bright, clean steel surface?
8. At what temperature does the first trace of reddish glow begin to appear?
9. What causes the first color to form on the surface of a piece of bright steel which has been heated?
10. What effect does light have on the appearance of the steel at various stages of red and white heat?
11. Why will cutting a panel cause the edges of the cut to pull out of shape slightly?
12. Why does failure of a gas weld on a sheet metal panel usually occur in the metal next to the weld rather than in the weld?
13. Why does heating a spot of metal on the surface of a panel cause warpage?
14. Why does bending a piece of metal rapidly back and forth cause it to heat up?
15. Why will a piece of metal that has been cold worked in any way be made stiffer?
16. After a piece of metal has been cold worked severely, then heated to orange red and cooled, can it be cold worked again? Why or why not?
17. Will major differences which will affect the metal man's work be found in the sheet metal used in the various panels of the same automobile? Explain.

18. Will major differences which will affect the metal man's work be found in the sheet metal used by different automobile manufacturers? Explain.
19. a. Why is a pattern of slight surface depressions often found on the inner panels of a body?
    b. Will this pattern of surface depressions affect the strength of the panel? Explain.
    c. What are these surface depressions called?
20. What causes the scale which forms on the surface of steel when it is heated into the red color range?
21. When sheet metal is heated red hot or hotter with the welding torch flame, why will much heavier scale form on the side away from the flame?

QUESTIONS ON BASIC SHAPES AND REINFORCEMENTS

1. What is meant by basic shape?
2. What are the basic shapes?
3. Are all basic shapes found on all panels? Explain.
4. Which crown is the most severely distorted when it is bent out of shape?
5. Why does turning a flange on an edge of a piece of sheet metal have a reinforcing effect?
6. Which offers the most reinforcement, the flange turned toward the load or the one turned away from it?
7. What are the advantages of box construction?
8. Is it necessary for a box member to be square? Why?
9. In what areas of the automobile body is box construction found?
10. What is a combination crown?

2

Collision Damage

The metal man's work in repairing collision damage is primarily a matter of undoing the effect of an impact force. Usually the impact is the result of a collision with some other object, often another automobile, but it can be anything with which an automobile can come into contact. When a collision occurs and damage results it is because the sheet metal was subjected to more force than it could resist.

The study of collision damage is complicated by the fact that it is the result of an accidental situation instead of normal wear. Being the result of an accident, each damage is an individual problem to be solved by the repairman. This is in sharp contrast to the repair of the operating units of the automobile, because similar units develop similar problems so that exact procedures can be prepared and handed to the mechanic. In solving his problems, the metal man must be guided by what he knows about the effect of impact force on sheet metal and the methods which may be used to restore it to original shape.

It is the purpose of this chapter to explain the basic damage conditions which result when impact force is applied to the basic shapes. By doing this it is possible to reduce a highly variable situation to a combination of basic conditions. The trained metal man or estimator sees the damage on any panel as an exact combination of these conditions instead of a tangled mess of sheet metal.

To understand these basic conditions, it is necessary to understand the relationship of shape to the effect of force on it. This is also a variable situation, because it involves different speeds, impact angles, size and rigidity of the impact object, and the construction of the area affected. This chapter has been arranged so that the relationship of shape to the effect of force on it is discussed first. This is followed by a list of the basic damage conditions and a discussion of the physical effects of each. The chapter concludes with an explanation of the variable factors of speed, angle, rigidity, etc., and how they are related to the severity of the damage conditions.

33

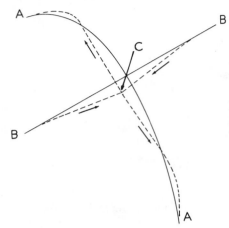

Fig. 25 Showing the flow of force from a direct impact on a combination high- and low-crowned surface.

EFFECT OF FORCE ON SHAPE

When any panel has been damaged by an impact, there must be a point or area where the impact object struck. On all damages of any consequence, the force will have traveled through the metal surrounding the impact, causing related damage. The exact nature of this surrounding damage will vary with the amount of force involved, whether it pushed or pulled, and the shape of the area on which it acted. These variable factors determine the exact nature of the basic damage conditions in every area affected. Also, similar forces acting on similar shapes can be expected to cause similar damage.

Fig. 25 shows the outward flow of force from a direct impact on a combination high and low crown. The solid lines, *AA* and *BB* represent vertical and lengthwise cross sections of a typical panel. The arrow, *C,* represents a direct impact on the intersection of these cross sections. The dotted lines show the effect of the impact on the original shape, and the arrows indicate the flow of force. Note that the arrows under the high crown point outward, indicating that the force following this path has pushed against the adjoining metal; and the arrows under the low crown point inward, indicating an exactly opposite effect.

An impact on a high crown always can be expected to push outward against the adjoining metal. The same impact on a low crown always can be expected to pull inward on the adjoining metal. When these crowns are combined, as they are on most body panels, the effect of pushing and pulling will act along lines which cross as shown in this sketch.

Any sheet material will react differently when subjected to force which pushes and force which pulls against it. Pressure on the opposite edges of a sheet toward the center will cause it to crumple because of its low resistance to bending. An outward pull on the same edges will draw it tight, and no further effect will occur unless enough force is applied to exceed its yield strength. For this reason, the damage conditions found in a high-crown area will be different from the damage conditions found in the adjoining low-crown area even though both are the result of the same impact.

THE BASIC DAMAGE CONDITIONS

Force spreading from the impact point into other areas of the panel or into other panels causes damage by changing the shape of the areas affected. The nature of such damage varies too widely to attempt to establish what could be called a typical condition. However, when a detailed examination is made of the damaged area, it will be found to be a combination of the following basic damage conditions: (1) displaced areas, (2) simple bends, (3) rolled buckles, (4) upsets, and (5) stretches.

In addition to these, there will be tears or rips and broken welds. However, these are not considered as basic conditions and are not considered further.

The damage found on any panel will be a combination of some or all of these conditions. The more severe the damage, the more likely it will be that all the basic damage conditions will be present.

Each of these conditions differs enough from the others to make it desirable to discuss them separately.

Displaced Areas. In almost every case, examination of a damaged panel will reveal that part of the area is not affected by bending or other distortion. Such areas are a part of the over-all damage only because they have been pushed out of position. Quite often they are under an elastic strain which, when relieved, will allow the area to snap back into shape. Such areas may be considered as displaced. Much of the center area of the door panel shown in Fig. 26 is displaced.

It is important to recognize all displaced areas and plan the repair procedure so that the buckles holding them out of place will be relieved properly. Large displaced areas often can be released so that there is little or no repair work except on the buckled areas which held them.

One measure of the severity of any damage is in the amount of displaced metal which makes up the damaged area. It is obvious that an area which can be made to snap back into shape will not require as much work to straighten as a similar area which is badly bent and distorted.

Simple Bends. As the surface of panel collapses under impact, it folds. Some of the folding is the result of simple bends, particularly in relatively flat areas. A simple bend is essentially a long, usually narrow area of metal which has served as a pivot for the movement of the adjoining

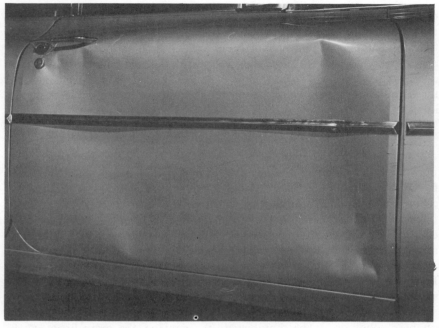

Fig. 26 Displaced metal. Much of the center area will snap back into shape when the sharp buckles are relieved.

metal. In doing so, it is changed in shape.

The deformation in a simple bend is due to the opposing action of tension and compression forces. As force which tends to cause bending is applied to a piece of sheet metal, it causes tension on the outside of the bend and compression on the inside. Bending occurs when enough force is applied to overcome the resistance the metal offers to this tension and compression. Under normal conditions, the metal on the inside of the bend is upset and the metal on the outside of the bend is stretched. The bending action is illustrated in Fig. 27.

The stretching and upsetting occur on the surface. It is quite obvious that somewhere between these surfaces, which are planes, there would be another plane which would be unaffected by either tension or pressure. This plane falls approximately in the center of the sheet, because the metal on either side of it is solid so that both tension and pressure are resisted equally at the start of the bending. When breaking occurs in a sharp bend, however, it starts on the outside because the action tends to pull it apart.

In studying the effect of bending, it is essential to direct the attention

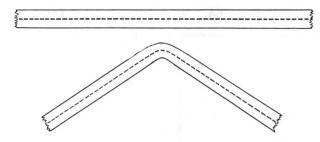

Fig. 27 Enlarged cross section of a piece of sheet metal before and after bending. The outer surface is stretched and the inner surface is compressed. The centerline remains unchanged.

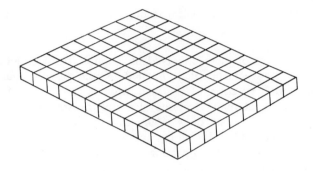

Fig. 28 Enlarged piece of sheet metal with lines scribed on the surface to represent cubes. The actual size of the cubes would be 0.037 inch.

to the very small unit of metal instead of being concerned with the entire panel. The drawing in Fig. 28 is for this purpose. This represents a piece of sheet metal slightly less than ½ inch long and ⅓ inch wide. The lines on its surface are spaced apart the thickness of the metal. Thus, each square formed by these lines represents one face of a cube which is joined on four sides to similar cubes.

The two sketches in Fig. 29, *A* and *B*, represent a cross section of one of these cubes before and after bending. In sketch *A*, the upper and lower halves are exactly the same size and shape. In sketch *B*, bending has distorted the square into the shape of a wedge. The upper and lower halves are still the same bulk, because nothing has been taken away or added, but they are different in shape, the upper being stretched and thinned and the lower being compressed and thickened.

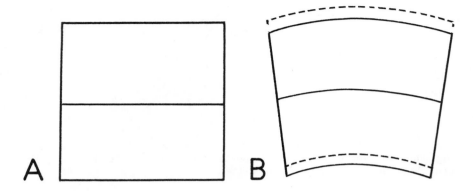

Fig. 29 The shape of a single cubical section *(A)* before and *(B)* after bending.

The total amount of metal involved in a simple bend is determined by its length and how sharply it is formed. Quite often an area several inches long and a fraction of an inch wide is affected. Such an area would be made up of many sections of metal the size of a cube such as this. The effect of bending on various sections throughout such an area would vary considerably. It follows logically that to straighten such an area, it will be necessary to apply force so that these effects are relieved, regardless to what extent each individual section was distorted.

Rolled Buckles. The rolled buckle is so named because of the rolling action which occurs in much of the area of a panel as it collapses under an impact. This action is similar to the pivot action of a hinge buckle except that the pivot point travels across an area instead of remaining in one place. An example of a severe rolled buckle is shown in Fig. 30, indicated by the arrow marked No. 1. Less severe rolled buckles are indicated by the arrows No. 2 and No. 3. The sharp dent between No. 1 and No. 3 is a direct impact area from which the force causing the rolling action spread.

The distinctive feature of a rolled buckle is two ridges running together at an angle. These ridges are generally sharply formed at the meeting point, which is usually in the area where a low crown blends into a combination low and high crown. On each side of the meeting point, the sharpness of these ridges will be reduced gradually, until in many cases they will blend into the shape of the adjoining surface. This is not true of the rolled buckles shown here, however, because they are in an area of metal which is quite high crowned in both directions, and the dent is quite deep.

The meeting point of the sharp ridges usually is raised above the level of the adjoining surface. This raised area is due to the stiffening effect of the ridges and the valley buckle which forms between them. The valley buckle forms a prop under the high point.

The damage caused by a rolled buckle can vary from a condition no more severe than a simple bend to one of the worst conditions with which the metal man will work. The severity of the distortion of the individual rolled buckle is governed by the amount of force which caused it. The rolling action starts as a curved ridge around the impact point and moves, or *rolls,* outward. The shape of this ridge is relatively smooth until some resistance point is reached, usually the point where the low crown blends into a combination crown. At such points, the inner surface of the ridge collapses, forming the valley buckle. If the rolling action stops at this point, the damage is not much more severe than a simple bend. If, however, there is sufficient force to push this rolling action farther into the higher crown, the damage will be severe. This is the case with the buckle indicated by arrow No. 1 in Fig. 30. Note that a path of flaked-

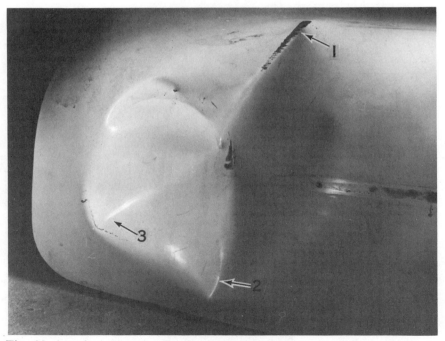

Fig. 30 A typical example of rolled buckles. Arrow No. 1 points to the break-over path of the most severe buckle. Arrows No. 2 and No. 3 indicate less severe buckles.

off paint has been left by the rolling action. This path is referred to as the break-over path because of the breaking or collapsing action it goes through in forming.

The metal in the break-over path will be upset. The next section deals in detail with the exact nature of upsetting, whether caused by a rolled buckle or otherwise.

Upsets. An upset occurs when opposing forces push against an area of metal and cause it to yield; in yielding, the surface area will be reduced and the thickness increased proportionally. The forces which cause an upset may act only from two opposite directions, as indicated in the

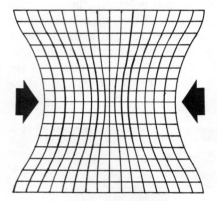

Fig. 31 Enlarged drawing showing the effect of force pushing from opposite directions on a section of metal approximately ½ inch square.

Fig. 32 Effect on a small, cubical section within the upset area. At *A*, the cube is shown before force has been applied. At *B*, pressure has been applied from four sides. At *C*, pressure has been applied from two sides.

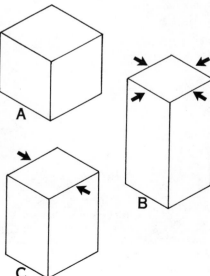

drawing in Fig. 31, or they may act against a central point from several directions. To identify an upset remember that one or both of the surface dimensions of the affected area will be reduced.

The effect and importance of an upset will be better understood if one remembers that it usually is restricted to a relatively small area. Fig. 31 can be considered as representing the same section of metal represented by Fig. 28. Reducing this enlarged drawing to the dimensions of most sheet metal found in the automobile body would indicate a piece about ½ inch square and 0.037 inch thick. Larger areas of metal can be upset, but the tendency to buckle and relieve the pressure limits the upsetting effect to areas not too much larger than this. The break-over path of a severe rolled buckle may be much longer but not much wider.

Many drawings of various shapes could be used to illustrate the effect of upsetting. However, each would be similar to the three drawings in Fig. 32. Drawing *A* represents a small cubical section of sheet metal before the upsetting force application. Drawing *B* represents the same section after force application from all four sides. Note that the top surface is shown much smaller, and the height, which would be the thickness, is much greater. Drawing *C* represents the same section after force application from only two sides. Note that only one side of the top surface is shown smaller, and the height, or thickness, is less than in *B*.

Upsetting a single section no larger in area than its thickness would not have a significant effect on the shape of a panel. When this effect is spread over an area ½ inch wide and much longer, it is an important factor. The series of photographs in Fig. 16, Chapter 1, showed that as little as 0.005 inch would cause an unacceptable bulge in a flat strip. The drawing in Fig. 31 does not represent any specific upset but the amount of upset shown would not be uncommon. Considering that this drawing represents an area of metal approximately ½ inch square, the

Fig. 33 Upset effect in the break-over path of a severe rolled buckle. The break-over action would reach the point where the solid and the dotted lines converge.

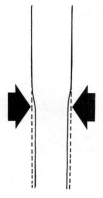

upset shown would be many times 0.005 inch. Such a spot anywhere on the surface of a low-crown panel would draw wrinkled-type buckles on each side of it.

Fig. 33 represents the upsetting effect of most rolled buckles. The offset in the lower section of these parallel lines represents the point reached by the break-over path. The resistance of the adjoining metal tends to force the metal together; lines scribed on the panel before the buckle was formed would have this shape after the break-over action passed between them.

Upsetting is not limited to the effect of the damaging force. The piece of metal shown in Fig. 34 has had a ridge formed in it by bending and straightening; this is a typical buckle left after any piece of metal has been bent double and the ends opened up again without work being done directly on the ridge which forms. The section in the center was flattened by hammering it down as it lay on a flat surface. Note that this section has been lowered until it is about level with the metal on either side. Flattening this section required far greater upsetting than would be found in almost any rolled buckle. Such upsets can be made by the repairman if he does not know that he should avoid hammering sharp ridges. This photograph also is used in Chapter 7 in the discussion of proper repair procedure.

Fig. 34 An upset section of a crease-type buckle, made by hammering the buckle as the piece lay on a flat surface. No heat was used.

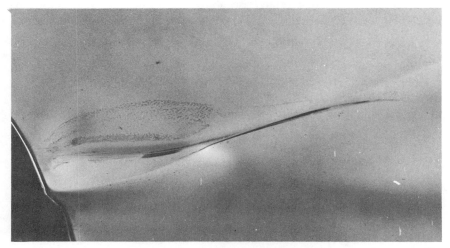

Fig. 35 A crease type gouge, the result of a high-speed impact by a small, rigid impact object.

A very common mistake is to confuse the effect of upsetting with stretched metal. An upset area will have a gathering, or drawstring, effect on the adjoining metal, particularly in a low-crown section. Such areas often will pop in and out; this often is called oilcanning. Oilcanning also can be caused by stretched metal, but, unless there is evidence that it has been subjected to tension or has been worked too much with the hammer and the dolly block, it is very probable that it is the result of an upset in an adjoining area.

Stretches. Stretch is the exact opposite of upset. Stretching occurs when an area of metal is subjected to force in tension greater than its yield strength. The result is an increase in surface area. Sheet metal is considered as being stretched whether the increase of area is caused by an increase of either length or width, or both.

Stretching also can be the result of the improper use of tools, particularly the hammer and dolly. (These are the metal man's most important tools, but it is important for him to learn how to use them properly.)

Stretching occurs under different conditions and usually in different areas than upsetting because it is the result of tension instead of pressure. The most common type of stretching is a gouge. Small point gouges may be seen in the impact area of the dented deck lid shown in Fig. 30. A much more severe crease-type gouge is shown in Fig. 35.

When the exact difference between stretched and upset metal is recognized, the problems of stretched metal become relatively simple.

Stretched areas of metal rarely rise above the surface level to cause unacceptable bulges. When they do, the metal man who has learned the proper technique of shrinking finds them relatively easy to repair. Gouged areas frequently are filled, because the fill can be blended into the surface area easily in most cases. However, the decision as to whether a particular gouge should be filled or straightened by shrinking should not be made without considering the conditions. In some cases filling is all that is required; in others filling can be a mistake for several reasons.

The term *false stretch* is used to identify the condition where an upset has caused an adjoining area to bulge so that it appears to be stretched.

VARIABLE FACTORS IN COLLISION

Even though all collision damage is made up of the same basic conditions, few damaged areas are exactly alike. This is because they are the result of an accidental situation. Because the damage from any collision is unique, the metal man is forced to determine his own procedure. He can do this best if he has been trained, or has trained himself, to analyze the conditions of the damage so that he can determine the fold pattern and apply force so that it has an opposite effect. An important part of a metal man's training is learning what to look for when he inspects the damage.

Analyzing the job consists of determining the area which received the impact, an approximation of the total force of the impact, and a check on the paths which the force might follow to cause related damage on points distant from the impact point. In making his analysis of the collision, the metal man should look for the following: (1) the angle of impact, (2) the relative speed of the impact object, (3) the size, rigidity, and weight of the impact object, and (4) the construction of the area receiving the impact.

These will be referred to in later discussions as the *variable factors* which determine the nature of the damage resulting from any collision. It is easy to determine the extent to which each factor has affected the damage. From this it is a simple step to visualize the actual movement of metal as it folded. The key to good repair procedure is simply a matter of reversing this movement.

Analysis of damage is done from the practical rather than the scientific viewpoint. For example: an impact on the forward section of a quarter panel might affect the alignment of the rear section to the deck lid. In the analysis, this should be recognized and the repair procedure planned so that the condition causing the misalignment will be relieved. Another impact on a similar quarter panel might not affect the alignment of the deck lid at all, so the repair procedure would be different. In either case, however, there would be nothing gained by knowing the exact amount of force of the impact or the engineering specifications of the panel.

There are two important reasons why the effect of the impact angle should be considered: (1) it determines whether the impact strikes a direct or a glancing blow; and (2) it determines the flow of force from the impact point or area to all other areas in which related damage is found.

With everything else equal, a direct impact will cause more damage than a glancing one on the same panel because the full force will be absorbed. It was shown by the sketch in Fig. 24 that the force which flows outward from a direct impact will be in tension on a low-crowned surface and in pressure on a high-crowned surface. A much more variable situation results when the angle of impact becomes much more oblique, as shown in Fig. 36. The sketch at *A* shows an impact approaching a panel at a relatively sharp angle. Sketch *B* shows the effect of a small rigid impact object which digs into the panel surface, pushing metal ahead of it and pulling metal behind it. Sketch *C* shows the effect of a larger, smooth impact object which glances off instead of digging into the panel surface, causing damage which is essentially the same as a direct impact.

Some of the damage conditions most difficult to repair are caused by the glancing impact which digs into the panel surface. Straightening the metal which has been pushed ahead of the impact is not simply a matter of driving out a dent. Usually the use of tension equipment is required, and frequently it is necessary to shrink the surface or use filling material to finish it.

Fig. 36 Showing the effect of an impact from a sharp angle. Sketch *A* indicates the angle of approach. Sketch *B* shows the effect when the impact object digs into the surface, pushing metal ahead of it and drawing metal behind it. Sketch *C* shows the effect when the impact object glances off instead of digging in; this is essentially the same as direct impact.

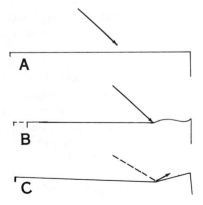

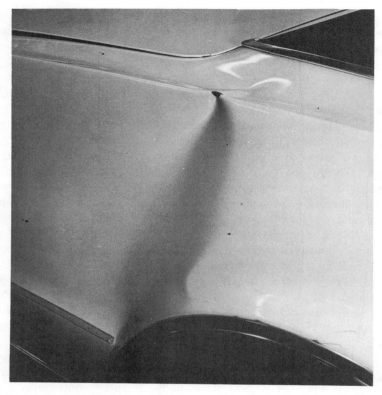

Fig. 37 Buckle formed by the collapse of a section of metal under pressure.

A quite different damage condition occurs when a panel having a combination crown, such as quarter panel, receives a direct impact on the end. In this case, most of the entire panel will be subjected to pressure which will tend to collapse any weak points. It is not uncommon to find sharp buckles formed where a flat surface has collapsed under such pressure.

RELATIVE SPEED OF IMPACT OBJECT

The speed of the impact object should be considered as relative because essentially the same damage results whether it moves against a standing automobile or it is stationary and is struck by a moving automobile. When both are moving toward each other, as in a head-on collision, the relative speed would be the combined speed of both.

The speed of impact is important because of inertia. Stated briefly, inertia is the tendency of any stationary object to resist being put in motion and of a moving object to continue moving. An excellent example of the effect of inertia is shown in Fig. 38. The hole in this piece of metal was made by a 22-caliber rifle bullet. It is possible to shoot a hole such as this in a body panel because of the speed at which the bullet travels. A much heavier object could exert the same amount of force at a much lower speed but, instead of piercing the panel, it would only dent the surface. The difference is a matter of time; under the impact of the heavier but slower moving impact object, the panel surface has more time to move inward and spread the effect over a larger area.

The speed of the impact is important to the metal man in making his analysis of damage, because it indicates the extent to which force has penetrated into the structure to cause related damage. A highspeed impact on the front end of a fender may cause severe damage at the point of impact but not affect the alignment of the fender to hood and door. Another impact by a heavier object traveling at lower speed may cause less damage at the impact point but break the fender loose from the cowl, causing the fender to move back against the door and cause additional damage. The trained metal man would know, by the appearance of the second damage, that he also should check the alignment of the cowl hinge pillar because it may have shifted enough to prevent proper door alignment.

Size, Rigidity, and Weight

In addition to the impact angle and speed, the size, rigidity, and weight of the impact object have a great bearing on the type of damage

Fig. 38 A .22-caliber rifle bullet hole in a piece of sheet metal.

which results from a collision. Again, as in the discussion of impact angle and speed, the metal man need not concern himself with the *exact* size, degree of rigidity, or weight. He is only interested in whether the impact object was large or small, rigid or yielding, or extremely heavy or very light.

The example of the bullet, used in the preceding section, serves as an illustration of the small, relatively rigid, but lightweight impact object. As a contrasting example, consider the effect of a roll-over accident in which the automobile lands on one side in soft earth. In such an accident, it is possible for the automobile to bounce as it continues to roll without causing severe visible damage. However, bends or misalignment may be found in the reinforced parts supporting the panels which received the impact. The reason is that the soft earth spreads the impact force over enough area of the panel surface to avoid severe overloading of any one point. Some of the impact force will be absorbed in displacing soft earth, but much of it will be transferred through the adjoining metal into the reinforcing parts.

An entirely different damage condition would result if the automobile were to roll onto something hard and unyielding, such as a tree stump or a rock. The effect of speed would be much greater, because the cushioning effect of the soft earth would not be present. Severe distortion in the impact area would absorb some of the force so that misalignments in adjoining sections would tend to be less; force expended at one point cannot travel on and cause additional damage elsewhere.

CONSTRUCTION

The rigidity of the area receiving the impact determines to a large degree the nature of the damage and the extent to which it spreads. For example: a direct impact on the center area of a door panel would spread over the entire area, but the same impact on the reinforced pillar section of the door would probably cover much less area. There is no easy way in which the severity of the one damaged area can be compared with the other, but it is obvious that the metal man should expect to find more misalignments caused by the impact on the pillar section. Similar examples would be pointed out over the entire surface of the body.

In analyzing any damage, it is essential to consider whether the impact has struck an area which is quite rigid or one which will yield readily. The effect on the rigid area will tend to cause severe distortion which spreads over a relatively small area; the opposite will be true of a similar impact on an area which will yield easily. However, to the untrained observer, the larger area of damage may appear to be the most severe because of its size. The trained metal man should never make the mistake of judging the severity of damage on the basis of size alone. This mistake is easy to make when the two conditions are combined.

QUESTIONS ON COLLISION DAMAGE

1. Why is it necessary to consider the repair of each damaged panel as an individual problem?
2. What is meant by impact object?
3. What is the impact area?
4. What is related damage?
5. On most panels damaged by impact, why will some of the area surrounding the impact be affected by tension and other areas be affected by pressure?
6. What is the effect of tension acting on the surface of a low-crowned panel?
7. How does the effect of tension acting on the surface of a low-crowned panel differ from the effect of pressure on a similar area?
8. What is displaced metal?
9. What is a simple bend?
10. What is a rolled buckle?
11. What is an upset?
12. What is a stretch?
13. Will all of the damage conditions—displaced areas, simple bends, rolled buckles, upsets, and stretches—be found on every damaged panel? Explain why or why not.
14. Where is the most severe distortion found in a rolled buckle?
15. Why is it easy to confuse stretched and upset metal?
16. In analyzing any damage, what can be learned by determining the impact angle?
17. A rifle bullet hole in a piece of sheet metal is shown in Fig 38; what would be the effect if an object of the same size and rigidity were pushed against an automobile door panel, using the full force of a 3-ton hydraulic jack?
18. What is the effect of inertia on a stationary object?
19. What is the effect of inertia on a moving object?
20. Why is the size of the damaged area not a dependable indication of the severity of damage?

3

Tools and Basic Operations

A knowledge of the proper use of the tools of the trade is necessary to understand the procedure of repairing even the simplest dent. Tools of some kind are required for every operation in straightening and preparing a damaged panel for repainting. Some of these operations require tools which normally are classified as shop equipment because of size and cost; others require only such items as may be classified as the metal man's hand tools. Both types of tools require the development of skill in their use. However, skill in the use of shop equipment is primarily in knowing where to use it. For example: comparatively little manual skill is required to set up a body jack, but it must be set up so that it will push against the right spot or it may do more damage than good. On the other hand, skill in the use of hand tools requires both knowledge and manual dexterity.

This chapter deals with the metal man's hand tools and the basic operations performed with them. The tools are discussed first, then the basic operations in which they are used. This has been done to explain the purpose of the individual tool and what may be expected of it before giving instruction for its use on an actual repair job.

The metal man's hand tools may be classified according to basic use, either straightening or metal finishing. Of course, some tools may be used in both basic operations but the primary use will be in one or the other. This chapter has been organized with this in mind. The first section deals with the metal straightening tools and the basic straightening operations. The second deals with the basic metal finishing tools and the basic metal finishing procedures.

METAL STRAIGHTENING TOOLS

To straighten damaged sheet metal, force is applied to restore it to original shape. This becomes a matter of straightening bends and relieving distortions. Tools used for this purpose are the means of applying the necessary force.

Metal straightening hand tools apply force by one or more of the following three ways: (1) striking a direct blow on the metal surface, (2) resistance to a direct blow struck on the opposite side of the metal, and (3) as a lever used to pry against the surface, usually on the inside.

It would be impractical to list every tool available for use in straightening sheet metal. The tools listed below may be considered as basic. They are: (1) bumping hammers, (2) dolly blocks, (3) bumping spoons, (4) body spoons, (5) pry or pick tools, (6) caulking tools, and (7) screw-equipped slide hammers.

Development of manual skill in the use of these tools is essential for the student who wishes to become a good metal man. This requires an understanding of the purpose of the tools and practicing to become proficient in their use.

Bumping Hammers

Bumping hammers are made in a wide range of styles, sizes, and combinations by the various manufacturers of body tools. Two very common styles are shown in Figs. 39 and 40.

The distinguishing feature of all bumping hammers is the one head which is quite wide and nearly flat on the working face. The width of this head may vary on different-style hammers, but most of the popular ones will be approximately 1½ inches. The most common shape for this head is round but some are made square. However, the exact size and shape of the hammer is not as important as having a hammer that is satisfactory to the person using it.

The large, nearly flat face serves to spread the force of a hammer blow over a fairly large area of the metal surface. This is essential in working with soft sheet metal. A smaller face or one having a high crown would tend to mark the metal when striking a hard blow on a spot backed up by the dolly block. The large, nearly flat face has the additional advantage of taking care of slight errors in aiming the hammer blow. This is particularly important in working on low-crown panels.

The shape of the slight crown on the large face is important. The ideal surface is almost dead flat in the center, blending into a crown around the outer edges. This flat center spot may be from ¾ to 1 inch in diameter. The outer edges should be rounded off enough to prevent making a sharp edge mark when a blow is struck with the hammer turned slightly from the proper angle.

In selecting a bumping hammer, it may be difficult to obtain one which fits this description exactly. In such cases, it is better to accept one which is nearly flat over the entire area because it is much easier to round off the edges than to flatten the center. This may be done by honing the edges down with a piece of fine, water resistant sandpaper wrapped around a stick of wood or a steel strap. Start with 220 or 260 grit and finish with 400 grit paper. A mirror finish can be put on the hammer face in this manner with very little effort. The same procedure can be used to maintain the hammer face when it becomes marked by rough use.

The opposite end of the bumping hammer is almost always different from the large head. The combination hammer, Fig. 40, is of the type most widely used. It is as much a metal finishing hammer as a bumping hammer. However, the hammer having the smaller round head, Fig. 39,

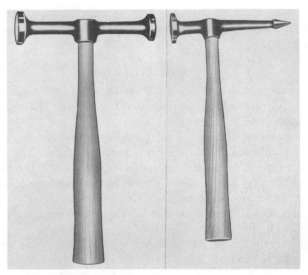

Fig. 39 General purpose hammer, sometimes called a dinging hammer.

Fig. 40 Combination bumping and picking hammer.

is an essential tool in straightening panels if its use is properly understood.

The small head is usually not used with the dolly block. It should have a much higher crown than the large head. It is used primarily to work out high spots and ridges in low-crowned panels. Light blows with this head, placed uniformly over the surface of a springy ridge, will straighten it easily. If the face of the hammer is properly polished, it is possible to work out many such areas so that they will require very little extra work to metal finish.

The same blow struck with the large head will not straighten springy areas nearly so well. The reason for this is that the large head spreads its force over too large an area. Instead of making a very slight bend at the point of contact, the force of the blow is wasted in flexing the surrounding metal. The smaller, higher crowned head reduces the area of contact enough to do more straightening and less flexing. It is simply a matter of straightening a large area a little at a time.

Much more detail in the use of the bumping hammer will be found in later chapters.

DOLLY BLOCKS

Dolly blocks vary so widely in size and shape that no general description can be applied to all of them. The purpose of all dolly blocks, however, is the same. They are used either as a striking tool or as a back-up tool for the bumping hammer. In both cases, the dolly normally is used on the underside, or inside, of the panel.

Four of the most common types of dolly blocks are shown in Figs. 41-44. Of these, the most frequently used will be the general-purpose

Fig. 41 *(Left)* General-purpose dolly block.

Fig. 42 *(Right)* Low-crowned general-purpose dolly block.

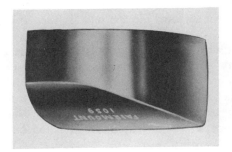

Fig. 43 Heel dolly block.

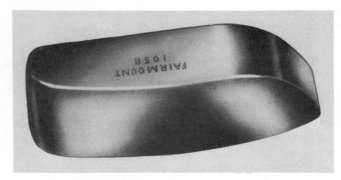

Fig. 44 Toe dolly block.

dolly shown in Fig. 41. This dolly has a variety of curves over its surface but its primary working face is the broad, smoothly curved upper section. The smaller, rounded lower section has some use as a working face but serves mostly as a hand hold.

The low-crowned, general-purpose dolly shown in Fig. 42 is similar to the one in Fig. 41 but its use is more limited. A dolly of this shape is very valuable when repairing low-crowned panels, but the working face will not fit into the shape of higher crowns.

The heel dolly, Fig. 43, and the toe dolly, Fig. 44, are both special-purpose tools. Being thinner, both of these may be used in narrow quarters where the larger general-purpose dolly cannot enter. They also provide a smooth, flat surface with sharp, right-angle edges for working flanges and sharp bends. Both of these are convenient tools to have; for various jobs, one of these will be better suited than the other.

Many other dolly blocks are available which are not discussed here. Many are as well suited to the job of metal straightening as the ones shown. Preference of a skilled metal man for a particular dolly block is a personal matter. It is much more important that the dolly block be satisfactory to the user than it is for him to use a particular one.

Used as a striking tool, the dolly is essentially a hand-held, handleless hammer. It is good practice to use a dolly in this manner to drive out simple dents. As the metal is brought out, the hammer is then brought into use as needed.

Used with the bumping hammer, the dolly is actually much more than just a back-up tool. Its primary purpose is to provide a reaction to the force of a hammer blow. When used properly, the dolly tends to raise the spot of metal which is in contact with its working face. This is true regardless of whether it is directly under the spot struck by the hammer or a short distance away. These operations are explained in detail in later sections of this chapter.

A very common misunderstanding of the use of a dolly block can be described as the anvil theory. Followers of this theory consider the dolly as a broad, smooth, anvil-like tool which is to be held on the underside of a buckle so that the metal can be driven down against it. The idea is very similar to the operation of straightening a bent nail by laying it on a flat surface and driving the bend down.

The rather widespread acceptance of the anvil theory accounts for the large number of dolly blocks available which have only one curve to the working face. In the cross direction, the working face will be flat. It is true that some metal straightening may be done in this manner, but it is not as effective as a properly shaped dolly used correctly. A dolly with the right crown on the working face will result in both faster and better work.

Two factors which must be considered in selecting a dolly block are weight and balance. For normal operation, the weight of the dolly block should be at least three times the weight of the hammer. This difference in weight is needed because the dolly is at rest when the hammer blow

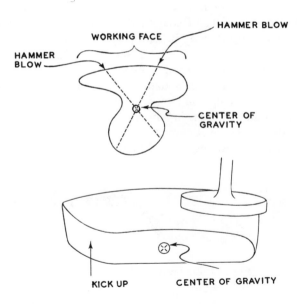

Fig. 45 *(Top)* Balance characteristics of the general-purpose dolly block. A hammer blow on almost any part of the working face will be directed toward the center of gravity.

Fig. 46 *(Bottom)* Balance characteristics of the toe dolly block. A hammer blow on either end will tend to cause the other to kick up because the center of gravity acts as a pivot.

strikes. The weight provides the inertia to resist the force of the hammer blow.

Balance is simply a matter of the distribution of the weight. This is illustrated in the sketches in Figs. 45 and 46. Note that the general-purpose dolly, Fig. 44, is shaped so that it is in balance regardless of where on the working face a hammer blow is struck. The toe dolly, Fig. 46, is only in balance when a blow is struck on its center area. A blow on either end will tend to cause it to roll, or kick, so that much of the effect of its weight is lost.

This is not to say that an unbalanced dolly is no good. Such dollies are special-purpose tools to be used where the better-balanced tools cannot enter. In the places where they are needed, they are the best tools available.

SPOONS

The term *spoon* is applied to so many body tools that it is difficult to define it accurately. However, a spoon is usually a bar of steel which has been forged flatter and thinner on one end, sometimes on both ends. It may be bent into a variety of shapes, depending on the use for which it is intended. The forged end, or ends, serve as a working face to use against the metal, and the rest of the bar serves as a handle.

Spoons are used for three basic purposes:

1. To spread the force of a hammer blow over a large area. Such spoons commonly are called dinging or bumping spoons.

2. As a dolly block in areas in which the inner construction limits access to the inner side. They are commonly called body spoons.

3. As a prying or driving tool. Heavy-duty body spoons are usually

Fig. 47 Low-crowned bumping spoon.

Fig. 48 High-crowned bumping spoon.

more satisfactory for this purpose than the lighter dinging spoons.

Bumping Spoons. A low-crowned bumping spoon is shown in Fig. 47 and a high-crowned spoon in Fig. 48. Both of these are light as compared to body spoons.

The primary purpose of the bumping spoon is to spread the force of a hammer blow over an area larger than the hammer face will cover. It is used to drive down long ridges which otherwise would require many more hammer blows. The job often will be done much faster by using a spoon, and a much smoother surface will result.

The low-crowned spoon is used more often than the high-crowned one, particularly on ridges which are quite stiff. The high-crowned spoon is a very worthwhile tool on springy metal. In many cases, it will work out a ridge which will only snap in and out if the low crowned spoon is used. This is because the higher crown concentrates force on a smaller area.

More detailed information on the use of bumping spoons will be found in the next section dealing with the basic operations.

Body Spoons. The body spoon must be quite heavy and rugged as compared with the dinging spoon. Body spoons are used for three basic purposes: (1) as a substitute for the dolly block, (2) as a driving tool, particularly where inner construction prevents a direct blow with a hammer or dolly block, and (3) as a pry tool behind inner construction.

The effectiveness of a body spoon as a substitute for a dolly block varies according to its shape and size. Balance is as important with the spoon as it is with the dolly block, but in many cases it is difficult to obtain. Balance is determined by the shape of the spoon, as shown by the sketches in Fig. 49. The shape is determined by conditions of the job rather than the preference of the user. Unless the spoon is shaped so that it can be

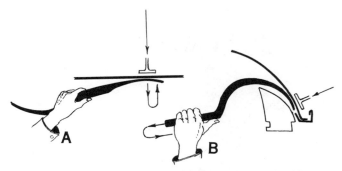

Fig. 49 Balance characteristics of body spoons. Sketch *A:* this spoon has no balance because the weight does not support the working face. Sketch *B:* this spoon has good balance.

put into operating position on the underside of the panel, it is useless. This creates a need for a wide variety of spoons of different shapes to fit the conditions found in various jobs. It is desirable to use a balanced spoon where possible. However, if the balanced spoon will not fit into the space under a particular panel, it will be necessary to use one which will. As with the unbalanced dolly block, the limited effectiveness of the unbalanced spoon is better than none.

Body spoons are used as prying and driving tools about as much as they are used as a dolly block substitute. In either driving or prying, it is a matter of working a panel on which the access to the inner side is obstructed. Such use will make it possible to work out areas which could not be straightened satisfactorily without cutting out inner construction.

This should not be interpreted as an attempt to establish the exact kinds of damage which can be worked with a body spoon. This must be done by examination of the individual job and making the best use of whatever tools are available.

The seven spoons shown in Fig. 50-56 are typical; some of these will be found in most metal men's tool kits. The basic features and general uses of each one are described separately in the following paragraphs.

The spoon shown in Fig. 50 is primarily a pry tool. The rather long, thin, curved blade can be inserted into very narrow spaces to pry out dents. It is not intended to serve as a dolly block, but it may be used as such when propped against rigid inner construction.

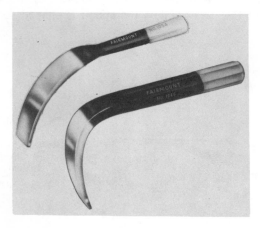

Fig. 50 *(Top)* Pry spoon.

Fig. 51 *(Bottom)* General-purpose body spoon, originally called a turret top spoon.

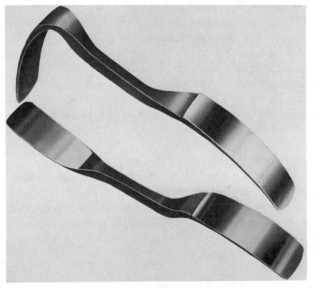

Fig. 52 *(Top)* General-purpose body spoon. Working faces on both ends and extra length make this spoon particularly useful on door and deck lid panels.

Fig. 53 *(Bottom)* Large offset spoon.

Fig. 54 Rough service spoon; also useful as a caulking tool.

The spoon shown in Fig. 51 is a general-purpose body spoon. It was originally called a turret top spoon because of the long working face which can be inserted between the roof rail and the roof panel. It may be used as a dolly block very satisfactorily because its shape provides good balance. It makes a very effective offset driving tool when held in a position so that the end of the handle can be struck with a heavy hammer. It can be used for prying also.

The spoon shown in Fig. 52 has working faces on both ends. The bent end serves very satisfactorily as a dolly block substitute. It is long enough to reach deep into restricted space where heavier tools cannot enter and heavy enough to provide considerable reaction to a hammer blow. The right-angle working face is particularly useful on door panels, and both faces are ideally suited to many deck lid jobs.

The spoon shown in Fig. 53 is both a dolly block substitute and a pry tool. It works very well in doors and deck lids, but it has many other uses, especially where the offset is needed to reach around inner construction. The chief disadvantage of this spoon is that it is completely out of balance. This is partially offset, however, by its extra weight.

The spoon shown in Fig. 54 is essentially a rough service tool. It has the best balance of any of those shown here when used as a dolly block substitute. The end of the working face makes an excellent caulking tool. When used in this manner, it is held by the short, curved end and the hammer blows struck against the raised pad on the handle. It is rugged enough to use with a hammer of any weight.

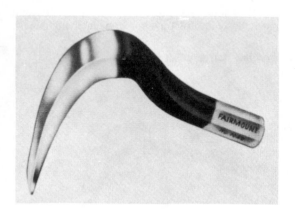

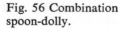

Fig. 55 Small general-purpose spoon.

Fig. 56 Combination spoon-dolly.

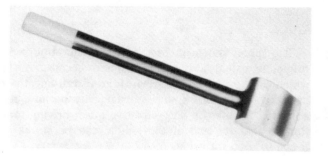

The spoon shown in Fig. 55 is a smaller general-purpose tool. The offset in the handle gives it excellent balance and makes it a fine driving tool. Being small and relatively heavy, it is a good dolly block substitute in any spot where it will fit.

The tool shown in Fig. 56 is a general-purpose tool which is actually a combination of spoon and dolly block. It is the ideal tool for use as a dolly block in areas which are beyond normal reach. It also serves well as a caulking tool in many areas. It is heavy enough to withstand the use of any weight hammer when used as a driving tool.

There are many other spoons in addition to those shown here. These have been selected as being representative but not necessarily the only suitable ones. The metal man who is interested in doing his job properly will be in constant need of new tools as the design of the automobile bodies changes. The man who only is interested in learning enough to "get by" and depends on panel replacement to solve all of his tough problems, regardless of cost to his customers, may not feel this need.

PRY OR PICK TOOLS

The use of spoons as pry tools has been discussed. Many other tools may be used for the same purpose in straightening panels where inner construction limits access to the inner surface. Usually such tools are made of tempered steel rods.

Although pry tools may be used on any panel, their most frequent use is on doors. By using pry rods, it often is possible to avoid removing the trim panel or disassembling other parts. Drain holes in the lower facing of the door offer convenient openings through which the tools may be inserted; other holes may be pierced in the facings where needed. Often there is much less work involved in closing such holes than is needed to disassemble the door trim or, sometimes, to remove the door from the body.

The set of pry rods shown in Fig. 57 is very satisfactory for most prying operations. The smaller ones are mainly punches which may be used both to pierce holes and to pry out small dents close to the edge of the panel. The two long bars which have handles formed on one end are for use on dents which are farther from the edge. The bar (lower left) which has the deep bend is for reaching around inner construction.

The special tool shown in Fig. 58 is for reaching deep into narrow spaces to raise metal. It allows close control of the position of the point because the two handles provide two-hand operation. The tool consists of a long, curved rod which has a lever rod clamped to it at a right angle. It may be used as a simple pry, but it is most effective when used by twisting it with the attached lever. In any panel where inner construction is close enough, the long, nearly straight section will lie against the inner

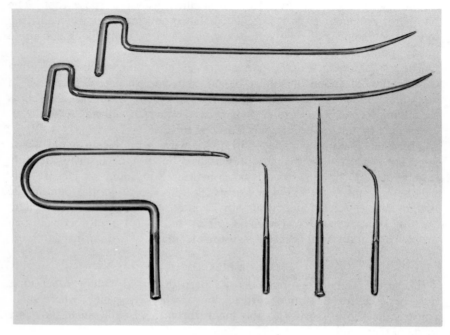

Fig. 57 Set of pry rods.

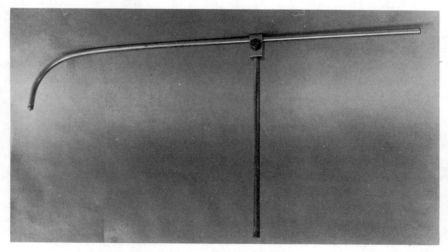

Fig. 58 Special twist action pry rod.

panel as the point is raised against the outer panel. The advantage is that it has the same leverage regardless of the depth to which it is inserted in the panel. Its greatest disadvantage lies in the size of the hole required for it to enter. This is not a disadvantage, of course, when it is inserted through a glass opening or other openings provided by the construction of the panel.

DENT PULLER

A slide hammer equipped with a sheet metal screw, Fig. 59, commonly called a dent puller, has come into common use. The dented area is pierced with one or more holes as needed; the tool is screwed into the holes; and the area lifted by operating the slide hammer. The action is similar to the use of a pry rod except that the lifting is done from the outside instead of from the inside. Unlike the pry rod, which does not pierce the metal, the surface must be finished by filling to cover and seal the holes.

Several reasons account for the growing popularity of the dent puller. Probably one of the most important is the growing popularity of the use of plastic body filler. When filling is substituted for metal finishing, the screw holes in the panel surface will be hidden automatically. Another reason is the growing complexity of automobile body construction. Access to the inside of many panels is blocked by welded-in inner panels and window mechanisms. Using a dent puller, the repair man can often repair a simple dent in less time than would be required to make the disassembly necessary to start the repair by other means.

The dent puller has a definite place in straightening sheet metal. However, it should be pointed out that its simplicity of use can lead to its misuse. It is senseless mutilation to pierce a large number of holes in the surface of a panel which could and should have been straightened by other means. The result can be an unsatisfactory job. Worse, it may be that more time was required to do it wrong than would have been re-

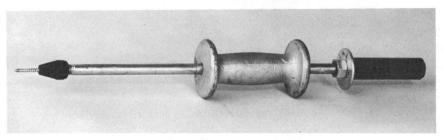

Fig. 59 Screw equipped slide hammer.

quired to do it right. The previous statement is based on the assumption that the repair man has developed the necessary skills.

Caulking, Driving, and Bending Tools

There are so many special-purpose tools used for straightening sheet metal that it would be impossible to list them all. The three tools shown in Figs. 60-62 are typical. Many others are used for the same or similar purposes.

The tool shown in Fig. 60 is for caulking. It looks as if it were a blunt, wide-bladed chisel. It is used for reshaping short radius bends or narrow, flat surfaces. A wide variety of caulking tools is needed to do the various caulking jobs normally found when repairing severely damaged panels. These tools may be of different lengths, and the shape of the working ends may vary from almost sharp to wide and flat.

The tool shown in Fig. 61 is a special-purpose caulking tool for straightening flanges. It is particularly suited to straightening the bead section of fenders, but it may be used on any flange which is turned away from the operator's side. In use, one end is hooked into the flange to be straightened, and the other end is held by the operator as he strikes hammer blows on the bar, close to the panel.

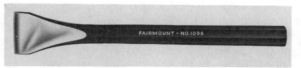

Fig. 60 Caulking iron.

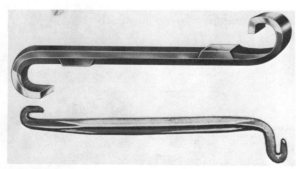

Fig. 61 *(Top)* Special flange straightening and offset caulking tool.

Fig. 62 *(Bottom)* Flange bender.

The tool shown in Fig. 62 is for bending narrow flanges, In use, the slot formed by the bend in the end is slipped over the edge of the flange, and the tool either is turned or twisted to make the desired bend.

BASIC STRAIGHTENING OPERATIONS

The purpose of this section is to explain and describe the uses of the straightening tools which have been discussed in the previous sections. These uses are basic, because they are essentially the same, regardless of the job. For example: the motions in using a hammer and dolly block would be very much the same on any panel on which they would be used. The difference between the procedure for panels having different kinds of damage is in the knowledge and judgment exercised in deciding where the basic operations should be used.

Two premises have served as guides in organizing this section. The first is that the student should be given a thorough understanding of the expected effect on the metal when the tool is used properly. The second is that the student must have an opportunity to develop a basic skill before using it to make an actual repair. The procedures and the effects which may be expected follow. Such knowledge is essential to rapid skill development. However, the responsibility for this development rests with the individual who wishes to gain the skill; both study and practice are necessary.

This section should be used as a guide for the student in studying and practicing the basic operations. Before actual repair work is attempted, these operations should be practiced until the motions become easy and the desired results can be accomplished. Such practice work can be done either on a piece of sheet metal mounted in the practice rack shown in Fig. 374, Chapter 9, or on undamaged areas of scrap panels. The knowledge and experience gained from such practice will enable the beginner to see the application of the basic operations to the conditions he will find on an actual damaged area. For example: having learned to raise an area of low metal by using the hammer and dolly block on a scrap panel, the student will find it easy to use this skill on a real panel.

USING THE HAMMER AND DOLLY BLOCK

The bumping hammer and dolly block are discussed first because they are the most important and versatile of the metal man's hand tools for straightening metal. They are also the easiest to misuse, because the difference between proper and improper use is often very slight. In most cases, misuse will tend to cause additional damage. Also, in many cases it is possible to restore the surface appearance of a damaged panel by picking and filing or by filling, even though the proper use of a hammer and dolly would do it better in less time. The fact that such work can be done "somehow" often leads the beginner to continue with less than the best methods. It is quite possible for a metal man to have good hammers and dolly blocks in his possession for many years without discovering their full usefulness.

The dolly block is used both with and without the hammer. Used alone, it is an excellent tool for striking the inner surface to rough out simple dents or to complete the roughing out of areas which are being jacked into place. Used with the hammer, the combination becomes a highly efficient means of smoothing the roughed-out surface.

There are two distinct and separate uses of the dolly in relation to the hammer. The dolly may be held directly under the spot struck by the hammer face, or it may be held to one side. These procedures should be classified as *hammer-on-dolly* and *hammer-off-dolly*.

HAMMER-ON-DOLLY

The first step in learning to use the hammer-on-dolly is to develop the skill necessary to place the dolly under the metal and strike a hammer blow directly on it. This often seems to be an impossible task to the beginner, but it is actually an easy one to master. Of course practice is important, and it is easier for some than for others, because it is essentially a matter of co-ordination between the hand and the eye. Even though the hand holding the dolly is out of sight under the panel, the student soon learns to bring any spot on the face of the dolly into contact with the spot he strikes. With practice, this can be done as easily as though the surface were transparent.

Light to medium hammer blows should be used when practicing to hit the dolly. The grip and swing of the hand and arm in striking the blow are important. Frequently, the beginner has learned to use a hammer to drive nails and on such tools as chisels and punches. If this is true, he has an unlearning process to go through before he can expect to use the hammer-on-dolly as it should be used.

The difference in using the bumping hammer and other hammers is in the follow-through at the end of the stroke. In most other uses, it is natural to maintain the same grip on the handle throughout the stroke so that when the head hits the surface the hand still will be exerting a downward effort. This is desirable when driving a nail or a punch because it adds to the effectiveness of the blow. However, this method is harmful when striking the surface of a panel directly over the spot supported by the dolly block. It upsets the timing of the operation by driving the dolly away from contact before the hammer blow stops; it can cause denting; and it will interfere with the rebound action of the dolly.

The bumping hammer should be held lightly, and the grip slackened as the blow descends on the metal. This is easy to do by forming the habit

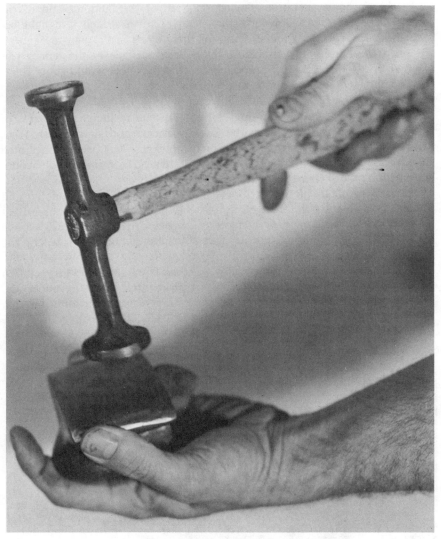

Fig. 63 Proper grip on hammer and dolly block.

of gripping the handle with only the third and fourth fingers. The thumb aids in starting the blow, and the first two fingers are used to snap the handle back after the blow is finished. The blow should be started with a snap action of the wrist rather than a full arm movement. The snap action will be made easier if the handle is held at a slight angle to the forearm. Proper grip of both hammer and dolly is shown in Fig. 63.

In the on-dolly operation, the action both of the hammer and of the dolly is concentrated on a very small spot of metal which is caught between the faces of both tools. Some of these spots are shown in Fig. 64. Before this photograph was taken, the painted surface of the fender was scuffed lightly with 320 grit sandpaper so that the spots would show clearly. Scuffing causes the spots to appear slightly larger than they would otherwise. The effect is the same, however.

The effect of a hammer-on-dolly blow is to *tend* to increase the area of the spot and to raise it above the level of the surrounding metal. This action is illustrated in Fig. 65. The metal thickness has been exaggerated so that the effect on it can be visualized better. The sequence of action, as shown by the sketches, is as follows:

1. The hammer blow is stopped by the inertia of the dolly and bounces off to start the next blow. At this point, the metal spot caught between the hammer and dolly faces is subjected to a compressive force which tends to spread and thin it. This spreading action is resisted by the surrounding metal.

2. Energy from the hammer blow is transferred through the metal to the dolly block, driving the dolly away from contact with the underside. Inertia of the dolly plus the hand pressure on it causes a definite time lag

Fig. 64 Contact spots made by a hammer-on-dolly on a sanded paint surface.

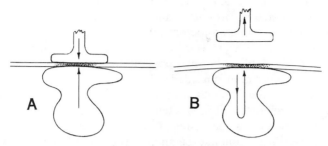

Fig. 65 Action of a hammer-on-dolly blow. Sketch *A* represents the instant of impact. Sketch *B* represents a fraction of a second later when the hammer is moving away and the dolly block has rebounded, lifting the metal surface.

between this movement and the hammer blow. It is this lag which permits the hammer to bounce away from the surface.

3. Hand pressure stops the movement of the dolly and snaps it back into contact with the underside of the metal. This is a definite impact which tends to drive the metal surface up. The effect of this is proportional to the amount of hand pressure applied to the dolly. It is very effective when heavy pressure is applied. This final lifting action, coupled with the spreading action which occurs first, can be used to raise large areas by spacing hammer-on-dolly blows over it properly.

Variable Factors. Three variable factors must be controlled or selected closely to obtain desired results when using the hammer-on-dolly. These factors are: (1) the force of the hammer blow, (2) the crown of the working face of the dolly block in contact with the underside, and (3) the amount of hand pressure applied to the dolly block.

The effect of the force of the hammer blow is the most obvious, but the others are of equal importance. For example: two hammer blows of equal force would have different effects on the same area of metal if different-shaped dollies were used with them. If a dolly with a working face that fitted exactly to the inside surface was used with the first blow, the force would be spread over the largest possible area. This would cause the minimum amount of spreading, or stretching, and almost completely eliminate the lifting effect of the rebound. If a dolly with a working face having a much higher crown was used with the second blow, the force would be concentrated on a much smaller area of metal; there would be a corresponding increase in the lifting action of the rebound because the smaller area would offer less resistance.

The effect of varying the hand pressure would be the greatest on the high-crowned working face, but there would be some difference noticeable with a low crown which fitted the inside surface of the metal. A lightly held dolly will cause the least lift; increasing the hand pressure will increase the lifting action proportionally. However, there is an effective limit to the increase that may be expected. Hand pressure past this limit will result in no extra gain and sometimes may be undesirable. This limit is difficult to establish, but it is possible for a man of average physical strength to apply more than is needed.

The tendency of the hammer used on-dolly to increase area and raise the surface is commonly called stretching. Technically, this is incorrect, because true stretching is the result of an application of force in tension. However, the result is similar even though the force is applied in exactly the opposite manner. Because it is widely accepted, the term stretching also is used here in referring to the effect on the metal of the hammer-on-dolly.

Stretching on-dolly is an important operation in the repair of at least some of the area of almost all damages because of the tendency of the folding action to cause upsets. This is particularly true in the break-over path of a rolled buckle. There are also other areas where this operation is equally important. Of course, it must be used carefully.

Many times, the beginner is cautioned against using the hammer-on-dolly at all because of the risk of overstretching. When overstretching occurs, it is the result of either using the hammer-on-dolly too much or where it shouldn't be at all. Rather than avoiding the procedure entirely, the beginner should practice until he learns to recognize where and how much the hammer should be used on-dolly; he also should develop enough skill to perform the operation correctly. Such knowledge and skill will show up both in the quality of the work he does and in the speed with which he does it.

HAMMER-OFF-DOLLY

The first step in learning the hammer-off-dolly operation is to develop the skill necessary to place the dolly in the right spot when the hammer blow strikes. This spot will be close to but away from the spot on which the hammer blow falls. The skill needed to find this spot is similar to that required to locate the spot under the hammer for on-dolly use. After the beginner has mastered the problem of placing the dolly under the hammer, it is relatively easy for him to learn to place it away from the hammer.

The next step is learning to judge exactly where the dolly should be placed to accomplish the desired result. This is a matter of locating high and low spots visually and moving the dolly under the proper one for each hammer blow. This is a continuing situation, because the spot must be chosen each time a hammer blow is struck.

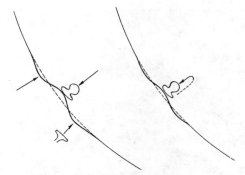

Fig. 66 *(Left)* Using the hammer-off-dolly. The dolly should be held firmly against the low spot before the hammer blow falls.

Fig. 67 *(Right)* The dolly rebounds after the hammer blow, increasing the lift effect on the low spot.

The action of the hammer-off-dolly differs from the action on-dolly in the first contact. Since it is not being supported by the dolly, the spot struck by the hammer is driven down. Movement of the metal transfers the force of the hammer blow to the dolly so that it rebounds in much the same manner as with an on-dolly blow. The result, as illustrated in Figs. 66 and 67, is to drive the high spot down and raise the adjoining low spot with a single hammer blow.

A small dent in a combination high- and low-crown area is shown in Fig. 68. The same dent, after straightening by use of the hammer off-dolly, is shown in Fig. 69. The only force applied to the underside of this dent to raise it back to the proper level was a firm hand pressure on the dolly and the rebound action which resulted.

The procedure for straightening this dent is explained in detail because it is the key to understanding the proper use of the hammer-off-dolly. It is particularly important to note that no hammer blows were struck on either side of the dent; all of the hammer work was done above and below it. The reason for this is that, being a combination high and low crown, metal was raised above and below the dent but not on either side. In striking the high metal, it was driven toward the proper level by the hammer blow; a fraction of a second later the rebound of the dolly returned a large part of the force of the hammer blow to the underside of the dent, lifting it toward the proper level.

Hammer blows on either side of this dent would have fallen on metal that was already pulled below the proper level instead of being pushed

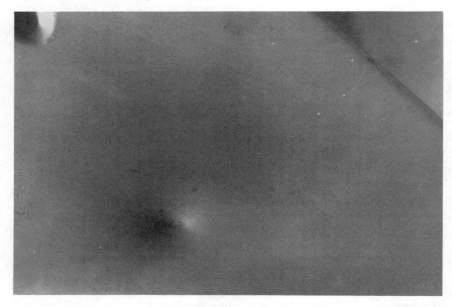

Fig. 68 A small dent in a combination high- and low-crown section of a fender.

Fig. 69 The dent in Fig. 68 after straightening by use of hammer-off-dolly blows.

above. This simply would be driving low metal lower. Instead of accomplishing a repair, hammer blows on either side would tend to add damage to that already existing.

It is recommended that any student learning to use the hammer-off-dolly should study the effect of small dents such as this on combination crowns. A pattern of high and low metal similar to that shown in Fig. 25 in Chapter 2 always will be found. This particular dent was made by striking a high-crowned section of a fender with the rounded end of the handle section of a general-purpose dolly block. This may be repeated on any scrap fender having the proper shape. Making such dents and working them smooth again without striking the underside is one of the exercises recommended for learning to use the hammer and dolly.

If this hammer-off-dolly procedure is understood properly, there should be no difficulty in recognizing the importance of the following rule: *when using the hammer-off-dolly, a hammer blow should never be struck except on metal which has been raised above the proper level.* This rule applies in every case. It is even more important to remember in straightening a severe rolled buckle than on this simple dent.

Following this same reasoning, the importance of this second rule should be recognized immediately: *the first hammer blows should fall on the high metal farthest from the dent, and following blows should work inward progressively.* When this procedure is followed, the affected area will be made smaller progressively. On the minor dent shown in Fig. 68, this is simply a matter of closing in from each side. When the same procedure is used on a long buckle, it is a matter of making it narrower progressively.

Variable Factors. Four variable factors must be considered when using the hammer-off-dolly. These factors are: (1) the force of the hammer blow, (2) the crown of the working face of the dolly, (3) the amount of hand pressure applied to the dolly block, and (4) the distance between the hammer contact and the dolly contact.

The first three factors are the same as those given for the use of the hammer-on-dolly. The reasons why these three apply to both procedures are not exactly the same however. Each of them is discussed separately.

When working off-dolly, the force of the hammer blow must be limited just enough to drive the high spot down to level. Less force will not accomplish the desired result and more will do damage. The student must learn to gauge this accurately by observation. Unlike when hammering on-dolly, the dolly is not under the hammer to stop the blow by inertia.

When striking a hammer blow close to but still slightly off-dolly, the result may be almost an on-dolly blow if a low-crowned dolly is used.

However, a high-crowned dolly will have a much smaller contact and permit use of the hammer without interference. In almost every case, when working off-dolly rather than when working on-dolly, it is better to use a higher crowned dolly, or a higher crowned part of the working face of the general-purpose dolly. When the hammer blows are intermixed, this is just a matter of shifting the dolly slightly to bring a different part of the face into contact—that is, if a dolly with the proper crown variations is being used.

The amount of hand pressure applied to the dolly is particularly important when working off-dolly because most of the lifting action is by muscular reaction. Since the dolly is not under the hammer, its inertia does less to stop the blow than it does when working on-dolly. The force of the blow is transferred through the metal to move the dolly outward against hand pressure, but there is a definite time lag because the hammer blow is not stopped instantly. The shock action of the dolly rebound is greater than the shock action of the inertia resistance offered to the hamer blow. It is the shock action which raised the metal. This can be proved easily by experimenting with more and less pressure on the dolly.

Any beginner who practices this properly will find that he can make a tremendous increase in the lifting effect of the rebound. This is because he becomes conditioned to the movement so that considerable muscular effort is added to the rebound by reflex action.

The distance between the points contacted by the hammer and dolly affect the operation in two ways. If the points are too far apart, the force of the hammer blow will not be transferred to the dolly because the flexing action of the surface does not reach that far. This varies with the surface condition being worked. In a relatively stiff area, a distance between the hammer and dolly contact of more than ½ inch may be ineffective. However, in a springy area, it may be possible to use the dolly effectively at much greater distances.

If the hammer and dolly contact points are too close together, there is a problem of interference. Interference means that, instead of striking off-dolly, the hammer strikes a blow which is in effect a misdirected on-dolly blow instead. Interference will be much greater with a low-crowned dolly than with a high-crowned one, which makes it desirable to do most off-dolly work with the high-crowned part of the dolly working face. Also, the effect of interference can be reduced by proper gauging of the force of the hammer blow. No damage can be done if the hammer face does not strike too hard against the dolly even though there is interference.

In some cases, interference between the hammer and dolly may be desirable. The metal man who has developed a high level of skill will have learned to combine the effects of hammering on- and off-dolly as he needs them. The beginner should not attempt to do this, however, until he has developed the necessary skill with the simpler operations.

BUMPING SPOONS

The skill required to use a bumping spoon with a hammer is relatively easy to acquire compared to the skill needed to use the hammer and dolly block. The primary difference is that the spoon works as a part of the hammer blow instead of proving a secondary reaction to it, as the dolly block does.

The purpose of the bumping spoon is to spread the force of the hammer blow over a much larger area than the bumping hammer face can cover. It is best suited to straightening long, relatively smooth buckles. The distortion in such buckles is comparatively light but is spread over a large area. Straightening could be done by using the hammer alone. However, many light blows would have to be spread over the area, and it would be difficult to avoid making damaging hammer marks. The larger contact area of the working face of the spoon is much easier to control, so that such damage is kept to the minimum or avoided entirely. Also, this method is faster in most cases.

The shape, or crown, of the working face of the bumping spoon determines the exact use to which it is best adapted. A flat or nearly flat face is best for high-crowned or combination high- and low-crowned areas. Such areas are quite stiff and require considerable force to relieve the distortion which causes the buckle.

A spoon with a higher crowned working face is best suited to buckles in low-crowned panels. The metal on either side of such a buckle will be springy instead of stiff, as on the high-crowned panel. The springiness reduces the support which the area provides for the buckle. The high-crowned spoon contacts only a small area, concentrating the force of the hammer blow on it. Thus, it actually will straighten such an area better than a flat-faced spoon. The larger contact area of the flat spoon will only tend to spring the entire buckle.

The procedure for using either spoon is essentially the same. Fig. 70 shows a bumping spoon in position. Note that the center area of the working face is in contact with the metal surface and the hammer is directly over this spot. Note also that a ball-peen hammer is used instead of the bumping hammer; a good bumping hammer never should be used for such a purpose.

The handle of the spoon should be gripped lightly so that the hand does not tend to resist movement. Even though the spoon is being used on metal which is quite stiff, there will be some tendency for the entire area to flex with the hammer blow. The spoon must be free for this

Fig. 70 Bumping spoon in position for the hammer blow.

movement. If the hand resists downward movement of the handle, Fig. 70, there will be a tendency to drive the opposite end of the working face down too far. This may cause damaging marks, particularly when using a spoon which has a flat working face.

Most of the damaged areas where a bumping spoon is the proper tool to use are too wide to be corrected with a single hammer blow. It will be necessary to strike a series of hammer blows as the spoon is moved back and forth across the buckle. On long buckles, work progressively down the length in a somewhat zigzag pattern.

In using a spoon on any buckle, start at the point of least distortion. On most buckles which remain after a rolled buckle has been worked out, this point would be as far from the break-over path as distortion could be detected.

The bumping spoon is most effective when it is used on a buckle which is under a strain that tends to straighten it. Such conditions will be found occasionally in minor damage on relatively flat panels. The experienced metal man learns to recognize the damaged panel that will snap back to shape after a buckle has been spooned down, leaving only minor damage actually to work out. However, such conditions are the exception rather than the rule. In most cases, the spoon should not be used until

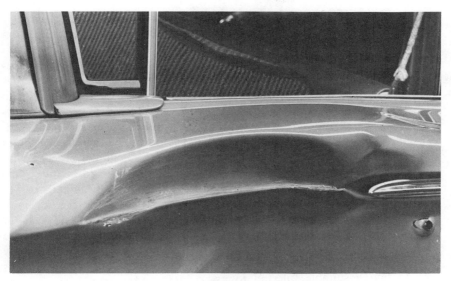

Fig. 71 Ridge which is too sharp for use of the bumping spoon.

most of the unfolding has been completed by other means. Spooning out remaining buckles is very often the final straightening operation.

A very common mistake of the beginner is to use a bumping spoon on a buckle that is too sharp. Metal that has been folded over so that the buckle forms a sharp ridge, as in Fig. 71, should not be spooned down because it is too rigid. Striking the top of such a ridge may cause upsetting. After such a ridge has been partly straightened by the proper methods, described in later sections, the spoon would be a very logical means of finishing the straightening operation.

Body Spoons

Skill in the use of body spoons is entirely different from the skill required to use a bumping spoon. And, in most cases it is more complicated. This is because the body spoon is used on the underside of the panel as either a substitute for the dolly block or as a pry tool.

The body spoon is never used for repairing any panel in which a dolly block has free access to the inner surface. Such a panel can be straightened better and faster with the dolly block. The use of the body spoon is made necessary by the inner construction found on many panels which limits access so that only a relatively long, thin tool may be used. Without such a tool, the metal man would be forced either to cut out the inner construction or to depend entirely on filling to repair damage on such panels. With a good set of body spoons, the metal man can repair many panels faster and with a minimum amount of filling or mutilation caused by cutting out and welding back inner construction.

Exact instructions for the use of the body spoons cannot be given because they are available in so many shapes for use in many different areas and damage conditions. The discussion of procedure must be limited to general suggestions. This is less of a handicap than it may seem, however, for the suggestions offered are simply variations of the basic procedure for using the dolly block. It is recommended that the beginner delay his practice with body spoons until he has had enough practice with the dolly block to develop some degree of skill. This should include some actual repair work on simple damage. At that time, the beginner's use of the body spoon will present far fewer problems than if he tries to use it before he develops the basic skill.

The body spoon may be used alone to pry out low metal or with the hammer. Used alone, it serves exactly the same purpose as the dolly block when the latter is used as a striking tool. Usually the main problems are to find a suitable fulcrum to pry against and to avoid making pry marks in the surface.

Used with the bumping hammer, the body spoon serves the same purpose as the dolly block. The difference is that the body spoon is more difficult to use and is less effective. This is because the working face of the spoon extends several inches from the hand; the sense of feel, which helps in locating the dolly block, is almost totally absent. The result is a tendency of the body spoon to wander after each hammer blow against it. This effect is greater from a hard hammer blow than from a light one. Thus an effective limit is placed on the force of the hammer blow, which in turn places a similar limit on the force of the rebound action of the spoon.

A second factor affecting the effectiveness of the spoon as a substitute for a dolly block is balance. This varies with the shape of the spoon, as was shown in Fig. 49. A spoon having the working face at or close to a right angle to the handle may be in almost perfect balance so that the only problem is the sense of feel. Another having the working face parallel with the handle will have practically no balance at all. The rebound action obtainable with such a spoon is limited for two reasons: one, the operator's grip is at a mechanical disadvantage; and, two, very little of the weight of the spoon is under the working face to provide resistance to the hammer blow.

As with the dolly block, the choice of a body spoon is governed by the conditions of the panel to be repaired. Only to a limited extent can it be determined by personal preference. In many areas of the body, a well-balanced spoon would be useless because its shape would prevent it from fitting into place. If work is to be done in such places, tools to do the job are needed. If it happens that a well-balanced tool can be used, fine; if it happens that an unbalanced spoon is all that can be used, it will be the best tool for the job.

PRY TOOLS

Skill in the use of pry tools is a matter of good judgment more than anything else. The judgment required is to recognize the spot or area which should be raised by prying and the proper tool to use. As with the body spoons, the reason for using any kind of pry tool is that access to the inner surface of the panel is limited by inner construction.

The use of pry tools is discussed here as a part of the basic operations of metal straightening. The same procedure is used in metal finishing. It is difficult to make a clear distinction between prying in straightening and in metal finishing, and there is no particular reason for doing so. The suggestions and cautions given here apply also to the metal-finishing operations and will not be repeated in discussion of that subject later.

Fig. 72 Use of a pry rod tool through an enlarged drain hole in the lower edge of a quarter panel.

The use of a pry tool should be considered as a last resort. If the area can be worked with other tools, particularly the hammer and dolly block or a pick hammer, it will be better to do so. A roughened surface always results when a blunt tool is used to raise the metal by prying against the underside. The extent to which the surface is roughened is determined by the shape of the tool and how carefully it is used. This is where the operator's good judgment is important.

Use of a pry tool is shown in Fig. 72. Access for the pry rod was made by enlarging one of the drain holes in the lower facing. These holes will be found on all door panels because they are needed to provide an escape for the water which enters beside the sliding door glass. They are always located so that the water drains to the outside of the weather strip.

In many cases, it is necessary to pierce holes in the facing of a door to permit use of pry tools where there is no drain hole. Such holes should be outside of the weatherstrip wherever possible. Whether a hole is made inside or outside of the weatherstrip, it should be closed in some manner to restore the door to its original condition.

On all jobs where pry tools are used, avoid using too much force. The area to be raised may be small enough to require prying at only one spot, but, if so, it will be the exception rather than the rule. Usually it will be necessary to move the point of the pry tool to several points rather than to pry on only one. The beginner often is tempted to pry too hard, making sharp bumps on the surface. Grinding or filing sharp bumps either can make a thin spot or even cut through the surface. It is a much better technique to lift a little at a time over a wider area than to pry up a sharp bump.

As with the body spoons, it is recommended that the beginner delay his attempts to use pry tools until he has had an opportunity to develop some skill with the hammer and dolly block and the pick hammer. He will find that any place on which he must use the pry tool, he will do as well or better if he uses the basic tools instead.

USE OF THE DENT PULLER

The primary purpose of the dent puller is to lift out dents. Restricted to simple dents which cannot be reached easily to be lifted out by other means, it is a valuable and almost essential tool. Simple dents, gouges, and creases which are too deep to fill without using an excessive amount of material can often be brought out so that only a moderate amount of filler is needed. The result is a saving in both time and material.

The creased gouge in Fig. 73 is an example of a damaged area which must have some straightening done before filling will be practical. A sharp object, probably the end of an automobile bumper, has been dragged across the character line, crushing it and making a deep dent

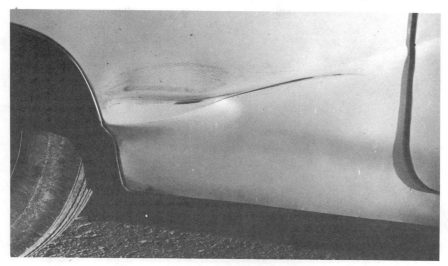

Fig. 73 Lower quarter panel, gouged and rubbed by a bumper.

just forward of the wheel opening. Formation of the dent has pushed an area of metal, just above it, much too high. Some straightening is essential before this area can be finished by filling because it is necessary to bring this high metal down to the proper level. Even excessive filling would not produce a satisfactory job under these circumstances.

Straightening this by removing the trim panel and working from the inside is not as satisfactory as it might seem because the access hole in the inner panel is not located over the dent. Furthermore, the window mechanism fills so much of the space within the panel that there is no room to work unless it is removed. Removing and replacing the window mechanism, plus cutting out and rewelding a hole for access to the panel amount to a lot of preliminary work in addition to the actual straightening. The preliminary work would take more time than would be required to straighten it from the outside with the dent puller and finish it by filling. This is the type of repair job on which the dent puller justifies its use in time saved.

The lifting operation is shown in Fig. 74. Using the disc sander, the paint has been ground off the deep part of the gouge and a row of holes pierced in it. Grinding off the paint before piercing the holes is always good practice. After piercing the holes and using the puller, the surface is roughened so that it is difficult to grind it without cutting through or leaving large areas of paint. The paint must be removed if good adhesion of the filler is expected. The holes can be drilled, but punching is prefer-

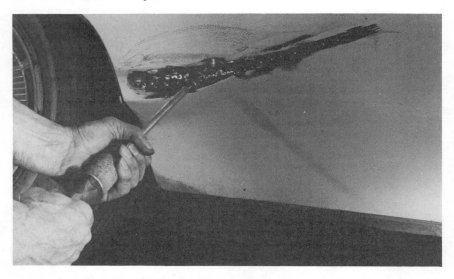

Fig. 74 Using the dent puller on the gouge. Paint has been ground off before piercing holes for the dent puller screws.

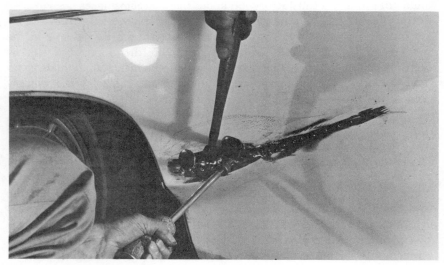

Fig. 75 Holding tension on the dent puller while the hammer is used on the high metal beside the gouge.

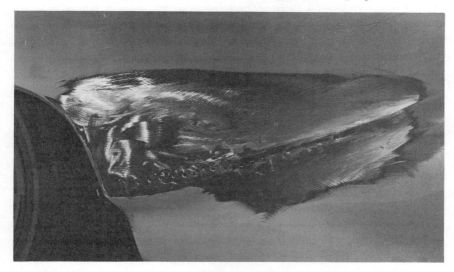

Fig. 76 The damaged area prepared for filling. Outer edges were filed lightly to outline the area to be filled.

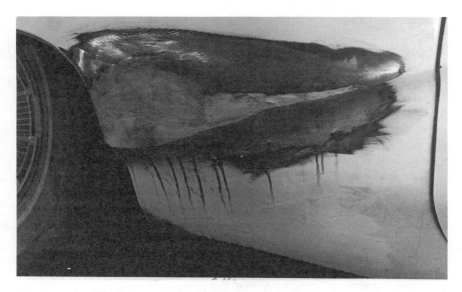

Fig. 77 The damaged area after filling with solder. Streaks are due to hot oil from paddle.

able because the small dent around the edge provides a better hold for the screw. A punched hole can be expected to lift a larger area than a drilled hole before the screw pulls out.

In Fig. 74 the repair man is holding tension on the puller while he works an area above the crease with the hammer. The combined action of the puller and the hammer has reduced the depth of the dent and lowered the high area above the spot being worked.

In Fig. 76, the paint has been ground off the surrounding area, and the surface filed enough to outline the edges of the area to be filled. This filing operation is often skipped by many metal men, but it is highly desirable to do it because it will insure that the edge of the filler material, in this case solder, will blend into the adjoining surface.

In Fig. 77, the surface has been solder-filled and is ready for finishing. Solder-filling was done in two steps. The area under the character line was filled first, using a rounded paddle. This was cooled, using a water soaked rag, and the rest of the area was filled and the cooling operation repeated.

The finished panel, ready for refinishing, is shown in Fig. 78. Most of the finishing was done with the body file. The sander was used only around the edges to buff off the file scratches. No refilling or further lifting was required because the surface had been prepared properly first.

BASIC OPERATIONS APPLIED TO A SIMPLE DENT

The purpose of this section is to explain the application of the basic hammer and dolly block operations to actual straightening. The dent selected to illustrate the operations is a very simple rolled buckle, Fig. 79. It is typical of the damage conditions that can be straightened by use of the hammer and dolly block. A more severe dent of the same type would require the use of tension to straighten it properly. (The use of tension is discussed in Chapters 7 and 8.)

Even though only one rolled buckle is involved in this damage, it is typical of much of the larger damaged areas. There are exceptions, but the area surrounding the impact point in most cases of extensive damage usually will have two or more rolled buckles similar to this. Whether such conditions are found alone, as here, or are a part of larger damage, the procedure for straightening is essentially the same. A much more severe rolled buckle, which would require the use of tension, still would require about the same hammer and dolly block procedure for the final straightening.

REPAIR PROCEDURE

It was pointed out previously that the metal man must examine the job to determine his procedure. In Chapters 8 and 9, which deal with much

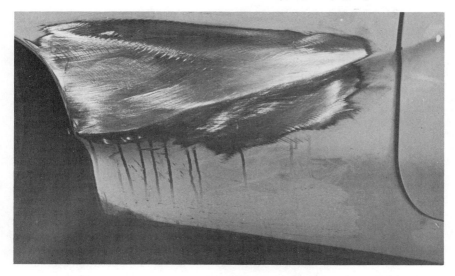

Fig. 78 The damaged area after metal finishing, ready for repainting.

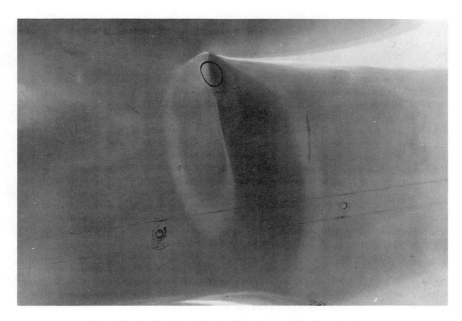

Fig. 79 Rolled buckle dent in the side of a fender.

greater damage, this examination has been done by separate discussions on the inspection of the damage and planning the repair procedure. Coverage of this damage is not carried to that length because it was selected to fit a predetermined procedure.

Careful attention should be given to the details of this damage because it is essential for the student to learn to examine every one closely. Slight variations from one damage to another may make considerable difference in the procedure to be followed. The ability to recognize such differences and to know how they govern repair procedure may be regarded as an inspection and analysis which enable the metal man to read procedure for doing the job. The beginner may require considerable study to recognize simple facts about a job which later will be recognized at a glance.

Whether the inspection of the job is done by a beginner or an experienced metal man, it is a matter of looking for the fold lines, displaced sections, and distortions caused by the impact and determining the order in which they occurred. From this information and the knowledge of what may be accomplished with the basic repair operations, it is a simple matter to apply force to the damage so that these conditions are relieved.

A quick examination of this damage reveals the following conditions:

1. It has been caused by a relatively light force.

2. It probably has been caused by a direct impact, but it could have been the result of force traveling through the length of the fender from a direct impact on the front end.

3. It is a minor but true example of a rolled buckle. A break-over point has formed, pushing a high spot ahead of it, but it has not rolled far enough into the high crown to cause a break-over path of severely upset metal.

4. There has been little or no tension lengthwise of the fender.

If a break-over path had formed, it would have been desirable to have used tension on this, as described in Chapter 8. As it is, it only will be necessary to drive the deepest part of the dent out to approximate level and smooth the surface with the hammer and dolly. When this is done, it will be ready to metal finish and repaint.

This straightening operation is fairly simple but it falls into two basic steps, just as all other straightening operations do. These steps also are called *phases* here and in the text following. They are: (1) roughing out, or roughing, and (2) bumping.

The *roughing phase,* in this case accomplished by a few blows of the dolly block, takes very little time, but it is the most critical of the entire operation. When it is done properly, it will be a simple matter to get the high spot at the break-over point down to level. When done improperly, this high spot can be very difficult to remove. Considerable extra effort will be required in the bumping and metal-finishing operations, and it is quite probable that traces of the high spot will show in the finished job.

The starting point of the roughing operation is marked by the black circle just below the break-over point, Fig. 79. The first blow will be struck on the underside of the circled area; the following blows will be progressively lower. This procedure is shown in much greater detail in the sketches in Fig. 80. These sketches represent cross sections through the deepest part of the dent in three successive stages: before starting, after the first blow with the dolly, and almost roughed out. In each sketch, the dotted line represents the original contour, and the solid line represents the damaged contour.

In sketch *A* the dolly block is shown in position to strike the first rough-out blow. Note that it is turned so that the highest crowned area of the working face will come into contact with the metal. This is necessary at this point because the blow will strike on the inside of a high-crowned surface. Three or four light blows were struck with the dolly before the action shown in sketch *B* was started.

Sketch *B* shows the hammer being used on the high break-over point and the dolly in position to drive out more metal at a slightly lower position. Use of the hammer is a follow-up operation. Driving the low metal out with the dolly block has pulled some of the high metal down. It also has left the area under a state of tension. The high spot will drop under the hammer blows until the tension is relieved. It is then time to drive out the surface more, as indicated by the dolly block in sketch *B*.

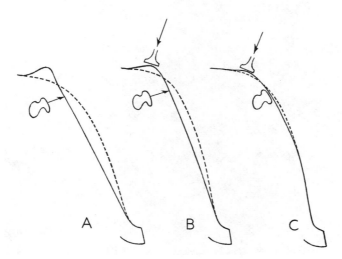

Fig. 80 Showing the basic rough-out procedure on a simple rolled buckle.

This action should be repeated several times to bring it to the condi-. tion shown in sketch *C*. Each time the dolly is used on the underside, it tends to pull the high spot down. The hammer being used on the outside works with this tendency by driving the high spot down farther and preventing too much tension from building up in the area. If too much tension is built up, it will stretch the metal between the high point and the spot where the dolly block strikes. If this occurs, it will be very difficult to drive the high spot down to the proper level.

To have attempted to drive the high spot down before striking the first dolly blows on the underside would have caused additional damage instead of straightening the dent. Note both in Fig. 79 and sketch *A* in Fig. 80 that the metal in the bottom of the deepest part of the dent is serving as a very rigid brace, or prop, under the highest point. This bracing effect always will be found in any rolled buckle. Instead of unrolling the buckle, hammer blows on the high spot would have caused severe upsetting. The result would have been a badly misshapen surface.

It should be recognized that this work was started close to the farthest point which the rolled buckle reached in the high crown. As the work continued, it moved progressively back into the lower crown area. The result of this first series of steps is shown in Fig. 81. This is a close-up view of the area circled in Fig. 79 and a portion of the sharply buckled area below it; a crayon line has been drawn around the remaining sharp

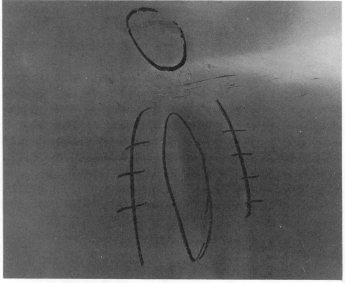

Fig. 81 Close-up view of a partially roughed-out surface.

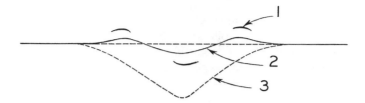

Fig. 82 Cross sectional sketch of the remaining buckles shown in Fig. 81: *1,* indicates strain left in buckle; *2,* roughed-out contour; *3,* original contour.

buckle in the center and two lines with cross marks drawn on the high ridge on each side. Note that the area within the original circle is quite smooth and unmarred, and the crayon line is still clear. This is the result of spending a few seconds polishing the bumping hammer with fine sandpaper.

The preceding explanations have dealt only with the vertical cross section of this rolled buckle. As the roughing-out operation progresses, it is also necessary to relieve the elastic strains which form on both sides of the deep valley section. Arrow No. 1 in Fig. 82 points to a short curved line used as a symbol to indicate a strain in the roughed-out contour below it, arrow No. 2. Note that two additional symbols are shown; one on the left-hand side in the same relative position, and the other in the center on the underside of the roughed-out contour. Under each one of these symbols, there is an elastic strain which is tending to draw the surface back toward the shape it had before it was roughed out. These strains are the spring back which always will be found when any piece of metal is bent. They can be found when any piece of metal is bent. Similar strains can be demonstrated by bending a piece of flat metal double and bending it back again. When the piece is released from the bending pressure, it will spring back some because of its elasticity.

There is one major difference between the strains in the loose piece of metal and those in a panel such as this. The loose piece of metal is free to move back into position to relieve the strain, but the strained metal within the panel cannot because the surrounding metal holds it. The tendency to move back is there, but it is not strong enough to overcome the surrounding metal.

The presence of strains in this area may be proved by cutting a crosswise section out of a partially roughed-out rolled buckle such as this. The cutting should be done with a saw which will not affect the strains in the metal. The piece cut should be approximately ½ inch wide and long enough to reach the unaffected metal on both sides of the buckle. When the piece is cut free, the elastic strain will cause it to change shape. Unless the ridge has been hammered excessively, it will spring back toward the damaged shape so that it will not fit the opening it was cut out of.

Referring again to Fig. 82, note that two strain areas are shown above the proper level. This is the typical condition found on any dent which has been driven out in this manner. It is caused by the stiffness of the work hardened valley buckle. This stiffness resists the opening action of the buckle and causes the high spots to rise on both sides.

The procedure to relieve this condition is indicated by the lines on the panel in the lower section of Fig. 81. The dolly is held firmly under the remaining buckle, indicated by the long loop, and the hammer is used to drive down the adjoining high areas, indicated by the lines on both sides of the loop. The procedure should be started at the upper section and worked progressively downward, keeping the hammer and dolly in step. The hammer blows either may be alternated from side to side or one side may be completed and then the other. In either case, the dolly should move with the hammer.

This action is not intended to complete the final straightening. It should be carried only to the point of relieving the strains which have been caused by the roughing operation. Then further roughing blows should be used to drive the deepest part of the remaining valley up to level, after which the hammer and dolly should be used again in the same manner.

When the hammer and dolly are used properly, there will be only a slight change in the appearance of the area. But, there will be a very noticeable difference in the resistance of the valley area to further roughing blows. This difference may be demonstrated by noting carefully the movement of the valley when struck with the dolly before and after the strains have been relieved. After the strains have been relieved, the valley will move much easier and be much smoother than when struck with the same force before.

Even though this was not a severe rolled buckle, the metal in the valley section has been subjected to enough compressive force to cause some upsetting. To restore the surface contour properly, this upset will require stretching. The easiest and fastest way to stretch this is to use the hammer-on-dolly. This is the operation which the beginner often is cautioned against because of the risk of overstretching. There should be no need for such concern, however, if the procedure and application are understood. Little or no hammer-on-dolly work should be done until the high spot at the break-over point has been relieved, leaving the area low but nearly smooth. Hammer-on-dolly spots should be placed over the low area to swell it into the proper shape. At any place where there are deep low spots, the dolly should be used to drive them out before the

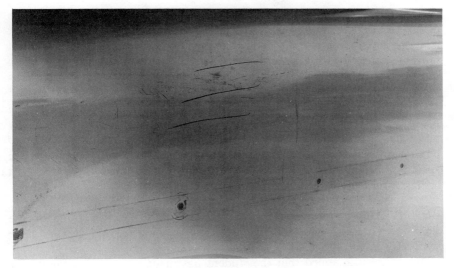

Fig. 83 The straightened buckle, ready for metal finishing.

hammer is used on-dolly to stretch the surface.

The finished straightening job is shown in Fig. 83. No hammer and dolly work has been done in the area of the molding. This area popped out of place in the original rough-out operation because it was only under an elastic strain from the buckles above it. Most of the straightening work was done in the area of the three parallel crayon marks. The upper mark is almost on the break-over point of the rolled buckle. This surface will metal finish with little effort.

METAL FINISHING

Metal finishing, as the term is used in automobile sheet metal repair, should not be confused with painting. Instead, it is the work of restoring final surface smoothness to damaged panels after straightening has been carried as far as practical. The primary need for metal finishing is based on the fact that perfect straightening would require more time and a higher degree of skill than the value of most panels would justify.

It is easy to make the mistake of considering metal finishing as simply a cutting operation to remove surface roughness. When done properly, metal finishing also serves as a means of locating the surface areas which are below the proper surface level so that the final straightening may be completed. In the process, the low areas usually are lifted by means of a pick hammer or similar tool, and the cutting operations, usually filing or disc sanding, are performed over the entire area.

Metal finishing requires a reasonably high degree of skill, but it is easier to learn than the basic straightening operations because the work is more nearly repetitive. There is much more similarity in the metal finishing operations of two entirely different damaged areas than there is in the straightening operations required to prepare them for metal finishing.

The basic cutting tools used in metal finishing are the 14-inch body file and the disc sander. One or both of these will be used in practically all of the metal finishing operations on any panel. Where other means of cutting are used, it is because of special surface contours which require specially shaped tools, such as bent files or drum sanders, to fit short radius curves.

Because of the importance of the body file and the disc sander, this section of the chapter deals with their use primarily. Coverage on the final straightening operations is interwoven where such operations are necessary on the actual job.

It has been assumed that the student has made an effort to familiarize himself with the basic straightening operations before attempting to develop skill at metal finishing. He should start practicing metal finishing as soon as he has learned to straighten simple dents. The usually more rapid skill development in metal finishing will enable the beginner to remedy some of his mistakes with the hammer and dolly block. He should not fall into the habit, however, of depending on metal finishing instead of learning to straighten properly. The least amount of metal cut away, the better and easier the job is.

The discussion of the use of the file has been placed before the explanation of the disc sander. The reason for this is that the file is the basic tool, and the sander is the power tool used to speed up the operation. The beginner who learns to use the file properly first will find that the use of the sander is much easier to master.

THE BODY FILE

A typical body file mounted on a wooden holder is shown in Fig. 84. Practically all files of this type are 14 inches long, have teeth on both sides, and have holes in each end so that they may be bolted to some kind of holder. Both wood and steel holders may be used; it is a matter of which the user prefers. Wood has the advantage of causing less dulling of the teeth on the unused side, which is held in contact with the holder. Some kind of padding material to serve the same purpose is desirable with a steel holder.

Special-purpose body files are used also. The most common of these is the half round, frequently called a shell file, which is used in reverse crowns. Specially bent files and shorter ones are sometimes needed. The

Fig. 84 A 14-inch body file mounted on a wooden holder.

use of these will be no problem if the basic procedure of filing has been learned.

Using the Body File. The beginner often attempts to use the body file in the same manner in which he uses a wood plane. The uses are similar in some ways but are not really alike. The difference lies in the fact that the wood plane has only one cutting blade which remains in a fixed position in relation to the plane bed. In contrast to this, the body file has cutting teeth along its full length, all of which should be used during the normal cutting stroke. This requires the body file to be manipulated in a manner entirely different from that of the plane.

To use the body file properly requires a thorough understanding of the purpose of filing. This has been stated previously, but it is repeated here for emphasis. When the file is used correctly, the cutting action removes minor surface irregularities and shows up larger ones by skipping over them (see Fig. 85). The show-up function is of greater importance than the cutting because it serves as a guide to the further straightening

Fig. 85 Low spots shown by file marks.

required to bring the surface to the proper level. When cutting only is needed to remove minor surface irregularities, it is better to use a power tool such as the disc sander.

Proper manipulation of the file is a matter of passing it across the area so that it has the maximum show-up effect. This is done by making it bridge across the low spots instead of cutting into them. Also, in the interest of efficiency, there is the problem of getting the most out of the effort required to push the file. To accomplish these results, it is necessary to consider the following: (1) the direction of the file stroke and (2) the side shift during the stroke.

The direction of the file stroke is important because of the differences in lengthwise and crosswise crowns which are found in almost all panels. The file should lie on the panel so that it has the maximum bridging effect over low spots. If there is any difference in crown, it is obvious that the one which is the nearest to flat will hold the teeth out of low spots better than a higher one will. This is the reason for the following rule: *the file should be stroked in the general direction of the flattest crown of the panel.*

The shift of the file during the stroke is important because it determines the area covered. This may be understood better by considering the result of filing without shifting. It would simply cut a single, narrow strip along the line on which it traveled. The area covered with one stroke would be small, and the length of the stroke would be limited by the distance across the area to be filed. When filing small areas, it would be necessary to use short, choppy strokes to avoid making file marks beyond the area where they are needed. This would be a good example of the "wood plane" method of filing. A job could be done in this manner, but it would be slow and ineffective because it would make use of only a few of the file teeth.

Much better results can be obtained by making two definite shifts of the file as it travels forward. The first shift is to make the contact area of the teeth to move from the front to the rear end of the file during the forward stroke. This should be done progressively so that the cutting action starts at the front end and has shifted to the rear at the end of the stroke.

The second shift is a side-slipping action which causes the file to finish the stroke a few inches to one side of the line on which it was started. Both of these shifts are illustrated in Fig. 86. This represents the stroke starting in the lower left, and moving to the upper right. Note that the lines representing file marks are shown starting at the front of the left position and shifting to the rear in the right position. The result is a relatively short, wide area of cutting instead of a long, narrow cut.

A slight curvature of the file blade is necessary to obtain the proper

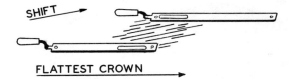

SHIFT

FLATTEST CROWN

Fig. 86 Showing the two shifts of the file during the stroke.

front-to-rear shift of the file when filing on a panel which is flat. If the file is also flat, all of the teeth will be in contact at the same time. This does not provide sufficient clearance for the individual teeth to bite into the metal, resulting in much slower cutting and preventing shifting of the cutting area. A flat file can be used on a flat panel if it is necessary to do the highest quality finishing job without consideration for the extra time required.

The side-shifting action should be alternated from side to side after every few strokes. This will improve the show-up effect on low spots, because the file will pass between high spots on one angle which it will bridge across on the other. It also aids in locating low spots by showing them up in sharper contrast than if the filing were done in only one direction.

The effect of side shifting is desirable on any crown, but it is more noticeable on combination crowns. This is due to the rather narrow contact of the file teeth as they bite into the surface. On a relatively flat panel, the tooth contact will be much wider, causing the low spots to stand out more sharply.

Picking. Lifting the low spot shown up by filing commonly is called *picking.* It can be done with any blunt-ended tool, such as a pick hammer or the end of the body file. The effect of filing and picking is shown in exaggerated detail in Fig. 87. Sketch *A* shows a wavy surface before filing. Sketch *B* shows the effect of passing a file across the surface. In sketch *C,* the point of a pick hammer is shown in position to drive the low spots up to proper level to be filed off. Note that these spots are above the level of the adjoining filed surfaces, otherwise the file could not cut them. Sketch *D* shows the finished surface after the filing has been completed.

The beginner's problem with picking is to hit the low spot on the underside. This is complicated by the fact that he is striking toward himself instead of away, as is usually done with a hammer. Howeaver, this can be learned with practice. A good way to develop this ability is to bring the tool (pick hammer or other) out into view and follow it with the eye as it is moved into position under the panel. After doing this a few times, the beginner will be able to co-ordinate the movement of his

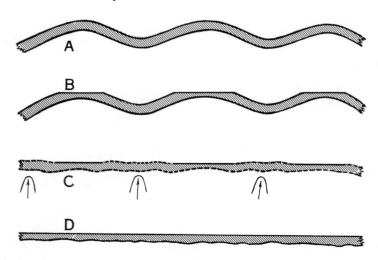

Fig. 87 Cross sectional sketch showing, in exaggerated detail, how filing and picking may be combined to produce a finished surface.

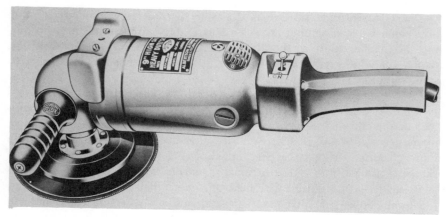

Fig. 88 A 9-inch heavy-duty disc sander.

hand and eye so that they both come to the same spot on the panel at the same time.

One word of caution to the beginner learning to pick: hold the tool in contact with the spot once it has been found. When the tool is brought to the spot, or as near as can be determined, it should first be touched to the underside of the metal and then a light pick blow struck. If there is any hesitation before the next blow is struck, the pick should be held in place against the surface. If it is allowed to drop away, the aim will be lost.

Once a pick mark has been located, there should be no trouble in hitting any other spot close by. However, until this ability to hit "where you're looking" has been developed, the beginner's work should be restricted to scrap metal panels to avoid the risk of serious damage to a good automobile.

The use of a sharp-pointed pick, hammer or otherwise, should be avoided except on very small spots. Much better results will be obtained by using a very blunt tool instead. The sharp-pointed pick will tend to pierce the panel rather than raise much of the area around the point of contact. The blunter tool spreads the effect of the blow over a much larger area, causing much less yield in the point of contact.

THE DISC SANDER

The portable disc sander commonly used in sheet metal repair is an electric unit operating on the 110-volt, 30-amp power supply used for lighting and other portable tools. Sanders are available which operate on the higher voltage power lines, but their use is restricted largely to factory production operations.

The sander shown in Fig. 88 is typical of those in body shop use. It consists of a lightweight electric motor of the commutator type which drives the spindle through bevel gears. The use of bevel gears permits the spindle to be at a right angle to the motor, making a long, easily maneuvered unit. The handle at the spindle end may be mounted on either side for either right- or left-handed operators.

Care of the Disc Sander. Proper care is an important factor in the life of a disc sander. Rough handling should be avoided, particularly dropping the machine or picking it up by the cord. Permitting it to lie on the backup pad for any length of time will tend to warp the pad so that it vibrates.

Overheating is probably the most common cause of serious damage to the sander motor. While it may be the result of too heavy use of a light-duty machine, it is most commonly the result of clogging of the motor ventilating system. All motors of this type have an air inlet at the commutator end and an outlet at the other. A continuous stream of air is drawn through the motor by a fan located at the outlet end. Clogging of either the inlet or outlet will interfere with the flow of cooling air and cause overheating.

The sander may become clogged if it is placed down on a dusty floor while it is still running. When the machine is lying on the floor with the spindle up, one air intake will be less than ½ inch from the floor. If dust or dirt is nearby, it will be picked up and drawn into the machine. However, a certain amount of clogging of the air passages will occur in normal use because the sander is normally operated under dusty conditions. Regardless of how the dirt is picked up, if the passages become clogged with it, the machine will overheat. The solution is, of course, periodic cleaning.

An accumulation of abrasive dust around the brush holders can cause a short circuit in the motor. The aluminum oxide abrasives used on sanding discs and the metal cuttings are both conductors. A build-up of such materials over the insulation at the brush holders will provide a path to the aluminum case of the unit. The result will be a motor that is "hot" to handle. A third wire is provided in the cord of all such portable electric tools so that the case can be connected to the ground. This ground connection should always be connected. It is dangerous to operate an ungrounded portable electric motor, particularly if standing on a damp floor. Severe electric shock or death can result.

SANDING DISCS

Sanding discs used in sheet metal repair work consist of a stiff fiber disc coated on one side with abrasive grit. The grit used almost universally is aluminum oxide. It may be bonded to the fiber by glue or resin. The resin bond is a little more expensive but is much more durable.

Several manufacturers of abrasive discs offer their products to the automobile repair trade. These products vary somewhat in special features, but all manufacturers have standardized disc sizes and the method of identifying grit size by number.

Disc size refers to the diameter of the fiber disc. Two sizes are in common use: 7 inch, and 9⅛ inch. Discs of smaller diameter also are used for special purposes, but they usually are obtained by cutting a larger disc down to the size needed. This is much more practical than purchasing smaller sizes, because they can be cut from the unworn center area of the larger size. However, smaller diameter discs are available when they are needed in sufficiently large quantities to justify their purchase.

The sanding disc is held in place by means of a special, wideflanged nut which passes through the center hole and threads either to the hub of the pad or the spindle. Most disc sanders require a ⅞-inch center hole, although some have been made which require a ½-inch hole. Discs are available having either size center hole, or a special nut can be obtained which will center the larger size center hole on the smaller spindle.

Grit size of the abrasive material used to coat sanding discs, and many other coated abrasives, is specified by number, such as 16, 24, 36, and 50, etc. This number refers to the size of screen which this grit will pass through. Screen size is determined by the number of mesh per linear inch. Thus, a 16 grit would pass through a screen having 16 mesh per linear inch but not through the next smaller size, 24.

Glue-bonded discs are made both in open and closed coats. The open-coated discs have the grit applied in very light layers, so that the fiber backing shows through. They are intended primarily for removal of paint and other soft material which will soften and cling to the abrasive coat. Although sometimes used for metal cutting, they are not as satisfactory as the closed-coated discs.

The closed-coated discs have a heavier layer of abrasive so that they will stand up under heavy-duty conditions. When the grit particles on the surface wear down or break loose, additional particles are uncovered to continue the operation.

Resin-bonded discs are made only in one coat. The much higher heat resistance of the resin serves to prevent much of the loading up due to melted paint clinging to the surface. For that reason, they may be used either on paint or for metal cutting, thus eliminating the bother of changing from an open to a closed type of coating. In general, the resin-bonded discs may be expected to wear longer than the glue-bonded discs.

The grit size for the particular job is the same for both glue-bonded and resin-bonded discs. The coarsest grit, 16, is intended primarily for paint removal and coarse cutting. It is not recommended for metal finishing panels because of the extremely coarse swirl marks left by the large grit. However, most paint can be removed by a 24 grit disc, and whenever possible it should be used. The 24 grit also can be used for metal finishing, but the panel will be left in much better condition if it is finished with a 36 grit. Buffing can be done with a worn 36 grit, but it will be better if a 50 or 60 is used.

Finishing Metal with the Disc Sander. The disc sander has two basic uses in metal finishing: the first is as a partial substitute for the body file; the second is to buff the filed surface to remove deep scratches. Each requires a different stroke of the sander to produce the required results.

To use the sander as a substitute for filing, it is important that the disc be applied to the surface so that it will leave a pattern of grit swirl marks which bridge across low spots. This can be done best by stroking the machine back and forth on the panel, following the direction which is nearest to flat, just as in filing. The pad should be pushed against the metal with enough pressure to cause it to flex but not enough to cause the machine to slow down. As the disc moves back and forth across the surface, the spindle should be tilted away from the direction of travel just enough to throw the cutting action to the following edge. At the end of the stroke, a fraction of a second is required to stop and start the back

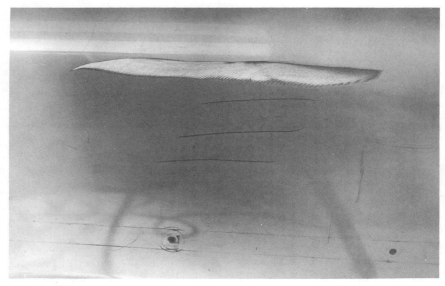

Fig. 89 First stroke with the disc sander, moving from left to right. Swirl marks show up low spots because they follow the flattest crown of the panel.

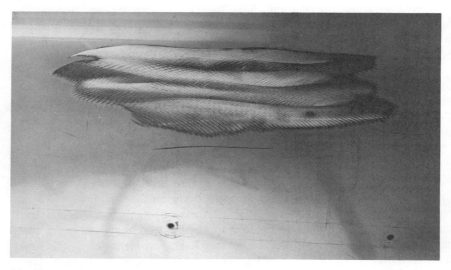

Fig. 90 Appearance of several back-and-forth strokes crisscrossed over an area. Low metal shows up as dark spots.

Fig. 91 Appearance of the sanded area after the low spots have been picked up and resanded. This surface should be buffed for the final finish.

stroke in the opposite direction. During this time, the spindle should be tilted to the opposite direction so that the cutting action will switch to the opposite edge, which will become the following edge. The pattern of swirl marks which this will produce is shown in Fig. 89

The swirl marks shown in Fig. 89 were made by stroking the sander from the left to the right. In Fig. 90, several back-and-forth strokes have been made. Note that the grit swirl marks show a definite crosscut action because of the tilt of the sander on each stroke. Also note that several dark spots show up. These are low spots which the disc has bridged over.

In Fig. 91, the low spots have been picked up and resanded over the complete area. This surface is smooth enough to be buffed and painted without further work. However, if there had been considerable rough metal, it would have been desirable to file the sanded area lightly and inspect for minor low areas before buffing.

The position for holding the sander conveniently so that it may be stroked back and forth easily is shown in Fig. 92. Note that the body of the machine is at a right angle to the direction of travel. However, it is not always possible to assume such a position when using the sander on various parts of the automobile. The beginner should start to gain his experience with the sander on a job which will permit him to assume an

Fig. 92 Proper position for easy stroking with the disc sander used in metal finishing.

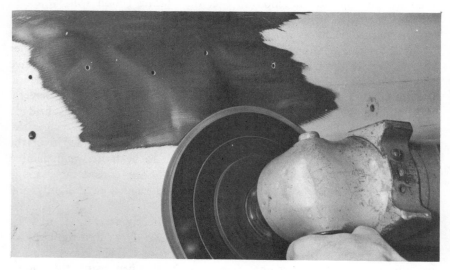

Fig. 93 Proper position for easy stroking with the disc sander when used for buffing. The direction of the stroke and the position of the machine are both at a right angle to the direction and the position used in metal finishing.

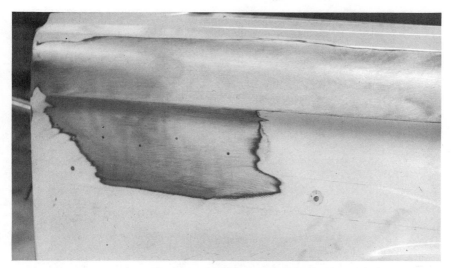

Fig. 94 Appearance of the buffed surface, ready for painting.

easy position. As he gains more skill, it will be easy to adapt to the various positions in which the sander must be held without upsetting the pattern of stroking.

Buffing with the Disc Sander. Buffing with the disc sander differs from the finishing operation in the direction of the stroke and the contact of the disc. The stroke should be at a right angle to the finishing stroke so that it follows the direction of greatest crown instead of the flattest. The machine should be held so that the spindle is straight instead of tilted to one side. This position permits the maximum area of the pad to lie on the panel surface. Fig. 93 shows the machine being held and stroked in the proper manner. Fig. 94 shows the finished job.

Best results will be obtained if most of the work is done on the down-stroke. This is done by relaxing the pressure on the machine as it is raised into position to make the next downstroke.

In many cases where a large area of metal has been sanded to re-move the paint and partially to finish the surface before filing, it will save filing to buff the area also. The reason is that the finishing stroke tends to leave ridges between strokes. Buffing off the ridges is just a means of cutting metal with the power tool instead of doing the work by hand with the file.

Use of Star-Shaped Discs. It is difficult to use a round sanding disc in a sharp reverse crown because the edge cuts a sharp groove in the sur-face. This can be avoided by cutting the edge of the disc into points, com-

Fig. 95 Disc sanding with a star-shaped disc.

Fig. 96 Trimmer for cutting star-shaped discs.

monly called a star disc. The number of points can vary from six to eight or nine. The sharper the radius of the reverse crown, the more points the disc should have.

The action of the star disc is to break the smooth outer edge of the disc so that it does not form the groove. Instead, the outer edge advances and recedes as each point passes a particular spot on the panel surface. The result is a smooth, polished effect which can be painted easily. Fig. 95 shows the finished job and the position of the pad. Note that it is being pushed into the work so that the disc is flexed to fit the curve of the panel. This disc will tend to slap the panel if it is not held firmly against it.

The operator never should use a star-shaped disc without full protection for his eyes and face. This disc tends to throw more grit than the round one. Also, it is particularly dangerous to allow the star disc to turn against an edge because the points can catch and tear off. A flying chunk of a sanding disc can blind an eye or cause a severe facial cut.

A cutter for making star discs is shown in Fig. 96. Essentially, this is a paper knife with a guide to hold the disc in position while cutting any of the different shapes shown in the illustration. It serves as a convenient method for cutting discs; however, they can be cut with an old pair of snips or even a straight edge and a sharp knife.

When cutting discs with a straight edge and a knife, the work can be done on the back side. A convenient method is to measure off a section equal to the radius of the disc. This will cut an even six-point star.

SAFETY MEASURES WITH THE DISC SANDER

The disc sander never should be used without proper eye protection. It throws off particles of grit and metal cuttings at tremendous speeds. The outer edge of a 9-inch disc driven by a highspeed sander will travel at speeds faster than 1½ miles per minute. Grit thrown at such speeds will injure and can cause the loss of an eye. Thus the need for adequate eye protection—either goggles or one of the many available types of transparent plastic face shields.

There is also serious risk of injury if any portion of the flesh comes into contact with the disc while it is in motion. The edge of a new disc will cut a deep gash in the flesh almost as rapidly as a power saw. Such cuts are slow to heal, because the action of the disc removes the flesh instead of making a clean cut. For this reason, the sander should be started or stopped only when it is in the proper working position. It is best to stop the motor before removing the sander from the job. Never under any circumstances lay the sander on the floor or hand it to another person while it is running.

QUESTIONS ON TOOLS AND BASIC OPERATIONS

1. What are the basic straightening tools?
2. Of the basic hand tools, which require the highest level of skill development?
3. What should be the shape of the working face of the large head of the bumping hammer?
4. On a hammer having a large and a small face, should the shape of the face of the small head be similar to the shape of the face of the large head? Why?
5. What is the proper use of the small head?
6. What are the two primary uses of the dolly block?
7. What is wrong with using a dolly block as an anvil?
8. How should the weight of the dolly block compare to the weight of the hammer to be used with it?
9. What is meant by "balance" of the dolly block?
10. What is a spoon?
11. What are the three basic uses of spoons?
12. Does the balance of a spoon affect its use? If so, how?
13. How does use of the hammer-on-dolly raise metal?
14. How should the hammer handle be gripped when striking an on-dolly blow?
15. How does use of the hammer-off-dolly raise metal?
16. In raising metal by both hammer-on-dolly and off-dolly, will the tendency to raise metal be increased or decreased by slackening the hand pressure on the dolly?
17. In using the hammer-on-dolly, there are two rules which determine where the hammer blows should be placed. What are they?
18. What determines the force of the blow when the hammer is used off-dolly?
19. Can the hammer be used effectively off-dolly on high and low spots which are as close together as ¼ inch? Explain.
20. Will increasing the distance between the hammer and dolly contact points reduce or increase the effectiveness of an off-dolly hammer blow?
21. Should the bumping spoon be used on sharp ridges? Why?
22. Should a crowned or a flat-faced bumping spoon be used on a ridge buckle in a flat or nearly flat panel? Why?
23. How should a bumping spoon be held?
24. What are the uses of a body spoon?
25. Where is the use of a body spoon required?
26. What shape body spoon has the best balance?
27. Why is it not always practical to use the body spoon which has the best balance?
28. What conditions make it necessary to use pry tools?
29. If holes are made in the lower edge of a door panel to permit use of pry tools, where should they be made?
30. What steps were performed on the simple dent used to show the application of the basic operations with the hammer and dolly?
31. Is straightening with the hammer and dolly block the best procedure on a dent which has formed a severe break-over path? Why?
32. In straightening a simple dent, where should most of the hammer-on-dolly block work be done?

33. In straightening a simple dent on a combination crown, where should the first blows be struck with the dolly?
34. In roughing out a simple dent, why should the straightening operation be started on the underside of the panel?
35. How can the hammer be used off-dolly to relieve elastic strains in a partially straightened area?
36. Why is metal finishing the practical method of restoring final smoothness to a straightened panel surface?
37. When used properly, the file has two functions. What are they?
38. In which direction should the file point at the start of the stroke?
39. In which direction should the file point at the finish of the stroke?
40. What purpose is served by shifting the cutting action from the front to the rear end of the file during the stroke?
41. What purpose is served by shifting the file to the side during the stroke?
42. Why should the side shifting action be alternated from side to side frequently?
43. How can skill at "hitting where you're looking" be developed?
44. Should the picking tool, hammer or otherwise, be sharp pointed or blunt?
45. What will be the result of a clogged ventilating system on the disc sander?
46. Which is the coarser abrasive grit: 24 or 36?
47. In metal finishing with the disc sander, why should the spindle be tilted slightly away from the direction of travel?
48. Why should the sander be kept moving and, when sanding small areas, removed from the work every few strokes?
49. Is it practical to sand an area using the back-and-forth stroke, then pick up the low spots and resand again? Why?
50. Why should the buffing stroke be at a right angle to the metal finishing stroke?
51. Why should a fine grit disc be used for buffing?

4

Shrinking Metal

Shrinking metal is simply a matter of making an upset where it is needed. It is the exact opposite of stretching. It may be needed on any spot on any panel where it is necessary to reduce surface area to restore the proper contour. However, not all upsetting should be considered as shrinking. The term, *shrinking,* is restricted by common usage in the body shop to mean only an operation in which heat is used to soften the metal to permit making the desired upset.

The shrinking operation is performed by heating a spot or area of metal, working it to shape with the hammer and dolly block, and cooling it. When done properly, gouges or raised areas will be brought back close enough to exact contour to be metal finished easily. The operation seems simple and easy to someone observing a skilled metal man, but it can be quite difficult for a beginner, particularly if he has not mastered the fundamentals.

It is essential to recognize metal shrinking as a precision job, particularly in flat or nearly flat areas where only a few thousandths of an inch will cause a bulge. Unlike most precision jobs, however, it must be performed by "feel" and judgment instead of working to exact measurements.

To master the shrinking operation easily, the beginner should learn the fundamentals first then develop skill through experience.

The fundamentals consist of:

1. Recognition of the types of damage which require shrinking.

2. An understanding of the basic shrinking operation.

3. An understanding of how heat may be used to obtain the required softening and stiffening effect.

4. An understanding of how controlling the rate of cooling by quenching can add to or reduce the amount of shrinking obtained with the individual operation.

In addition, it is essential to have developed previously sufficient skill with the hammer and dolly block to be able to use them with precision. The work is done on metal which has been softened by heating. A misdirected hammer blow which would be of no consequence on unheated metal can do serious damage on metal which is at high temperature.

108

TYPES OF DAMAGE WHICH REQUIRE SHRINKING

Shrinking may be required on almost any area of the sheet metal on the automobile damaged in a collision. The appearance of such areas may vary as widely as the locations in which they are found. However, when shrinking is done as a part of any straightening operation, it is because of a stretched condition, or it is necessary in order to blend a condition of false stretch into the surrounding contour. Both of these conditions were discussed briefly in Chapter 2, but a more detailed discussion is required to explain the application of basic shrinking procedure.

It should be noted that the same procedure for shrinking damaged metal can be used in forming metal parts by hand. Such operations are outside the scope of this book; however, the metal man who has learned the proper use of the hammer and dolly block in straightening and shrinking metal will find that it is easy to hand-form simple parts. Shrinking is particularly important in such operations, because it provides a method of eliminating excess metal easily.

STRETCHED METAL

Sheet metal is considered stretched when the dimensions which make up its surface area have been changed. In some cases the result will be an increase in actual area, but it is not necessary to consider area when determining whether a particular piece of metal is stretched or not. The

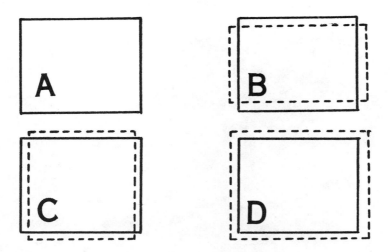

Fig. 97 Sketch indicating typical sketched conditions: *A* represents an area within a panel of any size. In *B* and *C,* the dotted lines show the effect of lengthwise and crosswise tension; *D* shows the effect of both lengthwise and crosswise tension. Any combination of these is considered to be stretched metal.

primary factor is whether length or width have been increased. Usually there will be a proportional decrease of the other dimension of area, length or width as the case may be.

The four sketches in Fig. 97 illustrate the varying conditions of stretched metal. Sketch *A* represents a small section of the surface of a panel. This section could be almost any size, from much smaller than the sketch shown to several times larger. If such a section could be laid out on the panel before the damage which caused the stretching occurred, the result could be measured afterward. In most cases, the result would be similar to the conditions shown in either sketch *B* or *C,* depending on the direction from which the force acted in causing the stretch. If force did act on the section from both sides, the result would be similar to the condition shown in sketch *D.*

The purpose of these four sketches is to illustrate that stretched metal may be found in a wide variety of conditions. In many instances there will be some combination of the two conditions represented by sketches *B* and *C;* however, it will be the exceptional condition which is exactly uniform, as represented by the dotted lines. Also, these sketches are simply flat, rectangular drawings on a piece of paper. Stretched metal will be found on the surface of a panel in almost any conceivable shape. Some stretched areas will be driven below the surface level, while others will be driven above.

The two most common stretched conditions requiring shrinking are gouges and stretched flanges. In both of these, the actual stretching is

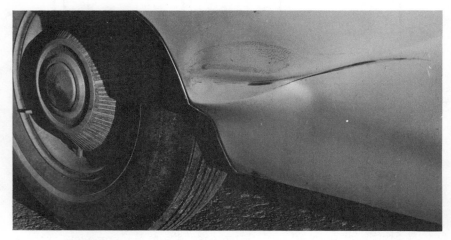

Fig. 98 Gouged quarter panel. Metal in the deep part of the gouge is stretched severely. Because of the problems of access and shape, this type of gouge is usually repaired by filling.

confined to a relatively small part of the panel surface. Stretched conditions which extend over a large part of a panel surface will be found occasionally on very severely damaged panels. Such conditions are very rarely repaired, however, because tremendous forces are required to affect a large area of metal in such manner. In most cases, there will be other severe damage which would require far more labor than justifiable when the price of replacement is considered.

The nature of a gouge introduces problems in shrinking it. Because most gouges can be repaired by filling, many steel repair men do not attempt to learn the procedure for shrinking them. The gouged quarter panel, Fig. 98, is an excellent example of one which could be filled much easier than it could be shrunk. The partial straightening and filling procedure on this was discussed in Chapter 3, Figs. 73-78. It is referred to here again to point out that not all gouges should be shrunk.

It is often good practice on gouges to use shrinking as a means of reducing the amount of filling; this procedure is explained in detail in Chapter 6, Figs. 106-119. Whether the shrinking operation is intended to remove the gouge condition completely or just reduce the amount of filling, it requires the development of a reasonable amount of skill to do it right.

The effect of shrinking across the width of a gouge is greater than it is lengthwise. Unless the shrinking operation is controlled closely, it will tend to affect length and width uniformly. The result is that the length is overshrunk as width is reduced to the proper dimension. Overshrinking the length of a gouge will have a drawing effect on the metal on both sides of it. On a long gouge running lengthwise of a nearly flat door panel, the drawing effect will pull wave buckles into the panel for a distance of several inches unless it is properly controlled.

The procedure for shrinking gouges to avoid the drawing effect is explained in detail in the section covering shrinking procedure.

Shrinking a flange is a simple matter compared to shrinking a gouge or a raised area. All that is required is to be sure that the adjoining metal is reshaped properly, then heat the flange and hammer it down against a flat surface on a dolly block. For that reason the procedure is not covered in detail.

The procedure for shrinking a surface which has been raised above the proper level is different from that for shrinking a gouge. There are many conditions which can cause such an area to require shrinking. Sometimes raised spots which require shrinking are left after a deep gouge has been shrunk. Another very common cause is an impact on a panel made by a large, rigid object. Such an impact often will cause slight stretching over an area much larger than the stretched area of a gouge. In the original damage, this type of stretched metal will be driven below the surface level.

However, it is often the best procedure to raise it above surface level before starting to shrink it. This is particularly true if it can be raised by driving the low area out without great difficulty by striking it with the dolly block.

Shrinking raised areas also is required in many cases to correct the result of errors in the use of tools, particularly the hammer and dolly block. Except in cases of extreme carelessness or inexperience, such stretching should present no special problem. If there is some difficulty, it is usually caused by an inexperienced metal man who needs assistance from someone with more knowledge. The procedure in such cases is essentially the same as for any other raised area. If the surface has not been mutilated badly, this type of stretched metal is often quite easy to shrink because the stretched condition affects the surrounding metal uniformly in all directions.

FALSE STRETCH

False stretch is the term used to identify a condition which often is confused with a true stretched condition. This confusion stems from the similarity of appearance. False stretch may vary from a simple *oil can* condition to a large, raised hump which appears to be stretched. The key to the identification of false stretch is that it will always be a smooth, unworked surface adjoining an area that has been upset. The raised area is caused by the gathering effect of the upset.

The most common cause of false stretch is failure to relieve all of the upset in a rolled buckle of the reinforced edge of such panels as doors, deck lids, or hoods; however, it can be found in any panel when the conditions are right. In many cases, it is difficult to avoid causing a little false stretch, but it is often the result of improper use of tools. Attempting to beat out stiff, unyielding buckles which should be straightened under tension is probably the most common cause of this condition.

A simple demonstration of a condition similar to false stretch can be made by folding a pleat in the edge of a sheet of paper. When the fold is held in place, the center area of the sheet will be raised into a sharp bulge. And, when the fold is released, the bulged area will drop back into place.

The ideal method of dealing with false stretch is to avoid it by planning the rough-out procedure to avoid making upsets. Emphasis on such procedures will be found in later sections of the book dealing with the roughing out of actual damage. However, there are some situations in which it is almost impossible to avoid creating some false stretch. In those cases, shrinking is the practical answer.

Shrinking false stretch is a blending operation. When done properly, the effect of the upset will be spread over enough area to relieve the bulge caused by the abrupt change of dimensions. The shrinking effect must not extend into the upset area, but it must blend to nothing in the adjoining metal. This presents a real problem because in any shrinking operation there is a tendency to overshrink. Unless very close control is maintained, there will be overshrinking and the upset will be carried farther into the unaffected metal. This is the condition sometimes described by metal men as "chasing a stretch across a panel." However, the metal man who has learned to recognize the difference between stretched metal and false stretch rarely will find himself in this predicament.

The actual procedure for shrinking false stretch is described in detail in later sections.

THE BASIC SHRINKING OPERATION

The basic shrinking operation uses the compressive effect of a blow on a crowned surface to make an upset. This is illustrated by the cross sectional sketch in Fig. 99. As the hammer blow strikes the crown it will tend to drive it down to the position of the straight dotted lines. As the crown flattens, it will tend to push outward against points *A* and *B*. The compressive effect produced is the result of resistance to outward movement of points *A* and *B*.

If an upset is to be made, the resistance to outward movement must be greater than the resistance to upsetting of the crowned area. Heat is required because without it the crown usually offers much greater resistance than points *A* and *B*. The proper application of heat to the crown section,

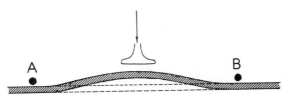

Fig. 99 Showing the compressive effect of a hammer blow on a high crown. Flattening the crown causes outward pressure on points *A* and *B*.

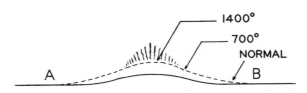

Fig. 100 Showing the softening effect of heat. A hammer blow on the heated spot will cause upsetting instead of forcing points *A* and *B* outward.

however, will soften it so that it will upset readily. It also will stiffen the resistance to outward movement of the *A* and *B* points by expanding the surrounding metal. Thus, heat tends to increase both conditions necessary for shrinking.

The effect of heat is shown in Fig. 100. In this particular illustration, the temperature range is from 1,400° F. at the center of the heated area to normal at, or close to, the *A* and *B* points. The expansion resulting from that temperature will raise the crown from the position of the solid line to the approximate position of the dotted line. The result is a low, cone-shaped hump which is much larger and stiffer than the original crown. This new shape offers much greater resistance to the hammer blow around the outer edges, points *A* and *B*, and much less resistance to upsetting in the center. Thus hammer blows on the center area will cause considerable upset because the conditions are right.

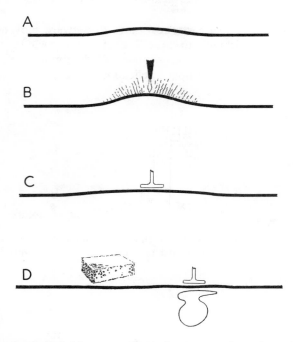

Fig. 101 The basic shrinking operation: *A*, cross section of spot to be shrunk; *B*, the same area expanded and softened by heat; *C*, the hammer being used to drive down the softened high spot; *D*, the hammer and dolly block being used to straighten the shrunk area. The wet sponge is used as needed to quench the hot metal.

Because cooling starts the instant that the torch flame is removed from the work, the effect of heating is only temporary. Cooling is rapid enough so that any work done with the hammer must be done as quickly as possible. The smaller the spot heated, the more important it is that no time be lost if the work is to be effective.

This explanation of basic shrinking procedure has been limited to the effect on a single cross section taken through the center of an area of metal raised above the proper surface level. In the simplest stretched condition which would require shrinking, a cross section taken at a right angle to this line would be approximately the same. The four basic steps of shrinking such a spot are shown in Fig. 101.

In Fig. 101, sketch *A* represents a cross section of the original spot to be shrunk. Since it is uniform, this may be considered as being the same as any other cross section taken at any other angle. Sketch *B* shows the application of heat from the welding torch flame, about 1,400° F. in this case. However, the exact temperature must be varied to suit the conditions. Temperature variations and the spread of heat are discussed in a later section.

The actual shrinking operation is shown in sketch *C*. The hammer has been used to drive the hot, expanded surface down to a much lower level. Although the hammer is shown in only one position, it would be necessary to strike several hammer blows over the heated surface to flatten the crown to this level. It should be noted especially that the surface is shown with some crown. It would be wrong to drive the surface down so that it was perfectly flat while it is heated because cooling will cause it to contract and be overshrunk. This slight crown will be reduced as cooling is completed.

The last two steps are shown together in sketch *D*. The hammer and dolly block are being used to finish straightening the shrunk surface, and the wet sponge is in position to quench the hot metal as needed. In this particular sketch the hammer is shown on-dolly. This often is necessary to relieve any overshrinking. The hammer also would be used off-dolly to finish straightening any noticeable waves. In this case, the use of the hammer and dolly is no different from that in any other straightening job, except that lighter blows and more care are required because the heated metal will yield much more readily than unheated metal.

The sponge is not always needed. If the surface has been lowered enough, the rest of the crown will drop into the proper level as the surface cools. If, however, the surface has not been driven down as far as necessary, quenching it with a wet sponge or rag will lower it much more than if it is allowed to cool slowly. The problems of quenching are discussed in much greater detail in a later section.

SHRINKING GOUGES

The procedure for shrinking a gouge is similar to that for shrinking an area of raised metal. In both operations the upset is obtained by softening the area with heat and applying force to flatten it. It differs in two respects, however: (1) the gouged area extends below the surface instead of above it; and (2) gouges tend to be stretched more severely than raised areas.

The dolly block plays a much more important part in shrinking the gouge, because force to accomplish the upset must be applied from the underside while the metal is hot. The more severe the stretched condition is, the more important it is that this be done. A very minor gouge can be driven up without heating and then shrunk as if it were a raised area instead. This procedure is recommended for large, lightly stretched areas which have been driven below the surface. However, it is not practical on any but the most minor damage, because it tends to spread the effect over a much wider area. It is a much better practice to use the hammer and dolly block as shown in the five sketches in Fig. 102.

Sketch *A* in Fig. 102 represents a cross section through a gouge with the proper surface level indicated by the dotted lines. In this case, the depressed area is shown as being smooth. Under actual conditions, however, this may be any shape. Quite often the bottom of a gouge shows the imprint of a sharp object. Regardless of the shape, however, the procedure would be the same.

The effect of heat application is shown in sketch *B*. Expansion has deepened the gouge by causing the metal on the surrounding edges to bulge inward. This is essentially the same as the effect obtained by heating a raised area, except that the movement is downward instead of upward. Here the temperature required would be relatively high, at least dull red heat and maybe hotter; the more severe the stretched condition is, the higher the temperature should be.

The first application of force is shown in sketch *C*. One or more blows have been struck with the dolly block on the underside of the deepest part of the gouge. This has driven the edges of the gouge above the level of the surrounding metal. On a small, single-point gouge, this high metal will form a ring around the low spot. On a long gouge caused by sliding impact, this high metal will form two lines on either side of the low spot.

The use of the hammer and dolly is shown in sketch *D*. The dolly block should be pushed hard against the underside of the gouge as the hammer is used to drive the high metal down to level. Usually these two operations will be repeated, sometimes several times. Each time they are repeated, the gouge and the surrounding high metal will be made smaller. However, there are too many variable conditions involved to attempt to establish the exact number of times that the operation should be repeated. The beginner is advised to try to obtain as much shrink effect as possible from his

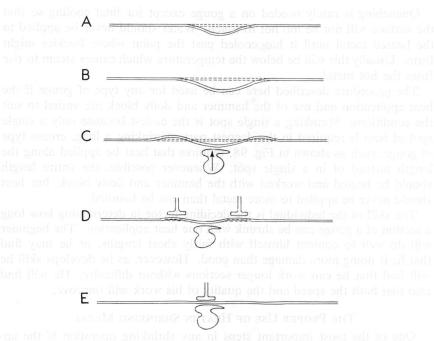

Fig. 102 Basic procedure for shrinking a gouge: *A*, a cross section through a typical gouge; *B*, the same cross section expanded and softened by heat; *C*, the heated area driven up by a blow of the dolly block; *D*, using the hammer and dolly block to level the high and low spots; *E*, using the hammer-on-dolly to relieve overshrinking.

efforts. It is simply a matter of using the hammer-on-dolly on hot metal.

The last operation is shown in sketch *E*. In this case, the hammer is shown on-dolly to stretch metal. Sometimes the beginner has difficulty understanding why metal should be stretched immediately after it has been shrunk. The reason is that the surface level must be restored while the temperature is still relatively high. After the surface level has been restored, the contraction due to cooling will cause the metal to buckle unless it is relieved by stretching. If the metal is allowed to cool without stretching, contraction will reduce the shrunk area so that it is too small, causing tension on all of the surrounding metal.

Probably the most important part of the procedure of shrinking a gouge is in the use of the hammer and dolly block to relieve excessive tension caused by cooling. The experienced metal man watches the surface closely and uses his hammer and dolly to relieve buckles caused by too much tension as soon as they begin to form.

Quenching is rarely needed on a gouge except for final cooling so that the surface will not be too hot to touch. Water should never be applied to the heated metal until it has cooled past the point where buckles might form. Usually this will be below the temperature which causes steam to rise from the hot metal.

The procedure described here can be used for any type of gouge if the heat application and use of the hammer and dolly block are varied to suit the conditions. Shrinking a single spot is the easiest because only a single spot of heat is required in the deepest part. Shrinking a long, crease type of gouge, such as shown in Fig. 98, requires that heat be applied along the length instead of in a single spot. Whenever possible, the entire length should be heated and worked with the hammer and dolly block, but heat should never be applied to more metal than can be handled.

The skill of the individual is the deciding factor in determining how long a section of a gouge can be shrunk with one heat application. The beginner will do well to content himself with fairly short lengths, or he may find that he is doing more damage than good. However, as he develops skill he will find that he can work longer sections without difficulty. He will find also that both the speed and the quality of his work will improve.

THE PROPER USE OF HEAT IN SHRINKING METAL

One of the most important steps in any shrinking operation is the application of heat. This is true whether the job is relatively simple or quite complicated; however, the more complicated the job, the more important it is that heat be applied properly.

Proper application of heat means that the proper temperature is applied to an area of the proper size. The problem is to apply just enough heat to do the job and no more. If not enough is applied, the metal will not be softened enough to permit the required upset. In such cases, the stretched condition will not be relieved, and the surface will be left rough or wavy.

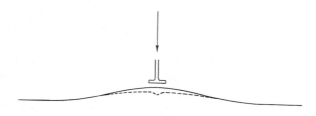

Fig. 103 Effect of overheating a small spot where a much wider area should be heated to lower temperature. The dip in the dotted line represents a collapse in the overheated spot instead of upset.

To a limited extent, extra work with the hammer can offset the effect of insufficient heat. Beyond this limit, extra work with the hammer will only tend to spread the crown instead of shrinking it. For example, in Fig. 99, the tendency would be to push points *A* and *B* farther apart instead of making an upset between them.

The effect of too-high temperature is shown in Fig. 103. This shows the result of heating red hot a small spot in the center of a large, slightly stretched raised area. Instead of shrinking uniformly all over, the hot spot collapses, forming a depression under the hammer. A lower temperature spread over the entire area would have produced a uniform upset and a smooth surface.

A common mistake made in shrinking metal is to heat every spot to red heat. No doubt this stems from the influence of the blacksmith. In the early days of the automobile industry, the first metal men were blacksmiths. An important rule of the blacksmith was that metal never should be forged at any temperature below red heat. This idea was carried over into any work done on automobile sheet metal, and it still persists, even among men who have little or no knowledge of the blacksmith's trade.

Steel such as used in automobile sheet metal begins to soften at the temperature at which the first color forms. The rate of softening increases progressively as the temperature is raised until the dark-blue color temperature range is reached. Past this point, the softening effect is directly proportional to the temperature increase until practically all mechanical strength is lost at bright red heat, close to 1,800° F.

The softening that results from heating to the blue color range is enough to permit considerable upsetting. On large areas which are not severely stretched, heating to the blue range or just slightly beyond will provide

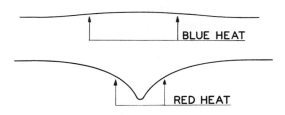

Fig. 104 *(Top)* Showing the approximate spread of low temperature heat over a minor stretched condition.

Fig. 105 *(Bottom)* Showing the approximate spread of high temperature heat over a severe stretched condition.

enough softening effect to permit the required upsetting as the surface is driven down with the hammer. Fig. 104 shows an application of heat in the blue temperature range over a wide area. This area could be any size from 1 or 2 inches in length and width to 5 or 6. Hammer blows spaced over this area will cause uniform upsetting instead of the condition shown in Fig. 103.

Low temperature shrinking, which includes any operation where heat is used below the red range, is not practical if the spot has any degree of work hardening. Severe work hardening requires heat up to the bright-red range to soften it completely. However, such areas also are stretched severely, otherwise they would not be work hardened. In heating work hardened areas, the high temperature should be confined as much as possible to the areas which are stretched severely, as indicated by Fig. 105. In a gouge having a cross section similar to this shape, most of the stretched metal, which also is work hardened, would be in the area between the two arrows. Red heat never should extend beyond this area.

QUENCHING

Quenching is a means of controlling the rate of cooling. The primary reason for quenching is to retain a greater amount of the upset than would be possible if the spot were allowed to cool slowly after shrinking. After the work with the hammer and dolly has been completed, the sooner the metal can be quenched, the more shrink effect will be obtained.

Quenching adds to the amount of shrinkage by stopping the yield of the heated area to the tension which results from contracting as the metal cools. Quenching is much more effective if the work with the hammer and dolly can be completed before the temperature has dropped below the color range. However, quenching still will have some effect if done while the temperature is above the point at which water will form steam on contact with the hot metal, particularly on relatively large areas.

Knowing when to quench is largely a matter of experience. The experienced metal man soon learns to judge visually when the surface will cool to the proper contour without quenching. If he sees that it will not, he will pass a wet sponge or cloth across the surface as he watches the effect. When the proper surface condition has been obtained, quenching should be stopped. Many times, quenching will show up minor buckles which can be straightened with the hammer and dolly block; then the surface can be quenched again. However, this must be done with the minimum loss of time. When reaching for the wet sponge, do not lay down the hammer or dolly where it will be difficult to pick up again. The best method is to hold both tools in one hand while the quenching is done with the other; this will avoid fumbling for tools if further straightening is needed.

Only in rare cases should a shrink spot be quenched rapidly without looking frequently at what is happening by moving the wet sponge away from the hot spot. If the spot is not checked as quenching is done, buckling of the metal in the surrounding area may result.

OVERSHRINKING

Overshrinking is the result of shrinking some of the temporarily expanded metal in addition to that which was stretched. When this occurs, it will have a drawing or puckering effect on the metal surface surrounding the overshrunk area.

A demonstration showing an effect similar to overshrinking can be made with a piece of cloth such as a handkerchief. With the cloth lying flat on a table top, gather a section in the center of it between the fingers. As long as this section is held it will be impossible to smooth the surrounding surface so that it will lie flat.

Overshrinking is more likely to occur when shrinking gouges than when shrinking a stretched condition which has been raised above the surface level. It can occur in either situation, however. A slight amount often is desirable because it will be relieved by the normal picking and hammer and dolly block work which will be done when the spot is metal finished. If it is too great, however, it will have a gathering effect on the adjoining surface, resulting in the formation of long wavy buckles in the metal. These can be relieved by using the hammer-on-dolly to restretch the shrunk area and, sometimes, some of the area immediately adjoining. When this is done, care should be taken to space the hammer blows over the affected area uniformly and to avoid pressing too hard against the dolly block. The desired effect is the spreading action of the hammer blow against the dolly. The rebound action caused by pressing the dolly hard against the inner surface will tend to raise the spot struck more than it should be.

SHRINKING PROCEDURE ON THE JOB

A typical example of the use of shrinking is provided by the procedure followed in straightening the gouged dents in the door lower panels shown in Figs. 106 and 107. Although the emphasis is on the shrinking procedure, all the straightening operations are explained so that the proper relationship of shrinking to the other procedures can be shown.

The damage on these two doors occurred in the same accident. The nature of the accident was not known, but the damage probably resulted from this automobile striking a glancing impact against a rigid, sharp object, probably a projection on the bumper of another automobile. However, the same damage could have been caused by another automobile striking this one while it was standing still. Whatever it was, the impact object approached from the front at a very sharp angle, contacting the front door almost at the front edge. As the impact object moved farther back, it

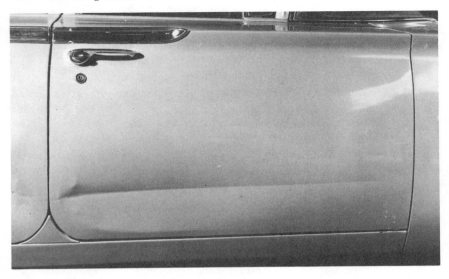

Fig. 106 Crease in a front door lower panel. The rear end of this crease will require shrinking.

Fig. 107 Crease in a rear door, similar to the one shown in Fig. 106.

dug deeper into the panel. Note that a sharp bend has formed along the lower edge from the center to the rear. The reinforced edges caused the impact object to bounce off the front door and strike the rear, causing a narrow, deep gouge all of the way. Probably the object came to rest at the rear end of the gouge on the rear door, Fig. 107. The second, lower gouge probably was caused by one of the automobiles being backed away from contact with the other.

There is nothing about the damages on these doors to make it desirable to repair one before the other. The procedure on the front is explained first, but the rear could have been done first just as well.

The inside of the front door is shown in Fig. 108. This shows the inside of the outer panel, partially covered with undercoating, and the loading hole. Note that easy access for hand tools is provided by this hole.

The first operation is shown in Fig. 109. Up to the point where the hammer is shown, the panel will not need shrinking. This operation was started as far forward as the metal man could reach with dolly block and both off- and on-dolly blows were used to straighten the dent to this point. The work would have been done much faster if the forward end of the dent could have been reached without too much difficulty; as it is, the forward end will have to be straightened by prying with rods passed through the hole in the inner panel or through the front drain hole.

Before the hammer and dolly block were used to straighten the dent, as

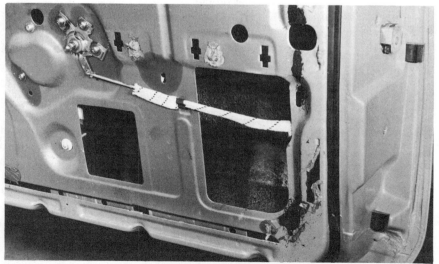

Fig. 108 Inside view of a front door, showing loading holes and part of the inner surface of the outer panel.

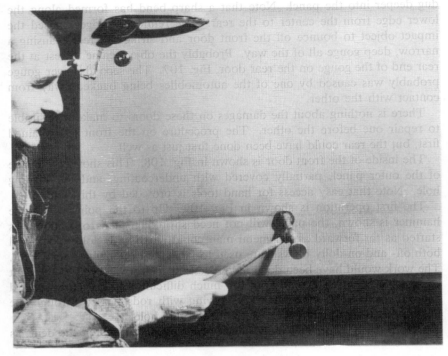

Fig. 109 Using the hammer-off-dolly to straighten the unstretched part of the crease. Most of the work was done off-dolly.

shown in Fig. 109, they were used along the lower edge to straighten the ridge formed as the panel bent over the flange of the inner panel. Hammer marks show along the ridge where this was done. The purpose was to relieve a strain on the metal above the ridge, permitting some of it to snap out, thus reducing the width of the dent. A similar operation is shown in Fig. 176, Chapter 6.

A word of caution concerning the use of the hammer and dolly block in straightening a light gouge, as shown in Fig. 109: use a high-crowned dolly block so that off-dolly hammer blows can be struck within ¼ inch of the point of dolly contact. The dolly contact should be kept on the underside of the crease and never allowed to wander off. Stiff hand pressure should be used on the dolly when striking off-dolly, and light hand pressure when striking on-dolly. Hammer blows should be relatively light. Used properly, off-dolly blows should be alternated from side to side, forming a double row of spots close enough together to nearly overlap. These should be carried along for approximately an inch ahead of the last on-dolly hammer blow, then on-dolly hammer blows should be made on the crease.

Fig. 110 Using a hand wire brush to remove paint after scorching it with an oxidizing flame.

The on-dolly blows should be carried forward almost as far as the off-dolly blows, and the entire operation should be repeated.

This work should be carried forward progressively, straightening the dent completely with one pass. The surface should be checked frequently to determine when enough stretched metal is being worked to cause the panel to bulge. The work was stopped at the point shown in Fig. 109 because a slight bulge was beginning to rise. The rest of the gouge was shrunk as it was straightened.

Part of the next step is shown in Fig. 110. Before using the wire brush to remove the paint, the surface was scorched with a strongly oxidizing flame. The flame was held almost on the surface of the panel and kept moving rapidly to avoid overheating the metal. By this method, paint can be burned very rapidly so that the brush will remove it easily.

The paint should always be burned on any surface where metal is to be shrunk. It enables the metal man to judge the temperature by color and leaves the surface smooth so that the level can be judged visually much more accurately. Also if the paint is not removed, the torch flame will burn it, leaving a gummy residue. Particles of this residue will be picked up on the hammer face, making it rough. If the hammer is used in this condition, it will make rough, choppy marks in the hot metal.

The first heat application for shrinking is shown in Fig. 111. This picture

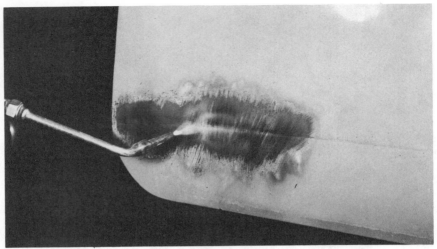

Fig. 111 Heating the gouge before shrinking. A temperature variation from faint color to bright blue was made by changing the speed of the moving torch from fast to slow.

was shot slightly late as the flame was being removed from contact with the surface. The flame first was played back and forth over the general area to spread enough heat to avoid a sharp break line betwen hot and cold metal. This was done with the tip of the inner cone about 1 inch from the surface. It was then lowered to about ½ inch above the gouge at the right end of the burned-off spot and moved steadily to the left to the point where it is shown. Because the stretched condition increases from the right to left, the torch was moved fairly rapidly at the start on the right, but slowed progressively as it moved to the left. This permitted a gradual increase in temperature from right to left. As an indication of the temperature, no actual color appeared in the first inch at the right end, but it had increased to slightly above bright blue at the left.

Shrinking this heated spot was done by using the hammer and dolly in the same manner they were used to straighten the forward section of the gouge where shrinking was not needed. (See Fig. 109.) As explained earlier in this chapter, only enough heat was necessary to permit the required amount of upsetting. However, in this case, the work had to be done rapidly because the spot was too small to remain hot long.

The remaining length of the buckle received one more heat application. Because the amount of stretch increased to the left, the temperature was allowed to rise further, up to cherry red in the deepest part. However, the heating method was the same, except that the flame was kept in place longer.

Fig. 112 Tools used in shrinking and metal finishing the gouge.

A body spoon and a spoon dolly were needed as the work approached the edge, because the shape of the facing prevented easy access with the dolly block. These tools and the others used on this job are shown in Fig. 112. The small screwdriver was used as a pry tool through the drain holes in the lower rear corner.

The end of the shrinking operation is shown in Fig. 113. This spot has been reheated and is being hammered down again because after the first operation it was left slightly high.

Two steps in the metal finishing operation are shown in Figs. 114 and 115. In Fig. 114, a heavy-duty disc sander with a sharp, 36 grit disc installed has been passed across the straightened and shrunk surface. Paint shows up in the low spots where it has not been burned off, and dark metal appears in the shrunk area. Note that there are few low spots. In Fig. 115, the low spots have been pried up and filed smooth. After buffing, the surface will be ready to repaint.

In Fig. 116, the gouge dent on the rear door has been roughed out and partially smoothed with the hammer and dolly block. Although this appeared to be stretched severely (see Fig. 107), most of the center part of the crease has straightened in the same manner as did the forward section of the front door.

The first step in roughing this panel was to relieve the sharp ridge along the lower edge with the hammer and dolly block. Then, by working through the loading hole, the dent was popped out and straightened with the hammer and dolly to the condition shown here. A pry rod was used to raise the forward end of the dent, because inner construction blocks

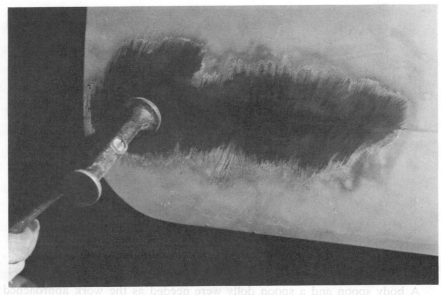

Fig. 113 The final shrinking operation on a high spot left after the gouge has been shrunk to level.

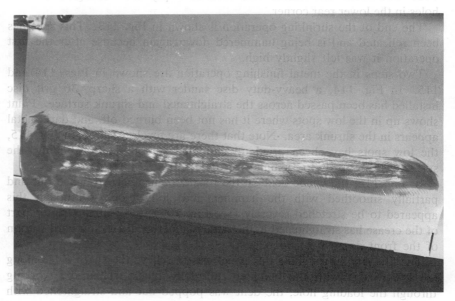

Fig. 114 Appearance of the straightened surface after disc sanding lightly with a sharp, 36-grit disc.

Fig. 115 The finished panel, ready for buffing. The low spots have been pried or picked up and filed smooth.

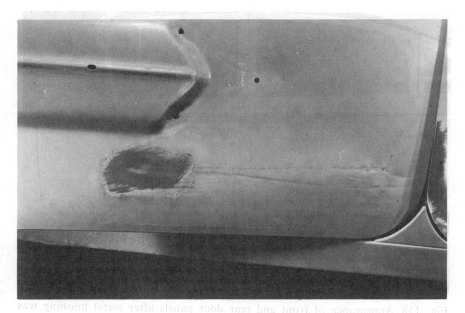

Fig. 116 Crease in the rear door, partially straightened. The rear end of the gouge has been prepared for shrinking by scorching and burning off the paint.

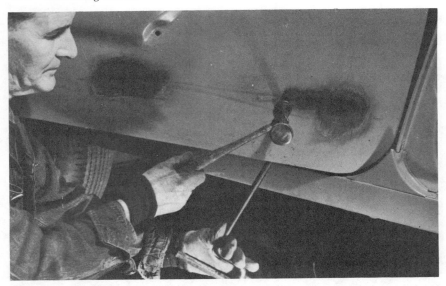

Fig. 117 Using a pry rod and hammer to partially shrink the front end of the rear door gouge. The inner construction blocks access with dolly or spoon.

Fig. 118 Appearance of front and rear door panels after metal finishing was completed.

Fig. 119 Appearance of the completed job after both lower panels had been refinished.

access to this area with either a dolly block or a body spoon.

The shrinking operation on the area where the paint is burned and brushed off was practically the same as performed on the rear edge of the front door. The front end of the dent was shrunk only partially because of the problems of access. The entire low spot could have been filled, but the shrinking operation shown in Fig. 117 reduced this enough to make the filling operation much easier and faster.

Shrinking over the end of a pry rod, as shown here, is simply a matter of warming the metal enough to make it upset when it is either pried up or driven down. By using the end of the pry rod on low spots as adjoining high spots are driven down, it is easy to shrink out most of the stretched metal in an area such as this. This results in the surface being drawn tight as the deeper parts of it are brought up to, or close to, level.

Shrinking over a pry rod is a very rapid operation because it is not done to exact limits. The purpose is to take out the slack and make the dent much smaller, not to restore the exact surface level. It requires less skill than is required to shrink a surface which is to be finished. It is important for the beginner to remember not to use heat much above the blue range and to select a rod which has a blunt point. In almost every case, a spot such as this should be quenched.

The completed metal finished panels are shown in Fig. 118. Both panels have been buffed with a fine grit sanding disc and are ready for painting. The solder fill on the rear door is relatively small and not deep. In soldering the door, there was very little tendency for the surface to distort with the heat because of the tightening effect of the partial shrinking operation.

The painted panels are ehown in Fig. 119. When the molding has been replaced on the rear door, there will be no evidence that either one had been damaged.

QUESTIONS ON SHRINKING METAL

1. Why is it that all upsetting of metal should not be considered as shrinking?
2. Why is shrinking a precision job?
3. Why does shrinking require well-developed skill with the hammer and dolly block?
4. What types of damage require shrinking?
5. When metal is stretched, is it necessary that both length and width be increased? Why?
6. When metal is stretched, can both length and width be increased?
7. What is the cause of false stretch?
8. Can all false stretch be avoided by proper straightening procedure? Why?
9. In the basic shrinking operation, how does the force of a hammer blow tend to cause an upset?
10. Why is it necessary to use heat to obtain the required upset?
11. Why must the hammer work be done rapidly when shrinking a relatively small spot?
12. Why should the dolly block be brought into use only after the upset has been made?
13. How does the procedure for shrinking a gouge differ from that for shrinking a raised area?
14. Why does the shrinking operation on gouges require the use of the dolly block in making the upset?
15. Why is the tendency to overshrink greater on a gouge than on a raised area of stretched metal?
16. Why is a relatively high temperature required in shrinking a severe gouge?
17. When shrinking a gouge, should the hand pressure on the dolly block be firm or light?
18. Why may it be necessary to use the hammer-on-dolly as a shrink spot cools?
19. On a long gouge, why is it best to work as long a section as possible with each heat application?
20. What is the result if an area being shrunk is not heated enough?
21. What is the result of using too much heat?
22. At what temperature, as indicated by color, will the metal be softened enough to begin to upset when hammered?
23. On what type of stretched metal can low temperature shrinking be done?
24. What type of stretched metal requires temperature in the red heat range?
25. What does quenching do?
26. How can the need for quenching be determined?
27. What is the result of overquenching?
28. What is the cause of overshrinking?

29. Why is a slight amount of overshrinking desirable?
30. On the door panel shown in Fig. 106, why was the forward part of the dent straightened without shrinking?
31. On the door panel shown in Fig. 106, why was the ridge along the lower edge straightened before the dent was?
32. On the door panel in Fig. 106, why was the paint scorched and brushed off before shrinking the gouge?
33. On the door panel in Fig. 106, why was the temperature gradually increased as the heat application approached the rear edge of the door?
34. On the rear door shown in Fig. 107, why was the front end of the gouge only partially shrunk and then filled?

5

Welding

Welding is a term which is difficult to define exactly because in the broad meaning it includes most of the processes of joining metal by the use of heat, including soldering. These processes vary widely in method and equipment. The original and the simplest method is the blacksmith's. He heated the pieces to be joined in the forge until they were plastic and then hammered them together on the anvil. Many modern industrial methods make use of the heat of the electric arc or heat caused by electrical resistance; even heat resulting from friction is used for some special applications. In newer methods, wide use is made of mechanical, electrical, and electronic control systems to make the process completely automatic. Manual methods, such as the oxyacetylene torch and hand-operated electric arc, are still used industrially; however, as progress is made in the development of more efficient mechanized methods, their use is becoming more and more restricted to repair and maintenance work.

Welding processes may be classified by whether the metal welded is heated to the melting point, so that it will flow together; or whether it is heated close to the melting point and joined by the application of force; or heated and joined by diffusion of a molten filler metal into the surfaces of the parts to be joined. The first usually is called *fusion welding* because the metal fuses and flows together; it includes both the oxyacetylene and the electric arc processes. The second usually is called *pressure welding* because of the pressure applied to make the joint. It includes the electrical resistance and forge welding processes. The most common of the electrical resistance processes is spot welding. It is used for almost all factory sheet metal welding because of its economy and the fact that it causes practically no heat distortion. The third is called either *soldering* or *brazing,* depending on the type and melting temperature of the filler metal used.

The nature of the welding required in sheet metal repair is such that a large part of it is best suited to the oxyacetylene torch processes. These include both the fusion welding of steel and brazing. In fusion welding of steel, the metal being welded is heated to the melting point

134

and usually a filler rod of similar metal is melted and added to the joint. In brazing steel, the metal is heated only to the temperature at which the brazing rod melts so that it can be deposited on the joint; the brazing material, usually a copper base alloy, flows onto the steel, making a strong joint for most purposes. Brazing requires the use of flux to clean the steel surfaces, but no flux is required for fusion welding mild steel with the oxyacetylene torch. It is essential for the beginner metal man to learn to do both types of oxyacetylene welding in any position, flat, vertical, or overhead.

Electric arc welding has some important applications in sheet metal repair work, but it is not a complete substitute for the oxyacetylene process. There is reason to believe, however, that the development of the shielded arc welding process may tend to change the situation. In time, this method could almost completely replace the oxyacetylene torch, leaving the torch as, primarily, a heating device.

The primary advantage of both the conventional and shielded arc weld-

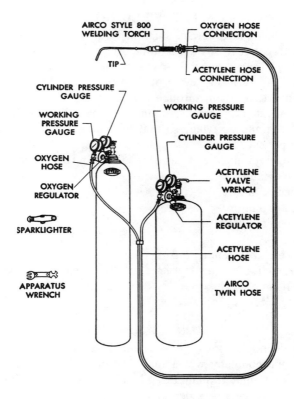

Fig. 120 Oxyacetylene welding outfit.

ing of sheet metal is the reduction of heat distortion. However, there are several disadvantages. An important one is the extra expense for the equipment. Another is that metal men have been slow to adopt arc welding because to do it properly on sheet metal requires a comparatively high skill. The last is less of a disadvantage than it has been in the past on both the conventional and the shielded arc methods. Better filler rods and better equipment have made considerable reduction in the skill requirements for conventional arc welding. Some of the equipment used in shielded arc welding can be operated more easily than oxyacetylene equipment. The advantages of less heat distortion and, in many cases, much greater speed, justify much greater use of both methods of arc welding.

It is common body shop practice to use the term *welding* when referring to the oxyacetylene welding of steel with a steel filler rod, because it is the method used most frequently. Other processes are referred to by name, such as brazing, arc welding, and resistance spot welding.

OXYACETYLENE WELDING EQUIPMENT

There are several different manufacturers of oxyacetylene welding equipment. Regardless of the manufacturer, however, all such equipment operates on a similar principle. The flame is produced by mixing the acetylene and oxygen in the proper proportions in the torch mixing chamber and passing them through the orifice in the torch tip where they are ignited. A steady flame is maintained by adjusting the pressure of both the oxygen and acetylene so that the mixture escapes from the torch tip at the proper speed.

Gas welding equipment consists of the following units:
1. Oxygen cylinder.
2. Acetylene cylinder.
3. Oxygen regulator.
4. Acetylene regulator.
5. Hoses.
6. Torch, includes handle, mixing chamber, and tip.
7. Eye protection for the operator, usually goggles or a face shield.
8. Spark lighter.
9. Hand truck for cylinders.

GAS CYLINDERS

The gas cylinders, sometimes called tanks or bottles, normally are supplied by the company which manufactures the gas. Except in operations where only limited quantities of gas are used, the cylinders are provided without charge for a period of thirty days; after thirty days a demurrage charge is made. Cylinders are also available for limited quantity users on various purchase or long-term lease plans. The exact nature of these plans varies from one manufacturer to another, but, in general, the user pays for the cylinders plus the normal maintenance which they will require. The user is guaranteed also that full cylinders will be available on an exchange basis when he presents his empties to the dealer. The price for the gas under this plan is slightly higher than for the large volume user.

Safety precautions require that the cylinders be attached to something which will prevent them from being knocked over. The common practice is to mount them on a specially designed portable hand truck. When portability is not required, they may be chained to something rigid, such as a wall or bench. The use of the hand truck is more desirable, however, because it simplifies the problem of removal in case of fire.

THE OXYGEN CYLINDER

This is simply a cylindrical, high-strength steel tank with a specially designed bronze shut-off valve and a safety device to release the pressure under emergency conditions. The standard-size cylinder, shown in Fig. 121, has a capacity of 244 cubic feet at 2,200 pounds pressure per square inch at 70°F. Smaller cylinders are also available. One common size holds 122 cubic feet; similar cylinders of approximately the same size are available from the various manufacturers.

The pressure in an oxygen cylinder varies according to the temperature. A fully charged cylinder will only show a pressure of about 1,780 pounds per square inch (psi) if it is kept outdoors in zero temperature. After it has warmed to 70°F., the pressure will increase to 2,200 psi and, if the temperature is raised to 120°F., the pressure will increase to 2,500 psi.

The high-pressure gauge on most oxygen regulators is calibrated to indicate the number of cubic feet of oxygen in the cylinder at 70°F. If the temperature varies from 70°F., an allowance must be made to determine the amount left in the cylinder. All such calibrations are approximate; however, they are close enough for ordinary use.

All oxygen cylinders are equipped with a safety cap which protects the valve. This cap should be kept in place at all times when the cylinder, whether full or empty, is not connected to the welding outfit.

Oxygen cylinders are subject to the Interstate Commerce Commission rules governing containers used for transporting compressed gases. These rules are intended to ensure that such containers are safe. However, the very nature of a container containing gas compressed to the pressure normally found in an oxygen cylinder makes it absolutely essential for the user to follow every possible safety precaution. These cylinders should never be stored near heat or highly flammable materials. The National Board of Fire Underwriters have rules for the storage of oxygen

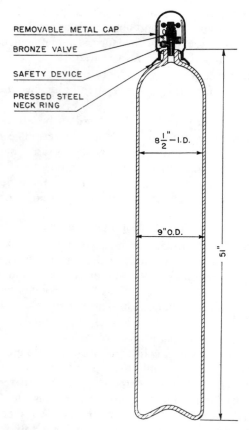

REMOVABLE METAL CAP

BRONZE VALVE

SAFETY DEVICE

PRESSED STEEL
NECK RING

$8\frac{1}{2}"$—I.D.

9" O.D.

51"

Fig. 121 Oxygen cylinder. Oxygen capacity 244 cu.ft. at 2200 lb. per sq. in. pressure at 70° F.

cylinders. In many communities, there are also local regulations. These should be followed.

A particular hazard is created when oil and grease are exposed to high-pressure oxygen. A small drop of grease in an oxygen valve can be the cause of a fire and an explosion. Under no circumstances should such material be allowed to get on cylinders or any other gas welding equipment. Other highly oxidizable materials may be equally hazardous. Greasy clothing or gloves should not be used around gas welding equipment, either.

Oxygen cylinders should never be used to support another object or as rollers to move something heavy. An electric arc should never be struck on the cylinder because it may cause it to rupture. The sudden release of oxygen under high pressure would cause tremendous damage; it would probably injure and possibly kill the operator and any other persons in the vicinity.

THE ACETYLENE CYLINDER

The acetylene cylinder differs in construction from the oxygen cylinder. This difference is made necessary by the nature of acetylene gas. It is dangerous to store it at high pressure in open-space containers. The danger stems from the fact that either heat or shock can cause it to separate into its more simple constituents, releasing tremendous amounts of heat as it does so. The fire and explosion hazards under such circumstances are so great that laws and regulations have been established governing the construction of acetylene cylinders.

The problem of storage of acetylene compressed to high pressure was

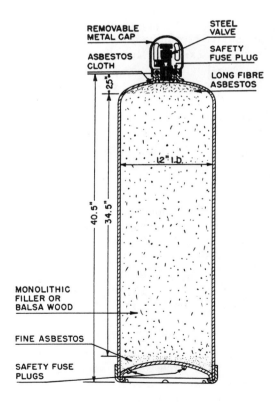

Fig. 122 Acetylene cylinder. Acetylene capacity approx. 275 cu.ft. at 250 lb. per sq. in. pressure at 70° F.

solved by the discovery that it can be dissolved readily into liquid acetone. Acetone can dissolve many times its own volume of acetylene gas. This knowledge led to the development of various porous filling materials for the cylinder. Such materials serve as a sponge to absorb the acetone and prevent the formation of open cavities. Thus, all of the acetylene pumped into the cylinder must be dissolved into the acetone. A cross sectional view of such a cylinder is shown in Fig. 122.

An acetylene cylinder 12 inches in diameter and 40.5 inches high can store approximately 275 cubic feet of acetylene at a pressure of 250 psi. Acetylene dissolved in acetone at this pressure in cylinders filled with suitable porous material can be handled with safety. Only a small fraction of this amount of acetylene could be stored safely in an open-space container. For this reason, no attempt ever should be made to transfer acetylene from the proper cylinder to another container.

Safety fuse plugs which melt at 220°F. are provided at the top and bottom of the acetylene cylinder. If the temperature of the area in which the cylinder is stored reaches this point, the acetylene will be released into the surrounding air and the possibility of an explosion will be avoided.

The extreme fire hazard of acetylene dictates rigid safety precautions. The acetylene cylinders should never be used to prop something up or as rollers. Being filled with liquid acetone, they always should be stored and used in an upright position. If a cylinder has been laid on its side, before it is used again, it should be allowed to stand upright for some time to permit the acetone to flow back away from the valve. If not, acetone may be discharged into the welding outfit, causing a void in the cylinder and damage to the equipment.

Pressure variations due to temperature changes are greater for acetylene than for oxygen. Furthermore, because the gas is dissolved in acetone, gauge pressure is not an exact indicator of the amount of gas in a cylinder. The only true indication is weight. Fourteen and 0.74 cu. ft. of acetylene gas weigh one pound. When necessary to determine the exact amount of gas in a cylinder, it is necessary to weigh the cylinder and subtract the tare (empty) weight to determine the weight of the gas. The cubic feet can be calculated by multiplying by 14.74. The tare weight will be found stamped on the cylinder.

The Oxyacetelyne Welding Outfit

Welding equipment consists of the two regulators for oxygen and acetylene, the hose, and the torch with an assortment of various-size tips. Goggles or other eye protection, a spark lighter, and a wrench having openings for all of the threaded connections are essential accessories. Most manufacturers offer kits which include all of these items in one package. The gas cylinders are not considered a part of this package because, as mentioned earlier, they usually belong to the company which manufactures the gas. A hand truck for the cylinders is an essential item also, but it usually is sold separately.

The Regulators. The regulators for both gases operate on the same principle, but they are made so that they are not interchangeable, for reasons of safety. The connections to the cylinders are of different size, and left-hand threads are used on the connections to the acetylene hose; left-hand threads also are used on the hose connection to the torch handle. This arrangement completely eliminates the possibility of making a wrong connection anywhere in the system.

A cross sectional view of a single-stage regulator is shown in Fig. 123. The important part of the regulator is the valve which controls the flow of gas as it is needed. This is done by the adjusting spring and the compensating spring. In use, the adjusting screw is turned in against the adjusting spring until the desired pressure shows on the low-pressure gauge. This action releases gas to the low-pressure chamber of the regulator, from which it flows through the hose to the torch. As long as the torch valve is open, the flow of gas will continue. Closing the torch valve causes a pressure increase in the low-pressure chamber which overcomes the pressure of the adjusting spring and closes the valve.

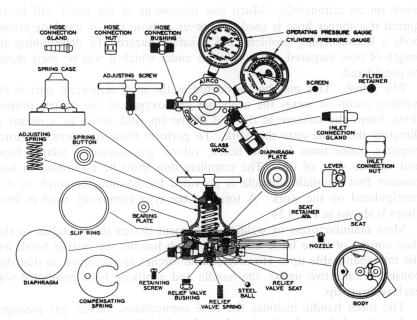

Fig. 123 Single-stage regulator parts.

The operation of a two-stage regulator is similar to that of a single-stage regulator, except that the pressure is stepped down in two stages instead of one. The first stage reduces the pressure to a predetermined level, and the second reduces it to whatever figure the adjusting screw is set. The two-stage regulator may be expected to provide more exact control of pressure and to last longer than a single-stage regulator.

The Hose. The hose used in gas welding is made especially for the purpose. It must be flexible, nonporous, and have sufficient strength to withstand the pressure of the gases. Under no circumstances should an air hose or hoses intended for oil be substituted for welding hose because of the danger of explosion.

Separate hoses may be used for acetylene and oxygen, but it is the usual practice to use twin, or coupled, hoses because they are easier to handle. Both hoses are of the same size, but they differ in color and the threaded connections with which they are fitted. The acetylene hose is usually red and always is fitted with left-hand threaded connections. The left-hand thread may be identified easily by a groove around the outside of the brass end fitting. The oxygen hose may be either green or black and is fitted with right-hand threaded connections. In replacing these fittings, which is sometimes necessary, it is important to make certain that the right fitting is used on the right hose.

Ten feet is about the minimum length of hose which is practical for work on an automobile. Much less movement of the outfit will be required if a longer hose is used. However, a hose that is too long creates both a housekeeping problem and a safety hazard. In determining the length of hose required, the conditions under which it will be used should be considered.

The Torch. This may be considered as the most important part of the welding outfit—it mixes the acetylene and oxygen in the proper proportions, burns the mixture at the end of the tip, and serves as a means of directing the flame onto the work. To perform these functions, the torch requires connections for the hoses, valves, gas passages, mixing head, and various sizes of tips. The complete unit must be assembled in such manner that a suitable handle is provided for holding the torch as it is manipulated on the work. A torch of the type commonly used in body shops is shown in Fig. 124

Most manufacturers of welding equipment design their torches so that they consist of three basic units: the torch handle, the mixing head, and the interchangeable tips. However, some torches are designed so that they consist of only two units: the handle and a mixing head combined with each separate tip.

The torch handle includes the hose connections, valves, gas passages, and is threaded on the front end so that the mixing chamber can be at-

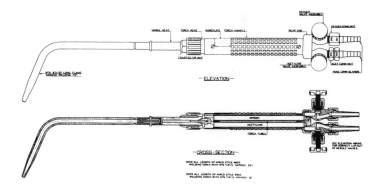

Fig. 124 Oxyacetylene torch assembly.

tached. Internal and external seats are provided on the handle and mixing head so that a tight connection is made for each gas passage when the mixing head is installed properly.

Most heavy-duty torch handles are designed so that the valves are at the rear end. Many light-duty torches are designed with the valves at the front end. Not all manufacturers of welding equipment follow this practice exactly, however. Some light-duty torches are made with the valves at the rear end, and some of the early heavy-duty torches were made with front-end valves.

The use of a single mixing head with all sizes of tips is an economy measure. For most work it is satisfactory and saves on the original investment. The use of separate mixers for each tip is desirable if the volume of work will justify the extra investment.

In addition to opening and shutting off the flow of gases, the valves provide a means of making fine adjustment of the flame. The adjustment of one valve is dependent on the other, because the flow of gases must be kept in proportion regardless of the size of the flame.

Common sense care, plus a few simple precautions, are all that are needed for trouble-free operation from any good torch. Rough handling should be avoided. The torch should never be used as a lever or bar to push metal into place for welding. When not in use, it should be hung up or put in a safe place to avoid accidental damage. Probably the worst abuse that a torch is exposed to in a body shop is laying it on the floor when working on the lower part of the body; it may be damaged either by being stepped on or by heavy tools being dropped on it. Such abuse can bend the valve stems or tip or even do worse damage.

In changing tips, care should be taken to avoid nicking or scratching the mating surfaces of the connection of the mixing chamber to the handle. Mixing chambers not in use, particularly on torches which have them combined with separate tips, often are damaged by not being cared for properly. They should have a storage place where they will be protected. When mixing chambers are being attached to the handle, they should be inspected to see that there is no dirt on the mating surfaces of the connection.

Torch valves should never be tightened so that they are difficult to loosen. To do so will damage the seat. After the seat becomes damaged, it may not be possible to shut off the gas completely even though the valve is turned too tight. The same rule applies to the sleeve nut which holds the mixing chamber in place.

SETTING UP THE OXYACETYLENE WELDING OUTFIT

To ensure safe operation and avoid troubles such as leaks or plugged orifices, a definite sequence should be followed in setting up a new outfit and putting it into operation. Essentially the same steps should be followed in returning an outfit to use after it has been disconnected for some time, or if there is the possibility that dust or dirt could have entered the passages. The sequence is:

1. Place the oxygen and acetylene cylinders on the truck and chain them securely. Or, if a stationary installation is to be used, be sure that the cylinders are fastened in an upright position.

2. Remove the safety caps and put them where they will be available when needed.

3. Inspect the end of the inlet gland on both regulators and the seats in the outlets of both cylinder valves. If any foreign material is found, wipe it off. The eraser on a lead pencil makes an excellent tool for wiping out the seat in the cylinder valve.

4. Open and close both cylinder valves to blow out any dirt or dust which may have entered the valve passage. Close the valves as quickly as possible to prevent the escape of an excessive amount of gas.

5. Connect both regulators. Do not attach hoses.

6. Be sure that the adjusting screws are released, then open the cylinder valves, note the pressure on the high-pressure gauge, and close the valves.

7. Check for leaks by watching the gauge for pressure drop. If time permits, the gauge should be left under pressure for a period of several minutes. If pressure holds steady, omit the next step.

8. If pressure drops, it will be caused by one of the following conditions: (a) leaking connection, (b) creeping regulator valve, or a (c) leak in the regulator. Retightening the cylinder connection may stop the

leak; otherwise the regulator should be serviced by a competent repairman before being used.

9. Blow out the regulator by turning the adjusting screw in far enough to release a small quantity of gas, then release the adjusting screw.

10. Attach the hoses to the regulators. Do not attach to the torch.

11. Blow out the hoses by releasing enough gas to carry any dust or dirt to the other end.

12. Attach the torch handle without the mixing head.

13. Blow out the torch handle. Open each valve separately to avoid possible fire hazard.

14. Check the hoses and connections for leaks by adjusting both regulators to maximum working pressures (acetylene, 15 psi; oxygen, 15 to 30 psi), then close both the torch and the cylinder valves and watch the gauges for pressure drop. This should also be left under pressure for several minutes. Retighten the connections if the pressure drops.

15. Attach the mixing head; if separate tip is used, leave it off.

16. Blow out the mixing head, using maximum oxygen pressure. Check both gases for smooth flow.

17. Attach separate tip, if used.

18. Light the torch.

This procedure normally would be followed only once, when the outfit is new. It will not take very long unless trouble is encountered with leaks. If leaks are present, however, they must be fixed. With a leak, there is more involved than just the loss of the gas—there is the danger of fire or explosion.

In cases where an outfit has been laid aside for some time and is being put back into use again, the need for blowing it out in the sequence listed above is greater than with a new outfit. This is particularly true if there is any doubt as to how it has been cared for. Even though the hoses have not been disconnected from the regulators and the torch, the complete outfit should be disconnected and each piece blown out separately. This will ensure that dirt in the regulator will not be blown through the hoses into the valves and mixing head.

Each time a full cylinder is installed in the outfit, the cylinder valve should be blown out and the mating surfaces of the gland inspected for foreign material, particularly oil or grease. After the regulator is installed, the adjusting screw should be checked to see that it is loose, then the cylinder valve should be opened and closed to check for leaks. If the high pressure drops without affecting the low-pressure gauge, it is probably because the connection to the cylinder is leaking. In such cases, it is best to remove the regulator and recheck the mating surfaces of the connection before applying excessive force to pull the connection tight with a big wrench. More often than not, the trouble will be dirt on the surfaces which has escaped detection. To leave it there and pull the connection tighter may not stop the leak, but it probably will damage the outfit.

In changing the cylinder, it is important to be careful with the regulator so that it will not be knocked around or dropped. It is especially important that the mating surfaces do not come into contact with any material which will contaminate them. Such precautions are only a matter of awareness of the problem and common sense.

Lighting and Adjusting the Torch

Lighting and adjusting the torch flame is a matter of making a series of adjustments in the proper sequence. Most of the sheet metal welding operations require the flame to be adjusted so that equal parts of acetylene and oxygen are being burned. Starting with an outfit which previously has been shut off and bled, the procedure for opening it up, lighting and adjusting the flame properly is as follows:

1. Check both regulator adjusting screws to see that they are released.
2. Open the oxygen cylinder valve; keep turning the hand wheel until the open seat position is reached. Several turns will be required.
3. Open the acetylene cylinder valve one-half turn.
4. Open the oxygen valve on the torch about one-quarter turn.
5. Turn the oxygen regulator adjusting screw inward until the required pressure is indicated on the low-pressure gauge.
6. Close the oxygen valve.
7. Open the acetylene valve on the torch about one-quarter turn.
8. Turn the acetylene regulator adjusting screw inward until the low-pressure gauge reads the same as the oxygen.
9. Use the spark lighter to light the escaping acetylene.
10. Adjust the acetylene valve until the yellow flame begins to push away from the tip. (See Fig. 125)
11. Open and adjust the oxygen valve until all but a slight trace of the long, feathery flame disappears, leaving a clearly defined, intense blue cone of neutral flame burning on the end of the tip. (See Fig. 126)

The exact pressures to which the oxygen and acetylene regulators should be adjusted are determined by tip size. The reading on the gauge always will be at least equal to the number of the tip, and with some makes of equipment it may be higher. Many welders use approximately 5 pounds of pressure for the tips up to number 5, and increase the pressure to the tip number when larger tips are used. Higher pressures, unless excessive, will do no harm except to make it more difficult to adjust the torch flame.

The size of the neutral flame produced with any tip can be varied to

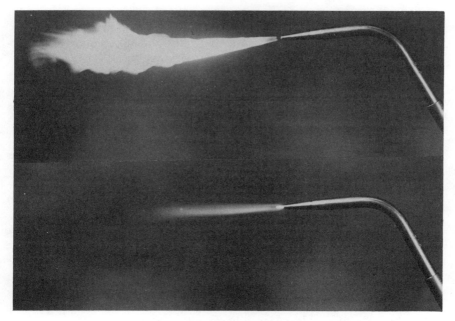

Fig. 125 Adjustment of the acetylene flame before the oxygen valve is opened.

Fig. 126 The neutral flame.

some degree by adjusting the amount of gases released. The variation in size that can be obtained in this manner is not as much as the difference in size of flame produced by the next larger or smaller tips. For any one tip size, changing the flame size can be done only by changing the speed of the gas flowing through the orifice. If the gas flows too fast, it will blow the flame out, because the gas will be moving faster than the flame can consume it. If it flows too slowly, there will be backfiring, making it difficult to weld.

Some tendency to backfiring is always present in a gas welding operation because of the molten particles of metal which fly from the puddle. When one of these flies into the tip orifice, it extinguishes the flame momentarily by blocking the flow of gas. In most cases, the blocking action is only momentary, because the particle is cooling and shrinking and gas pressure is building up against it. As the flow starts again, the gas is reignited by the molten metal in the puddle. The result will be a minor explosion having sufficient force to blow molten metal out of the puddle; it will make a sound much like a rifle shot. All of this action takes place within a fraction of a second. Occasionally, backfiring will be repeated with almost machine-gun rapidity.

Slowing the gas too much also can permit the flame to enter the tip orifice and follow the passage into the mixing head, making an angry, buzzing sound. When this occurs, the valves should be shut off immediately. It is best to shut the acetylene off first because the fire cannot burn without fuel. Before relighting, the tip should be inspected for partially blocked orifices and both valves opened separately to be sure that the gas flows freely. The flame should be adjusted so that it is large enough to prevent the condition from recurring, or, if a smaller flame is needed, a smaller tip should be installed.

Adjusting the flame for paddle soldering and some other heating operations is simply a matter of using less oxygen so that a long feathery flame is produced. The flame may be used at any adjustment that is desired, but it is best to avoid using a yellow flame because it will tend to deposit soot on the surface being heated.

Acetylene burning alone will give off a large quantity of sooty, black smoke unless it is forced out of the tip orifice fast enough to mix with the air. This soot will rise into the air and later settle, making a very undesirable mess. This condition may be avoided by opening the valve wide enough to cause the gas to mix with the air and burn clean as soon as it is lighted. It is not uncommon for the beginner to leave the torch smoking while he tries to decide which adjustment to make next. He should be trained to open the valve past the point of heavy smoking as soon as he strikes the light. Proper flame adjustment cannot be made until the acetylene valve is opened to this position, so it is simply a matter of doing it without hesitation to avoid the unnecessary soot.

The Oxyacetylene Flame

The primary characteristic of the oxyacetylene flame which makes it suitable for welding is its intense, high temperature—about 5,850°F. when adjusted properly for welding. Temperatures up to 6,300°F. can be developed by adjusting the flame to an excess of oxygen; this higher temperature is not suitable for welding steel, however, because of the ill effects it has on molten steel.

The oxyacetylene flame actually consists of two flames: the intense blue inner cone and the sheath flame. The highest temperature is produced in the blue inner cone. The temperature of the sheath flame, which extends several inches beyond the inner cone, is much lower. The high temperature of the inner cone is used for practically all torch operations.

There are three basic torch flames which are made by adjusting the torch valves to vary the ratio of oxygen and acetylene which is being used. These may be considered as flame types. They are: (1) neutral flame, (2) carburizing flame, and (3) oxidizing flame.

The neutral flame is used for practically all welding operations on mild steel. In most cases, either the carburizing or the oxidizing flame will be harmful to steel. Only a very slight resetting of either valve will change the flame from one type to the other. For this reason, it is essential for the beginner to be familiar with the characteristics of all three.

The Neutral Flame. The term *neutral flame* indicates a flame which has been adjusted so that it does not throw off either carbon (from the acetylene), or oxygen to contaminate the molten metal. When the flame is neutral, the torch valves have been adjusted so that the volume of acetylene and oxygen entering the mixing chamber is in the exact ratio needed to produce complete combustion. When adjusting the flame setting, this condition can be recognized by the disappearance of the feathery streamers, leaving a sharply defined, intense blue inner cone.

The neutral flame will produce a clear, clean appearing puddle which flows easily. It does this because the surrounding sheath flame has nothing in it to affect the molten metal. The sheath flame then serves as a protective mantle to prevent burning of the molten metal by oxygen in the surrounding air.

The temperature of the neutral flame is approximately 5,850°F. at the tip of the cone. This temperature drops rapidly in a very short distance; the midsection of the sheath flame will be about 3,800°F., and at the outer end about 2,300°F. Thus, it is obvious that the inner cone should be held quite close to the puddle to obtain rapid melting.

The Carburizing Flame. The term *carburizing flame* indicates a flame which has been adjusted so that it throws off unburned carbon into the sheath flame. The presence of this condition can be recognized easily by the feathery streamers which extend from the tip of the inner cone.

The carburizing flame will cause the molten metal to boil and lose the clear appearance it has under the neutral flame. This is caused by the addition of carbon to the molten metal from the flame. A weld made with a carburizing flame will be brittle when cold.

An experiment to demonstrate the effect of the carburizing flame can be made very easily. Adjust the flame so that the feathery streamers extend at least ½ inch beyond the inner cone. Then, play this flame on one corner of a piece of sheet metal, keeping it in the position it should be for the neutral flame, so that the feathery streamers actually strike the heated surface. While the piece is at bright red temperature, plunge it into cold water. A file test will prove that the metal is much harder because carbon has been added.

This experiment can be varied by keeping the carburizing flame on the hot metal for different lengths of time. If the flame is kept on long enough before quenching the metal in the water, the heated spot will become so hard it will snap like a piece of glass.

A slight amount of carburizing may not be particularly injurious to a weld in mild steel, but it is not desirable. If there is excessive carburizing, the weld definitely will be weakened. On some of the nonferrous metals, such as nickel and Monel metal, the carburizing flame sometimes is used without ill results.

Using a carburizing flame to heat metal for the shrinking operation can cause considerable trouble because hard spots will result. When the file strikes these spots, it will chatter instead of cut, and be damaged in the process.

The Oxidizing Flame. The term *oxidizing flame* indicates a flame which has been adjusted so that it throws off excess oxygen into the sheath flame. There are no visible streamers, but it may be recognized easily by the harsh hissing sound it makes, and the excessive foaming and sparking it causes in the puddle. It can be recognized also as the flame is being adjusted by a shrinking of the inner cone and a purplish color.

The oxidizing flame has no use in welding steel. The excess oxygen will cause the molten metal to burn. The slightest trace of excess oxygen should be avoided, because the weld will be weakened proportionally.

The oxidizing flame sometimes is used for heating heavy parts to temperatures below the bright red heat range. It develops approximately to 6,300°F., which is slightly more than the 5,850°F. of the neutral flame.

OXYACETYLENE FUSION WELDING PROCEDURE

The oxyacetylene fusion weld is made by manipulating the torch flame so that a puddle of molten metal is started and carried along the seam. Normally, a bead is built up by depositing molten metal from a filler rod as the puddle moves along. The use of a filler rod is not always necessary, however, if there is enough metal on the edges to be welded so that they will flow together and make a bead of sufficient strength without it.

Making a good weld is a matter of manipulating the flame properly and depositing the filler metal in the proper position at the proper time.

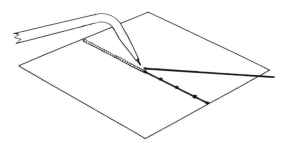

Fig. 127 Angle of the flame to, and its distance from, the work.

To do this, the following conditions must be kept under control by the operator: (1) distance of the end of the flame from the work, (2) angle of flame to the line of the seam, (3) rate of travel, (4) side motion (weaving) of the torch, and (5) position of the filler rod end in relation to the puddle and flame.

Each of these conditions is discussed separately in the following sections.

FLAME DISTANCE

The distance of the flame end from the work can vary to some degree for different welds. In most cases it should be quite close, but it should never touch the molten metal. The approximate distance is shown in Fig. 127.

The actual distance is determined by the temperature and the spread of heat. The closer the flame is to the work, the higher the temperature will be, and the more it will be concentrated on a very small spot. If the flame is moved back from the work, the drop in temperature is quite rapid. For example: the temperature of the inner cone of the neutral flame is 5,850°F., but the temperature at the end of the sheath flame is only 2,300°F. When a small tip suitable for welding sheet metal is used, this drop occurs in a distance of 2 or 3 inches.

In welding sheet metal, it is desirable to raise the temperature of the puddle to the melting point as quickly as possible. It also is desirable to prevent the spread of heat into the surrounding metal as much as possible. This would seem to indicate that the flame should be held so that the inner cone almost touches the metal. However, it is quite difficult to hold the flame in that position without actually touching it to the molten metal occasionally. There is the additional problem of the blast of the hot gases in the sheath flame which blow against the molten metal in the puddle. A much safer distance is to hold the inner cone away from the puddle just slightly less than its length. Thus a smaller flame would be held closer to the puddle than a larger one. At this distance, the blast effect of the flame is slowed down, and the possibility of accidentally touching the hot puddle is avoided.

Distance affects penetration to some extent. Even on light sheet metal, time is required for heat to flow through from one surface to the other. On heavier metal, time is even more important. By holding the distance about equal to the length of the inner cone, this needed time is provided. If it is held much closer, it may be difficult to obtain full penetration—only the upper surface will be melted.

Greater distance may be required when welding light to heavy metal. In such cases, the flame must be directed so that the heavy metal is brought up to the melting point without overheating the light so that it melts away. However, other factors as well as distance must be considered when such welding problems are encountered.

FLAME ANGLE

The angle of the flame to the work will vary to some degree according to the job. Actually, two angles must be considered: (1) the angle of the flame to the surface and (2) the angle of the flame to the line of the seam.

In making a simple butt weld on relatively flat stock, the angle of the flame to the puddle should be somewhere between 30° and 45° and pointed directly down the line of the seam. This angle is shown in Fig. 127. If increased penetration is needed, the angle should be increased. If less penetration is needed, the angle should be reduced.

Pointing the flame directly down the seam line on a butt weld will preheat both sides evenly. If the torch is turned to either side, that side will be heated more than the other. This will cause unequal expansion and tend to separate the edges even though they are tack welded together.

On lap welds or when welding light metal to heavy, a different condition will be found. If the torch is pointed down the line of a lap weld seam, the flame will tend to melt the exposed edge of the upper piece faster than it melts the metal which it covers. The answer to this is to hold the flame so that it is turned slightly away from the edge, and to hold the filler rod so that it acts as a shield for the exposed edge. This position of flame and filler rod is shown in Fig. 128. Note that the opera-

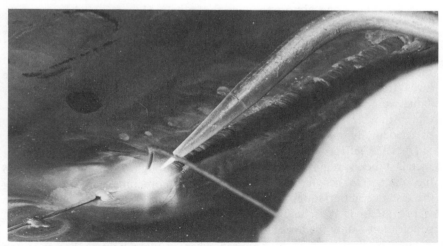

Fig. 128 Position of the flame and filler rod in welding a butt joint. Bending the rod permits the operator to keep his hand away from the heat.

tor has bent the filler rod so that his hand will be away from the heat of the hot blast from the torch.

In welding light to heavy metal, it always will be necessary to hold the flame so that it points toward the heavy piece. The greater the difference in thickness, the more the flame should be pointed toward the heavy piece. In such cases, it is a matter of experimenting to find the angle and distance from the puddle which will bring both edges to the melting point at the same time.

RATE OF TRAVEL

The rate of travel governs the width of the puddle and, to some degree, the depth of the penetration. Holding the flame on one spot without moving it will cause the puddle to grow larger until it melts through; moving it along the seam too fast will not heat the metal fast enough to make a puddle. Obviously the proper speed is somewhere between these two extremes.

With the torch held at the proper angle and distance, the rate of travel can be adjusted easily by watching the width of the puddle. If it becomes too narrow, travel should slow down; if it spreads too wide, the forward movement should be speeded up.

Lack of confidence many times prevents a beginner from determining the proper rate of travel. Just as soon as the puddle grows a little too large, the novice will pull the flame away from the puddle completely. This disrupts everything. All that is needed is to move along the seam a little faster.

WEAVING THE FLAME

Weaving the flame from side to side will spread the heat over a wider path and slow the forward travel. The result will be deeper penetration and more time to add filler metal if a heavy bead is desired.

The weaving motion may be either a straight back-and-forth motion which, when combined with the forward motion, creates a zigzag effect, or it may be a spiral motion. In either case, the result is essentially the same.

When welding light gauge metal such as is found in body panels, it is largely a matter of operator's choice whether the flame should weave or follow a straight line. Mostly, it is only necessary to hold the flame steady and move forward just fast enough to permit the puddle to spread to the desired width. This spreads the heat into the adjoining metal less than weaving will. The result will be slightly faster travel and less heat distortion.

Many welders weave the flame whether it is necessary or not, because they find that they can hold it steadier that way. If so, it is better to weave than to attempt to hold the torch in a straight line.

When welding heavy metal, such as some of the brackets and structural members, weaving is necessary to obtain the required penetration.

FILLER ROD POSITION

The position of the filler rod in relation to both the puddle and the flame varies according to the type of weld being made. In making a simple butt weld, the rod must only be in such a position that the end of it may be melted and deposited in the puddle. The best position for this is to hold the rod at an angle to the surface of approximately 45°, and in line with the seam. The end should be kept quite close to the puddle so that as molten drops form on the rod, they may be deposited with a slight downward motion. As the weld progresses along the seam, the rod will describe a continuous up-and-down motion. This motion should never raise the rod above the flame so that the end cools. The approximate position is shown in Fig. 127.

The use of the filler rod as a shield to prevent melting away of the exposed edge of a lap weld was mentioned briefly in the discussion on the torch angle. This practice is necessary in many cases where the edge of one piece is exposed more than the other. In making many such welds, the end of the rod will have to be kept in contact with the edge instead of raising it. In such cases, the filler will be fed into the puddle continuously instead of by a series of drops deposited by raising and lowering the rod.

BUTT WELDING

In learning to make a butt weld, one of the problems is to manipulate the torch and filler rod as described in the preceding sections. It is also necessary to position the pieces to be welded so that the edges are in the proper alignment and spacing, and to tack weld them so that they will stay in alignment while the welding operation is in progress. When these steps have been performed properly, making the weld becomes a simple matter of making the weld bead.

Although neither the alignment of the edges or the tack welding of the seam present any difficult problems, they are important enough to justify separate discussions. Failure to perform either one properly can result in a very difficult welding problem.

Small pieces of metal have been used in the illustrations in the following section dealing with these subjects. Such pieces make satisfactory practice material for the beginner. Until he has developed skill on such material, he should not be permitted to work on a valuable automobile.

Alignment of the Edges. Alignment of the edges of the pieces to be welded means that they should be spaced properly and flush. In the case of sheet metal of the thickness used in body panels, proper spacing is primarily a matter of making certain that the pieces are not separated too widely. Full penetration of such metal is not difficult to obtain when the edges are butted together tightly. Some space between the edges will make very little difference; however, a gap wider than the thickness of the filler rod is difficult to fill because of the tendency to melt back the edges. Extra-wide gaps will result in extra-heavy beads which overheat and warp the surface and require excessive time.

When welding butt joints in heavier metal, it will be necessary to provide some space between the edges to get full penetration. A good rule is that for metal ⅟₁₆ inch thick or thicker, the space between the edges should be about the same as the thickness.

The importance of having the edges to be welded positioned so that the surfaces are flush is much greater on thin metal, such as body panels, than it is on heavier material. If one edge is much higher than the other, it will be exposed to much more heat. Unless the flame is diverted to heat the lower, less-exposed edge, it will melt the exposed edge away, leaving a hole which will be difficult to fill. Diverting the flame will change the angle so that more heat will be directed to the piece which was low, overheating and expanding it more than the other. The result will be uneven heat distortion which will leave the finished job in a warped condition that will be much worse than if the edges had been heated properly.

Tack Welding. This is necessary for any seam of any type that is more than an inch or so long. Without tack welding, the preheating effect of the flame ahead of the puddle will cause the edges of the pieces being welded to expand and force them out of alignment. Depending on the circumstances, the misalignment may be either a wide separation of the edges or an overlap. In either case, the result will not be an acceptable job.

The torch manipulation in making a tack weld is essentially the same as for making a seam weld, except that the torch angle should be more nearly vertical. Tack welding always should be started and carried out so that it causes the least possible heat distortion. In the operation shown in Fig. 129, the first weld was made in the approximate center and the third one is in the process of being made. Note that the flame is being pointed so that most of the preheating effect is directed toward the welds which have been made. These welds hold the pieces together so they cannot separate. If the torch were turned in the opposite direction, the warpage ahead of the flame would be much more because the edges are not held.

Tacking of the other end of this seam will require the angle of the flame to be in the opposite direction. If these pieces had not been held

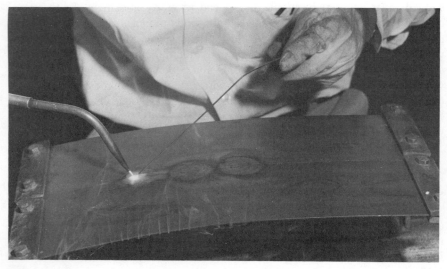

Fig. 129 Tack welding. The flame should be directed toward the tack welds made previously. The smoke is caused by oil in the panel.

securely in the practice fixture, it would have been necessary to have tacked the ends first. When tacking an end, the flame always should be directed off the edge so that the surfaces will be heated as little as possible.

The size of the tack weld should be kept as small as possible to that it will cause the least possible amount of heat distortion. Heat distortion which has been avoided does not have to be corrected. This is particularly important if the final weld will be finished to a smooth surface.

Controlling heat distortion can be done best with the hammer and dolly block—note the dolly in Fig. 129. However, they never should be used on a tack until it has cooled well below red heat. In many cases, it is better to wait until the metal has cooled to nearly normal temperature. It is difficult to establish rules which can be followed to avoid trouble, however, because so much depends on experience. If the tack weld is worked too hot, it will tend to shrink too much; if it is not worked hot enough, it may leave some distortion in the panel. The beginner must learn to judge the conditions for himself.

Welding the Seam. Welding the seam after tack welding simply involves running a bead so that it overlaps the edges of both pieces. This should be just a matter of maintaining the torch at the proper angle, distance, and rate of travel as the rod is fed into the puddle. No weaving motion of the torch was necessary in making the seam shown in Fig.

130. Weaving on a seam such as this only would slow the forward motion and heat the adjoining metal more, which would create more heat distortion than necessary.

The seam shown being welded in Fig. 130 was made without stopping. Note that the area of the puddle has bulged upward sharply, and the area at the start of the seam already has started to draw out of shape. This will be warped badly after it finally cools. This could have been reduced considerably by welding only a short distance and stopping so that the metal could cool. The idea would be to avoid excessive heat in the panel by allowing it to escape into the air.

Use of the dolly and hammer to work the area as it was being welded could have prevented most of the drawing action in this weld. This operation is partly one of straightening and partly a matter of stretching the upset effect of the hot metal. Both are necessary on a weld such as this if it is to be left in a smooth condition.

Fig. 131 shows a close-up view of a short length of the upper side of the weld in Fig. 130, while Fig. 132 shows the underside of the same section. Note that the ripple action is relatively uniform and raised very little above the level of the surfaces on each side. The cracks which show on each side are in the weld scale. These will be found adjoining any weld. Also note in Fig. 132, that the weld scale is heavier and more cracked and blistered than on the upper surface. This is due to the lack of a sheath flame on the underside to protect it from the oxygen in the air. This condition also will be found on any weld.

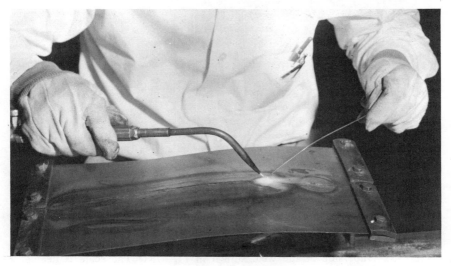

Fig. 130 Welding the tacked seam. Warpage is due to heat.

Fig. 131 Rippled appearance of the weld being made in Fig. 130.

Fig. 132 Underside of the weld shown in Fig. 131. The scale is heavier because this side does not have the protection of the flame.

The weld bead shown here is a good example of the type which the beginner should try to make. Many authorities have recommended that the weld bead should be built up above the surface level as a guarantee against breakage. Such a bead is a disadvantage on a weld which must be finished smooth, even though the final finishing will be done by filling to cover the weld. Also, the experience of most welders is that breaks occur in the metal beside the weld rather than in the bead. For these reasons, it is recommended that the weld beads used on sheet metal be made as nearly flush with the surface as possible. They will be made faster, will hold, and will be easier to finish.

Making a Lap Weld

A lap weld is similar to a butt weld in that it requires tacking and a bead to be laid down on the joint. It requires more care and skill to make, however, because tacking must be done more carefully and the upper edge must be protected throughout the operation.

The tacking requires more care because of the overlapped position of the pieces. In a properly aligned butt joint, inward movement of one piece is blocked by the other; in the lap joint, there is nothing to block movement of either piece. The result is that there will be enough movement to change the alignment before the puddle forms. Unless care is taken with the following tacks, this movement will increase with each one.

This tacking problem is severe enough so that on a long lap weld on a body panel it is necessary to hold the metal by means of rivets or metal screws before starting to tack weld. If this is not done, it will be very difficult to prevent movement that will affect the shape of the panel. Screws 2 or 3 inches apart usually will be sufficient.

The tack welds shown in Fig. 133 were made without the aid of metal screws, but this job is not representative of the problem on a body panel because the pieces are free on the ends and relatively narrow. This tack welding operation was done in the same sequence as the tack welding shown on the butt weld. (See Fig. 129.) The only difference is in the flame angle and the filler rod position. Note that the flame is turned toward the exposed edge of the upper piece, Fig. 133, instead of pointing down the line of the joint, as it is in Fig. 129. This flame angle requires the filler rod to be kept between the flame tip and the exposed edge of the upper piece to serve as a shield. If the flame is not held at this angle and the filler rod held in this position, either the puddle will be too far from the edge of the upper piece or the edge of the upper piece will melt back faster than the puddle can be started in the lower piece. In either case, too much filler rod will be required to make the tack. The result will be a rough weld and excessive heat distortion because the flame will be kept on the work too long.

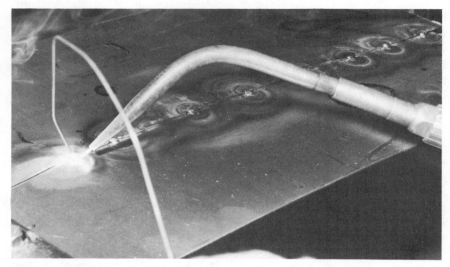

Fig. 133 Using the filler rod to protect the upper edge of a lapped seam being tack welded.

In welding the joint shown in Fig. 133, the rod is kept in the same position it was kept in for tack welding because the exposed edge of the upper piece must be shielded from the flame continuously. The flame should be turned more nearly down the line of the seam so that the puddle will be kept moving forward. In most cases, it will be better not to raise and lower the rod into the puddle, as is commonly done in welding a butt joint. Instead, the rod is fed into the puddle as it melts away. If the rod is raised only momentarily, the exposed upper edge may melt away faster than the gap can be filled.

Sometimes it may be desirable to weave the flame slightly in making a lap weld, but usually it will be best to hold it steady as it moves forward.

Making an Outside Corner Weld

The outside corner weld is the easiest of all welding operations to make with the oxyacetylene torch because the angle of the surfaces prevents excessive pickup of heat from the sheath flame. To practice, simply prop two pieces of metal together to form the corner and fuse them together. Tacking will be required on long pieces, but short lengths, up to 3 inches, can be welded without it.

Unless it is desired to build up the bead to keep a square corner, the use of the filler rod is usually not necessary in making a corner weld. The edges will fuse and run together easily, leaving a rounded corner without filler.

The flame should be directed down the line of the seam so that the preheating effect is divided evenly on both pieces. Turning it to either side will cause that side to expand more than the other and separate the edges, making the welding operation much more difficult.

Making an Inside Corner Weld

The inside corner weld is the most difficult to make because the corner restricts the flow of hot gases from the torch, causing overheating. Unless extra care is taken, the tendency will be to burn through the surfaces on one or both sides of the joint before the puddle can be made and filled in the corner. Because of this condition, it is recommended that the beginner wait to start practicing on this joint until he has developed a fair degree of skill in making the more simple welds.

In most instances, the inside corner will be made with one piece in the flat, or horizontal, position, and the other vertical. It will be much easier to make a smooth, even weld if the torch tip is held at an angle much closer to the horizontal piece, and the end of the rod is held above the end of the flame, as shown in Fig. 134. Tacking and welding should be done in approximately the same positions.

Care should be taken to avoid undercutting the upper edge of the bead. The metal at the edge of the puddle will tend to thin if it is too hot. If the thinned section is not filled with molten metal from the rod, it will be

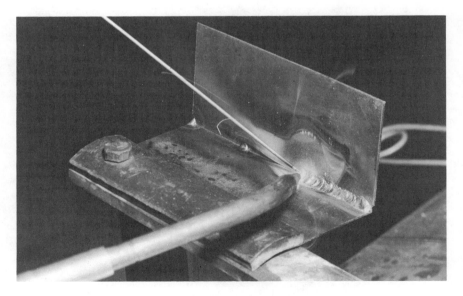

Fig. 134 Torch and filler rod position for welding an inside corner.

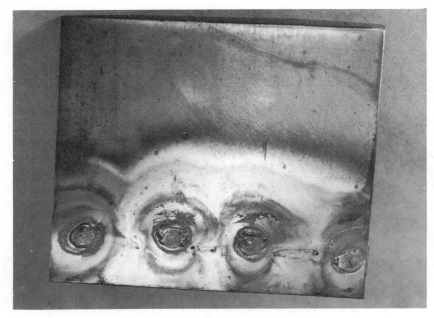

Fig. 135 Buttonhole welds.

Fig. 136 Underside of the buttonhole welds shown in Fig. 135.

left weak. Undercutting does not present a problem on the lower edge of the bead because the hot metal will flow down and fill any thin spots.

Holding the tip of the flame as close to the puddle as possible without actually touching it will simplify the problem slightly because the heat will be concentrated where it is needed, deep in the corner. It also will be desirable to use a smaller tip than required for welding metal of the same thickness in a lap or butt joint.

Making a "Buttonhole" Weld

A "buttonhole" weld is made by melting a hole in the upper piece of a lapped joint, starting a puddle in the lower piece, and adding filler metal to refill the hole. It requires careful manipulation of both the torch flame and the filler rod. However, the beginner who has learned to make a lap weld should not have particular difficulty in making the "buttonhole." An example is shown in Fig. 135.

The problem in making a weld of this type is in preventing the hole from enlarging too much as the puddle is started in the lower surface and the hole is being refilled. This can be kept to a minimum by using as small a flame as possible and keeping it almost vertical to the surface. The rod should be kept close to the flame as the hole is being melted so that filler material can be melted into the hole instantly when needed. As the hole is being filled, the filler rod should be shifted to shield the edge of the hole at any point where the metal begins to melt away too fast.

Fig. 136 shows the underside of the welds shown in Fig. 135. Note that there is much less evidence of the puddle than on the upper side. This is the way it should look. If too much metal is added to the puddle, it will only sink through below the surface where it will do no good.

BRAZE WELDING AND BRAZING

Braze welding and brazing are similar in that both require a nonferrous filler rod which melts above 800°F. but below the melting point of the metal to which it is applied. The two welding methods are frequently thought of as being the same, but there is a technical difference. In braze welding, the filler rod, usually brass or bronze, is used to fill an open, groove joint or to build up a bead. Capillary action, or sweating in, is not involved. In a true brazing operation, the filler metal is drawn into a closely fitted joint by capillary action. The joint is actually a film of filler metal between two surfaces instead of a fill on the outside.

Silver base alloys are used also as brazing material on both ferrous and nonferrous metals. They are seldom used in body repairing, however, because of cost.

It is common practice in the body shop to call both braze welding and brazing by the same name: brazing. Actually, most of the welds made with these filler materials are more nearly braze welding than brazing. To obtain the capillary action required to fill the braze joint properly requires clean surfaces, a few thousandths of an inch space between the surfaces, and uniform heating over the entire joint area. These are difficult conditions to control accurately when welding sheet metal, particularly when the metal is subjected to the distortion effect of the oxyacetylene torch. In most cases, the metal man obtains some penetration of the point by capillary action and makes up for the rest of it by building up filler metal on the surface.

The primary use of the brazed, or braze welded, joint in repairing automobile bodies is to reweld seams which have been electric spot welded originally. Even though electric spot welding equipment is available, it is not always practical to use it on every rewelded seam because other sheet metal parts prevent access. In such cases, the brazed joint may be as satisfactory as any, and it is often the best. Even though the full strength of the properly brazed joint is not obtained, the strength of the joint will be satisfactory if reasonable care is observed in making it.

In the rest of this chapter, the term *brazing* is used instead of *braze welding*. For one reason, it is the term most commonly used in the body shop; and another reason is that wherever possible the use of copper base alloys in welding sheet metal should be limited to joints on which a reasonable degree of penetration by capillary action can be obtained.

PRINCIPLES OF BRAZING

Brazing is made possible by the property of many of the nonferrous metals which allows them to diffuse or penetrate into other metals when the proper temperature and surface conditions are available. The proper temperature conditions are that the copper base filler material must be melted but not heated above the melting point, and the metal to which it is applied must be heated to approximately the same temperature. Brazing is only done on metals which have a higher melting point than the brazing material; the metal being welded is never heated to the melting point.

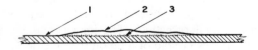

Fig. 137 Cross sectional sketch of a deposit of brazing material on sheet metal: arrow No. *1* indicates the sheet metal; *2*, the deposit of brazing material; *3*, the interface.

To obtain the proper surface conditions, simply clean to remove foreign material, and use flux to clean the surface chemically and exclude atmospheric oxygen while the molten metal is being deposited. Cleaning to remove paint, rust, or other foreign material may be done mechanically by grinding, scraping, wire brushing or similar means, but it also can be done by means of a strong flux. Usually, such cleaning is done mechanically because of the problem of neutralizing the chemicals in the flux residue after they have been used. After the surface has been cleaned mechanically, it can be brazed with fluxes which will not cause corrosion after use.

When brazing is done properly, the molten brazing material wets and penetrates into the surface to which it is applied. This penetration is sometimes called diffusion because the two metals intermix to cause an alloying action at the interface where they join. The alloy thus formed is, in many cases, stronger than either metal which combined to make it. Fig. 137 represents a cross section of a deposit of brazing material on a piece of sheet metal. Arrow No. 1 indicates the metal, 2 the brazing material, and 3 the alloy at the interface.

The strongest brazed joints are made by reducing the space between the surfaces so that the alloy layers join. The space necessary for this action when brazing steel is from 0.003 to 0.005 inch. To understand how joints of this type can be made, it is essential to understand the action of the flux and capillary action which draws the molten material into the joint.

BRAZING FLUX

Brazing flux serves as a chemical cleaner for the surface to be brazed and as a protective shield for the heated metal surface, thus making it possible for the molten brazing material to wet and diffuse into the surface on which it is applied.

Brazing flux usually is applied in the form of a powder or paste, or it may be a solid coating on the filler rod. Some flux is in the form of a liquid which is applied through the oxyacetylene flame by adding it to the acetylene gas. The use of liquid flux in this manner is almost altogether restricted to factory production operations where the equipment is in constant use. The presence of the liquid flux in the flame turns it to a brilliant green instead of the usual bright blue.

All fluxes melt and run onto the surface. The usual method of applying powdered flux is to heat the end of the filler rod and dip it into the powder. The hot rod will melt the flux with which it comes into contact so that the end of the rod will be coated with flux when it is withdrawn. As the filler rod is used to add molten metal to the puddle of brazing material, the flux melts and runs ahead.

Paste flux differs from powdered flux only in that it can be brushed onto the surface before the welding operation is started. This relieves the operator of the time-consuming operation of dipping the end of the rod into the flux to obtain a new supply. It is quite effective also when it is essential to have a supply of flux in the joint before the operation is started.

Filler rods that are precoated with flux also relieve the operator from having to dip the rod as he works. Coated filler rods cost more than the bare rods and separate flux, but the convenience often justifies the extra expense.

Capillary Action. This is caused by the attraction of any surface for any liquid which will wet it. An everyday example of this action can be seen in a glass tumbler partly filled with water; a thin film will rise on the sides of the glass about ⅟₃₂ of an inch above the level of the rest of the water. This film of water rises against gravity because the surface of the glass attracts it. It rises only a short distance, however, because the attraction of the single surface is limited. A similar attraction will be found on the surface of other liquids in other containers. Molten brazing material would have a similar action in a steel container if the surface is clean and was fluxed properly.

Two glass tumblers can be used for an experiment to show how proper spacing of surfaces can be used to fill a weld joint with molten brazing material. The tumblers used may be either cylindrical or tapered, but the sides must be straight and one should be small enough to fit into the other. Put a little water in the bottom on the large glass and lower the small one into the larger until the bottom just touches the water. Capillary action will draw water on it above the surface level just as it has on the side of the larger one. This is the same action described in the preceding paragraph. Now, press the outside of the small glass against the inside of the larger one; a film of water will rise to the top of the small glass instantly in the narrow space between the surfaces of the glasses. This occurs because the combined attraction of both surfaces is so much greater than gravity. The action of molten brazing material in a properly spaced joint which is clean and heated to the proper temperature will be similar.

In making this experiment, the effect of different spaces between the two tumblers should be noted. Moving the small one away from contact ⅟₁₆ inch will permit the water to drop almost to original level. As the space is closed, however, a point will be found which permits the water to rise almost instantly. This point will be only a few thousandths of an inch away from contact.

A similar result is obtained when brazing is done under ideal circumstances. Fig. 138 represents a cross section through an ideal brazed point. Note that the surfaces are shown as having been very close together but not actually touching—0.003 to 0.005 inch would be ideal. At this distance, the molten brazing material will flow into the joint in the same manner that water can be made to rise between the glass surfaces in the experiment just described.

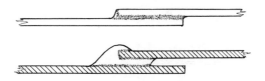

Fig. 138 *(Top)* Cross sectional view of an ideal brazed joint.

Fig. 139 *(Bottom)* Cross sectional view through a widely spaced brazed joint, showing the effect of reduced capillary action.

Fig. 139 represents the effect on capillary action of wide spacing and uneven heating. Note that this is the same as the joint in Fig. 138 except for space between the surfaces. The brazing material is shown as being drawn only part of the way into the joint. Also, it has followed farther on the upper piece than on the lower. This is to be expected when brazing a seam which can be heated from one side only—usually the case with body seams which can be brazed satisfactorily. In many cases, there will be practically no penetration of the seam. This should not be accepted as unavoidable, however, because a good welder will learn to manipulate his flame and filler rod so that he obtains enough penetration to make the joint much stronger.

Uses and Advantages of Brazing

The primary use of brazing is in panel replacement to reweld joints which were originally electric spot welded when assembled in the factory. The advantage is that brazing causes less heat distortion than fusion welding, because the melting temperature of the copper base alloys used as filler metal is much lower than the melting temperature of steel. Many such welds are located in low-crown sections where the extreme heat of fusion welding with a torch flame will cause severe distortion. More often than not, there will be more work involved in relieving the heat distortion than in making the welds. Brazing sometimes will offer a means of preventing serious heat distortion and save the extra time required to relieve it.

There may be no advantage in brazing on a relatively high-crown section which will not distort as readily. Also, if the proper electric welding

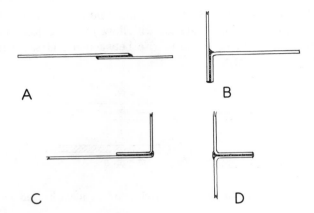

Fig. 140 Four common variations of the lapped joint. Joints *A* and *C* are essentially the same, as are joints *B* and *D*.

equipment is available, it may be better to use it than to use brazing.

Another advantage of brazing is that it can eliminate the need for sealing if the joint is brazed full length.

Brazing on automobile sheet metal repair should be restricted to over-lapped seams. There are some materials and methods which may be used to make good butt joints, but they are not satisfactory or practical for repairing automobile bodies.

Four sketches of joint types suitable for brazing are shown in Fig. 140. Joints similar to these will be found throughout the body structure of any automobile. Sketch *A* is a true lapped joint. Sketch *C* is actually a varia-tion of *A*. Likewise, sketches *B* and *D* are variations of the same basic joint in which the flanges extend away from the surface.

To braze joints such as these so that the entire overlapped area is filled is often impractical when using the welding torch. In most cases, the metal man has to be satisfied with a partially filled joint and some build-up of brazing material on the surface. The problem is to heat both sides of the joint uniformly so that the filler metal will flow by capillary action. If two torches are available, and there is reason to devote the extra effort to the operation, it can be done, however. Usually, though, only partial penetration into the joint will serve the metal man's purpose.

A brazed joint of the type usually made on sheet metal panels is shown in Fig. 141. This joint is overlapped about ½ inch. It was tested for penetration by cutting narrow strips across the joint and pulling them apart. The penetration was approximately one-half of the overlap, or ¼ inch. This amount of penetration would be adequate for any body joint welded satisfactorily by brazing.

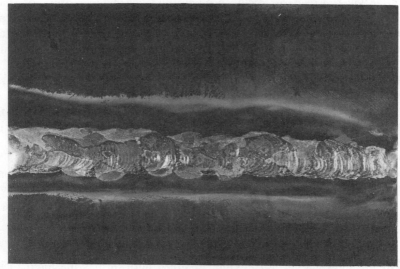

Fig. 141 A typical brazed joint with a low bead built up over the overlap. Testing showed penetration to one half of the depth of the overlap.

The built-up bead over this joint makes the operation a combination of brazing and braze welding. The irregular deposit on the surface of the bead is flux. This may be chipped off if it is on a surface where it is undesirable. However, it will do no harm to leave it in place.

STRENGTH OF THE BRAZED JOINT

Care in fitting up the joint and in manipulating the flame are both very important in making a satisfactory brazed joint. Before the pieces of metal are put together, they should be clean so that flux and molten brazing material can penetrate. It is useless to expect penetration if the joint is filled with sealer, rust, or other material which would prevent tinning.

If everything else is equal, the joint in which the pieces are spaced just wide enough to permit the brazing material to be drawn in by capillary action will be stronger than one in which the pieces are much farther apart. This is illustrated in Figs. 138 and 139. Note in Fig. 138 that the bond between the surfaces is made by the alloy formed on the interface. This material is much stronger than the pure brazing material which fills the wider space between the surface in Fig. 139.

Proper torch flame manipulation is a matter of watching to see that the temperature is just right so that the tinning action is continuous. When it is right, the molten brazing material will flow or spread at the leading edge of the puddle. If the temperature is not high enough, the molten material will run over the metal in much the same manner drops of water will roll over an oily surface. This also will occur if the surface is contaminated so that the flux is ineffective, or if no flux is used. If the surface is too hot, the brazing material will be damaged by burning the tin, which is a part of the composition of the copper base alloys used for brazing.

Appearances are sometimes deceptive, but a good and a poor brazed joint usually can be determined by inspection. The good joint should be smooth and bright, and the edges should blend into the surface of the metal on which it is applied. In contrast to this, a pitted or blistery surface, or an edge which appears to stand on top of the metal, usually is evidence of an unsatisfactory brazing job. An excessive amount of fine, white, powdery material on both sides of the joint indicates overheating; sometimes there will be a considerable amount of such powder even though the joint does not look as though it were badly burned. This is always evidence of a rather poor job.

BRAZING PRACTICE FOR THE BEGINNER

The beginner should not attempt to braze until he has mastered fusion welding to the extent of making a good lap joint. His first attempts at brazing may be either on a lap joint or simply the laying of a bead on the surface of a piece of sheet metal. In either case, it is important to adjust the rate of travel, distance of the flame from the work, angle, and amount of filler rod added so that the bead is of uniform width and height. In most cases, the flame should be held slightly farther from the work than for fusion welding. Otherwise, the procedure is about the same, except that the operator must be more alert so that he can notice and correct wrong procedure.

Some welding authorities recommend that the flame be held at a distance considerably farther than recommended here. If this recommendation is followed, the flame will heat a larger area of metal and tend to aid the penetration into the joint by capillary action, but the primary advantage of brazing sheet metal will be defeated. Unless brazing can be done so that it causes less heat distortion than fusion welding, there is no advantage to be gained by brazing and the joint should be fusion welded.

The beginner should test the quality of his practice joints by cutting narrow strips across the seam and pulling them apart. There should be enough penetration to make a strong bond. If no penetration is being obtained, it will be necessary to experiment with flame angle and manipulation until satisfactory results are obtained.

As soon as the beginner has learned to make a reasonably good brazed joint in the flat position, he should practice on vertical work. Much of the brazing needed in repairing a body, particularly in welding in new panels, will be on vertical seams. Much more care and attention to detail are required on the vertical seam, because the brazing materials tend to run much more freely when molten than steel does. This is not a problem on a flat seam, because the molten metal cannot run off, as it will on the vertical seam.

RESISTANCE SPOT WELDING

Resistance spot welding takes its name from the method used to generate the welding heat. The weld area, always two or more overlapped sheet metal surfaces, is gripped between the electrodes of the spot welding machine and a low-voltage, high-amperage electric current is passed through it. The current-carrying capacity of the electrodes and the conductors of the machine is much greater than that of the sheet metal which is between the electrodes, forming part of the circuit. Thus, by the use of the proper current and pressure on the electrodes, the metal can be heated almost to the melting point and joined under pressure in a very short period of time. A cross sectional sketch showing the relationship of the electrodes to the weld they produce is shown in Fig. 142. Note that this indicates that the highest resistance, and therefore the highest temperature, is found between the surfaces of the pieces to be joined.

Resistance spot welding is the primary welding method used in assembling automobile sheet metal parts because of its speed, economy, and freedom from heat distortion. Its use in automobile sheet metal repair work has been limited, however. There are many reasons for this, but probably the most important has been a lack of suitable equipment

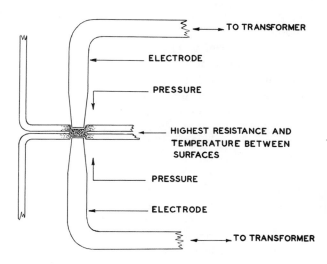

Fig. 142 Cross sectional view of spot welder electrodes in welding position.

priced within the range of justifiable cost for the shop in which it will be used only intermittently. Another important reason has been the lack of familiarity of metal men with the possibilities of spot welding. Also to be considered is the amount of preparation required to reweld a seam which has been painted and sealed. However, as more suitable equipment becomes available, and metal men learn more about the possibilities of spot welding to rebuild damaged automobile bodies, there may be increased use of this method.

To gain skill in the use of a spot welder requires knowledge rather than manual dexterity. For that reason, discussion here will be limited to an explanation of the operation of the machine and the requirements for its use. If these are understood properly, almost no one should have difficulty in making good spot welds. Safety measures will be considered separately.

The Spot Welder

A spot welder of the type suitable for use in body repair work is shown in Fig. 143. A machine of this type is made up of the following units: (1) air cylinder to operate electrodes, (2) control switch (hidden), (3) electrodes, (4) step-down transformer, and (5) heavy-duty conductors.

This particular machine is equipped also with a stand to support the transformer and relatively long conductors to carry the welding current to the electrodes. Other spot welders are made by different manufacturers which have the electrodes connected directly to the transformer; such transformers are designed to be carried by the operator instead of being supported on a separate stand. There are both advantages and disadvantages to both types.

The Step-Down Transformer. This is required because the current required for spot welding must be very much higher in amperage and lower in voltage than that supplied by the utility line. The exact current values vary with the metal thickness and the diameter of the spot weld. Amperages may vary from 5,000 to as much as 20,000; the voltage is rarely more than 5 volts and some machines are designed to work with as low as 1 volt.

The transformer must be relatively heavy to supply the high amperage current required for welding. This presents a problem to the designer of such equipment because he must also make it light enough to be used in almost any position. He is limited also by the power source available in the repair shops in which his equipment will be used. Most shops are equipped with a 220-volt, single-phase power line from which 15 to 30 amp can be drawn for the operation of a welder. By reducing such current with a step-down transformer, it can produce sufficient amperage for spot welding.

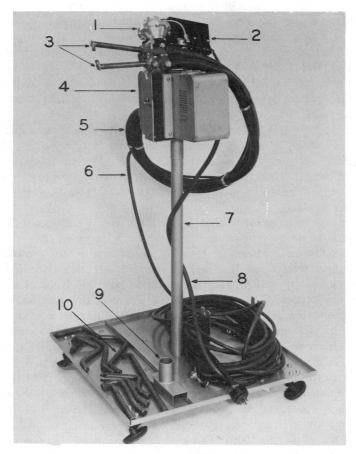

Fig. 143 Electric resistance spot welder: *1,* air cylinder to operate electrode clamp; *2,* control switch (hidden); *3,* electrodes; *4,* step-down transformer; *5,* heavy-duty conductors; *6,* air hose; *7,* portable stand; *8,* cord with plug for 220-volt outlet; *9,* support bracket; *10,* extra electrodes.

The Heavy-Duty Conductors. The heavy-duty conductors must be capable of carrying sufficient current to make the weld without excessive overheating. At the very low voltage of the welding current, the resistance offered to its flow is great enough so that the conductors must be as short as possible. For that reason, the conductors are made of heavy copper and are no longer than necessary to reach the work on the various parts of the body requiring spot welding.

The conductors are insulated to protect against short circuits, but there is little or no danger of electric shock to the operator if he comes in contact with them. Care in handling any spot welder is essential, however, because the primary of the transformer, operating on 220 volts, is extremely dangerous if handled improperly.

The Electrodes. The electrodes are simply solid copper, or copper alloy, bars which serve as extensions of the conductors to carry current to the metal to be welded. The strength of solid bars is required, because the spot to be welded must be gripped with sufficient pressure to make the weld.

Some spot welding electrodes are equipped with replaceable copper alloy tips which will stand more wear than soft copper. However, satisfactory welds can be made with a soft copper tip, although it will require more care than the alloy. Whether the extra expense of removable tips is justified depends on the amount of welding to be done with the particular machine.

In general, any seam should be welded with electrodes that are as short as possible because current and pressure losses on the weld will be proportionally less. However, some of the seams on the various bodies where a spot welder may be used are located in places difficult to reach. If these are to be welded, it is necessary to have electrodes long enough and shaped properly to reach the seam. To meet this need, most manufacturers offer an assortment of electrodes. Additional electrodes may be made by the operator if he has the proper copper bar stock available.

The Electrode Clamping Device. This is an essential part of the spot welder. It may vary in design from a simple toggle operated by a hand lever to a cylinder operated by compressed air. Regardless of the design, the clamping device must have sufficient holding capacity to make the weld when the metal is heated. The machine shown in Fig. 143 is equipped with an air cylinder operated clamp.

The Control Switch. This is located in the primary circuit of the transformer. It serves to energize the transformer to start and stop the welding action. Control switches may vary from a simple toggle device to an elaborate electronic device which can time the input current flow to an exact number of waves. Most of the welders suitable for use in body repair shops are equipped with simple switches, however.

When power-operated electrode clamping devices are used, the operation of the control switch usually is made a part of the power system. Thus, the operator only energizes the air cylinder with a tripper-type valve. This also operates the electric switch so that it will be closed and opened at the proper time.

Spot Welding Requirements

The following conditions are necessary for the resistance spot welder to make strong welds:

1. Both surfaces of both pieces to be joined must be clean.
2. The pieces to be joined must fit together.
3. The electrode points must be clean.
4. Current, time, and pressure must be right.
5. Pressure must be held on the weld until the temperature has dropped sufficiently to restore strength.

Clean surfaces are essential because of the very low voltages used in spot welding. Voltage, which corresponds to pressure, causes the current to flow just as pressure will cause water to flow. Paint, sealer, rust, grease, or other foreign material on or between the surfaces will serve as an insulator and prevent the flow of current through the weld. Unless the current flows, there will be no heat and no weld.

The usual result of dirty surfaces is that only a partial contact is made, particularly if the surface has been cleaned carelessly. Partial contact will concentrate the current flow on a smaller area than the electrode tip will cover. The result is overheating, causing molten metal to spatter out of the weld spot. White-hot metal particles can shoot away from the electrodes for a considerable distance. Such metal is lost from the weld, weakening or even burning holes in one or both pieces. There is also the hazard of injury to the person, particularly the eyes, or the danger of fire if flammable material is present.

Proper fit is important because there is always a tendency for the electrodes to sink through the metal when they are used as a clamp to draw the surfaces together against a spring resistance. This tendency is greatest when the tip diameter is small. Unfortunately, most of the spot welders suitable for use in the body shop are limited to electrode tips with small diameters because of limited current capacity—about ⅛ inch is common.

The effect of spring resistance in the pieces being welded is illustrated in Fig. 144. These sketches, *A, B,* and *C* represent the same cross section through a spot at different stages in the welding operation. The separated condition before welding, shown in sketch *A,* could be caused by a bend holding the surfaces apart. In sketch *B,* the clamping action of the electrodes has pushed the surfaces together against the spring action. In sketch *C,* the welding heat has softened the spot between the electrodes, and the spring action of the surrounding area has lifted the metal around them. In effect, the electrodes tend to shear the weld spot out of the surface. The smaller the tip diameter, the greater this tendency will be, because the clamping pressure is concentrated on a smaller area.

Clean electrode points are as essential as clean metal surfaces for the same reason. The points tend to burn and pit due to the temperature and pressure conditions under which they are used. Excessive burning and pitting, indicated by sparks flying from the weld, is caused by arcing

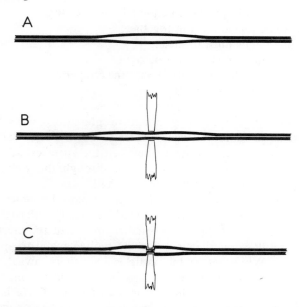

Fig. 144 Effect of improper fit of surfaces to be spot welded: *A,* cross section of two pieces held apart by a bend; *B,* the pieces clamped together by the electrodes; *C,* electrodes sink through hot metal as they spring apart.

between the points and the surface. When this occurs, the points should be cleaned.

The points can be kept in proper operating condition by filing and sanding. Common sense will indicate when to clean the points before making more welds.

If not properly cared for, the points will burn away more rapidly than necessary. When they have been burned too badly, they must be replaced. Some electrodes are available with replaceable points made of copper alloy which will withstand much more wear than the softer copper used in the electrode bars. These offer considerable savings if the welder is in frequent use.

Current, time, and pressure are the most important factors in making a spot weld. Sufficient current must flow through the metal spot to heat it almost instantly. The larger the weld spot area, the more current must flow because the resistance of the spot will decrease as the area is increased. This is the reason that spot welders having limited capacity must be used with small diameter electrode points.

The operator can recognize when the tip diameter is too large for the current which the machine produces by the size of the discolored area surrounding the weld. This should be small. With the proper current values and controls, a weld ¼ inch in diameter can be made with the dis-coloration extending less than ⅟₁₆ inch outside the spot. Good welds can be made with discolored areas larger than this, but it is desirable for them to be as small as possible. Any spot weld having the discolored area several times larger than the weld spot should be considered as not de-pendable. It is probably the result of the current being left on too long because there was not enough amperage to make the weld. Unless there is sufficient amperage to produce welding heat almost instantly, there is little to be gained by more time. Current sufficient to produce only bright red heat will never weld, even though it is left on until the discoloration spreads to any width.

A spot welder can be equipped with a timer which will control the time to a fraction of a cycle of the alternating current. Such timers are used for production operations and are available for smaller machines suitable for body shop use. However, a timer is not as necessary on the smaller machine, because it must be used under variable conditions, making a certain degree of operator control necessary. Without a timer, the operator holds the switch on until the proper heat is reached. He must depend on his knowledge of the conditions, the appearance of the spot, and his na-tural sense of timing.

Pressure being an essential part of the resistance welding operation, it must be controlled properly. A spot weld cannot be made unless the heated surfaces are pressed together with sufficient force. However, if pressure is too great, the electrodes will sink into the heated metal too far, partially piercing it. The three sketches in Fig. 145 indicate the results which may be expected when the pressure is correct, when it is too low,

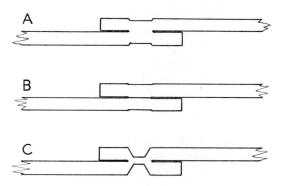

Fig. 145 Effect of electrode pressure on a spot weld: *A,* proper pressure pro-duces a slight depression in forcing the metal to join; *B,* low pressure leaves the surface smooth and the piece unwelded; *C,* too much pressure cuts through the metal.

and when it is too high. In each case, it is assumed that both the current and time are right.

The slight but noticeable depressions in sketch *A* always will be found on a good weld. Practically no depressions (sketch *B*), probably means that the weld has not been completed, as indicated by the line separating the upper and lower piece. Depressions extending deep into the metal (sketch *C*), indicate a weld which may fail because it is almost cut through.

Either bodily injury or property damage can result from improper use or maintenance of a spot welder: flying sparks, which are white-hot particles of metal, can cause fire, burns on the body or face, or blindness if they strike an unprotected eye; short-circuited wiring can cause severe electrical shock to the operator, or start a fire if flammable material is present.

Even under perfect operating conditions, the electrodes will throw off white-hot particles of metal. These can cause severe damage to the eye at a distance of several feet, yet the operator usually must use the machine not more than 2 feet from his eyes to enable him to see what he is doing. Therefore, his face should be covered by a transparent shield large enough to provide full protection, his collar should be buttoned, his sleeves buttoned, and he should wear gloves.

Protection against electrical hazards is equally important, particularly with portable machines which operate on a 220-volt input. The fact that the electrodes operate at such low voltage they can be handled without risk often leads to carelessness with the rest of the machine. Any damage which might cause short circuits in the high-voltage lead wire or transformer windings should be repaired before the machine is used again.

The use of a ground wire connected to exposed metal parts of portable electric equipment is demanded by most electric codes, state laws, and is a requirement of most insurance policies covering the hazards of such situations. A spot welder never should be used without such a wire. Even with it, the operator never should stand on a wet floor when using the machine.

ELECTRIC ARC WELDING

The electric arc is used as the source of heat in arc welding. The basis of the method is that an electric current flow can be maintained across an open space after it has been started under the proper current and voltage conditions. Temperatures well above the level required for welding result because of the high resistance of the open space. All arc welding systems make use of this characteristic of the electric arc.

In the original method of arc welding, a carbon electrode was used to maintain the arc, and the filler rod was fed into the puddle in much the same way it is fed into the oxyacetylene puddle. There is still the occasional application of the carbon arc, but it has been almost completely replaced by other, more efficient methods.

A later development on arc welding was the consumable electrode. In this method, the filler rod is used as the electrode by feeding it into the puddle as it melts off. Bare steel wires have been used for this purpose, but they have been replaced almost altogether by the coated electrode. The coating burns off, creating an inert atmosphere over the puddle area to protect the molten metal from attack by oxygen in the air. The result is a better weld which is much easier to make than with the use of a bare wire electrode. This method is in wide general use for most manual arc welding, particularly repair work.

The arc-spot welding gun is a specialized application of the coated electrode welding method which has been developed specially for the body repair industry. It is similar in operating principle but different enough in detail to be discussed separately in the following pages.

In searching for better methods of welding nonferrous and light gauge sheet steel, welding engineers have developed several methods of so called *shielded arc* welding. In shielded arc welding, the inert atmosphere is provided by feeding an inert gas to the area of the weld puddle to exclude atmospheric oxygen. The original gas used for this purpose was helium, which accounts for the name, *heli-arc* welding. However, other gases, particularly argon and carbon dioxide, have largely replaced helium for this purpose.

Shielded arc welding methods have been developed which use both consumable and nonconsumable electrodes. In the consumable electrode method, the electrode is usually a continuous wire which is fed into the puddle automatically. This is particularly adapted to high speed, production welding. Some machines have been built which can weld a continuous seam at speeds measured in a good many feet per minute. Other equipment of this type is intended for hand operation in much the same manner of use as the acetylene torch, except that the operator uses only one hand.

A tungsten electrode is used in the nonconsumable electrode method. Although tungsten will burn away, the process is very slow. The tungsten electrode and equipment for releasing the inert gas are combined in what serves as a torch. The operator uses this torch in one hand and feeds the filler rod into the puddle in the same manner that he would use an oxyacetylene torch and filler rod.

MIG (metallic, inert gas) and TIG (tungsten, inert gas) are terms used for consumable and nonconsumable electrode, shielded arc welding methods. Both MIG and TIG methods would offer the body shop considerable improvement, if they were available. However, few body shops have installed such equipment, probably in part due to the high price of such equipment and in part to the general lack of knowledge of the methods.

The discussion of arc welding methods which follows is limited to the conventional, coated electrode type. MIC and TIG are mentioned because it seems that they will find their way into the body shop eventually, but the extent of their present use does not seem to justify extensive discussion. Also, the discussion of conventional arc welding is less extensive than that given for oxyacetylene welding. It seems obvious that all arc welding methods will remain in a secondary position until better equipment, designed for body shop use, is made available and adopted by the majority of body shops. Given such equipment, the torch would still be needed for heating operations.

ARC WELDING APPLICATIONS

The chief drawback limiting the use of arc welding on sheet metal is the difficulty in filling wide openings. The intense heat of the arc tends to melt away any exposed edge faster than filler metal can be deposited.

Butt joints can be made with the arc, but the edges of the pieces must be fitted together tightly to avoid burning large holes. It is never necessary to leave a gap between the edges for penetration, as it is with heavier metal. Even with a perfect fit, it is necessary to be extremely careful to avoid burning through. This practically eliminates the use of arc welding for the butt joint for all but the most skillful welders, except where the extra care may be justified.

The arc weld has two particular advantages when it is compared to the acetylene flame which justify its use wherever it is practical. The first is that it tends to cause less heat distortion because it welds faster and without the blast of superheated gas. The second is that it is less of a fire hazard when used close to materials which are only moderately flammable, such as fabrics and rubber. However, the second advantage is partially offset by the tendency to throw off sparks which will cause burned spots on anything they touch, even though they may not cause an actual fire.

The advantages of arc welding make it especially well suited to rewelding seams which have been welded originally by the resistance spot method. In replacing damaged body panels, there are many seams which are difficult to weld with the resistance spot method even though the machine is available. Many such seams also are difficult to reweld with the torch because of heat distortion and the risk of fire from the blast of hot gases from the flame. The arc welder offers a better substitute for resistance spot welding in many but not all cases. When it can be used, it often will save considerable labor by avoiding heat distortion.

When the arc is used on a lapped sheet metal joint, the surfaces must fit tightly together. If an attempt is made to fill a wide space between two surfaces, holes will be burned in one or both. The amount of heat distortion will be increased also, because the arc will be held in one place for a longer period of time; this defeats the purpose of using the arc. If the surfaces do not fit, they should be fitted before arc welding is begun; or, if they cannot be fitted without too much effort, another method of welding should be adopted.

It is always desirable to use the arc instead of the torch when welding any metal which is heavier than sheet. The arc causes much less spread of heat into the adjoining metal so that there is much less heat distortion and loss of stiffness. However, when the welding is done as a part of a straightening operation which requires the use of heat, the arc may be impractical because it is not as satisfactory as a source of heat.

The Arc Welding Circuit

In arc welding with any type of equipment, the metal to be welded is made a part of the electric circuit. This is done by using two cables running from the output terminals of the machine. The electrode holder is attached to one cable, and the other is attached to the work. Thus, when the electrode is touched to the work, the circuit is completed.

Starting the arc is a matter of touching the electrode to the work and pulling it away a short distance, in most cases less than ⅛ inch. As the electrode is pulled away, the current continues to flow across the gap, giving off tremendous heat and a brilliant blue light which is very injurious to the eyes unless they are protected by a suitable glass screen. In arc welding with the conventional, flux-coated electrode, the arc melts the electrode and deposits it on the surface of the puddle of molten metal which it creates. In any arc welding operation with a carbon or other nonconsumable electrode, the filler rod must be fed into the arc separately.

Starting the arc is referred to as *striking the arc* because the motion usually is completed by scratching it on the surface in a manner similar to striking a match. The operator must become skillful in striking, holding, and manipulating the arc so that the filler metal is deposited where it should be. To do this requires a knowledge of how to adjust the machine so that the proper current values are obtained and how to select the proper electrodes for the various operations. When these conditions are met, the arc can be maintained continuously. In manual arc welding, the arc can be maintained until the electrode is used up; in some automatic welding operations, the arc can be maintained for the length of time necessary to complete the seam.

Arc Welding Equipment

Two basic types of arc welding equipment are in general use: the alternating current transformer type and the direct current generator type. Each has its advantages and disadvantages.

The advantages of the alternating current, or AC, machine are that it is a relatively simple device, costs less, will last a long time, and is adequate for most simple welding jobs. For these reasons, it is the machine most commonly used in automobile repair shops, particularly body shops.

The chief disadvantage of the AC welder is that there are many welding operations for which it is unsuited—for instance, those jobs which require the use of direct current so that the polarity of the electrode will be either positive or negative. Such jobs cannot be done satisfactorily with an AC machine. However, most such jobs are on alloys or nonferrous metals which the automobile repairman usually is not required to weld. The alternating current of the AC welder is more difficult to weld with in a vertical or overhead position as compared to the direct current generator type. This is due to the change of polarity of alternating current, which occurs 60 times per second. However, this is not such a drawback to the repairman as it might seem, because he can learn to operate the AC machine in either position with a little practice. Most of his welding will not require work in a difficult position, anyway.

The advantage of the direct current generator type welder, or the DC machine, is in its greater versatility, as compared to the AC machine. With few exceptions, the DC welder will do any job that can be done with the AC machine, plus those which either cannot be done or are difficult to do without direct current.

The DC welder normally is driven by an electric motor drawing current from a utility power line. However, it may be driven by any type motor having sufficient power and flexibility to carry the load. Except in rare instances, when other motors are used, they are either gasoline or Diesel. The operating costs and maintenance problems of using either motor are much greater than with electric drive, so they are used rarely except where portability is needed. However, when it is necessary to take the welder to a job where an electric power line either is not available or connection to it would be difficult, the gasoline engine driven welder provides a satisfactory and efficient means of doing the work. There is no difference in the quality of the work done with either the electric or other type drive.

A complete AC welding outfit is shown in Fig. 146. This consists of

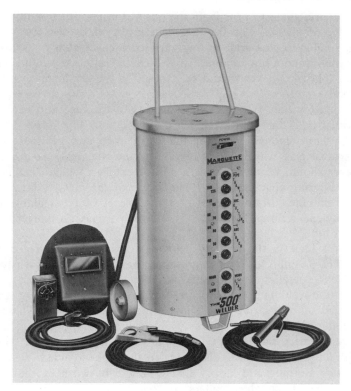

Fig. 146 Alternating current arc welder.

the welding transformer, the electrode holder and cable, the ground clamp and cable, welding helmet, and a plug-in receptacle to be attached to the power line. The cables on this machine are equipped with plugs on the ends which fit into outlets on the case to vary the output of the machine. Other machines may be designed to vary the machine output by other devices, but the end result will be the same.

A chipping hammer, to remove the slag deposit from the weld, is an essential tool for any arc welding operation. This is normally considered as a hand tool rather than as part of the equipment. It is a light hammer with a chisel-shaped end.

ARC WELDING SAFETY

The problems of safety in arc welding fall into two classifications: protection for the operator and avoidance of fire hazards. Both of these should be considered when doing arc welding.

The operator needs protection from the ultraviolet light given off by the electric arc, against burns from the hot metal, and the possibility of injurious electric shock. The brilliant light given off by the arc will cause burning, similar to sunburn, on any exposed area of skin if the exposure lasts for more than a few minutes. It will cause serious eye injury in much less time. The eyes never should be exposed to the arc for even a fraction of a second.

Protection for the eyes and exposed parts of the face and neck should be provided by a face mask, shown on the left in Fig. 146. The mask should be large enough to cover the entire face and neck. It is fitted with a special glass which filters out the ultraviolet light. If broken, this glass never should be replaced with any other glass which does not have the same filtering characteristics. The shade of the glass is no indication that it is suitable. Many glasses of the same size are available for use in oxyacetylene welding helmets. Use of such a glass is dangerous, even for a short time.

The glass filter in the welding helmet is covered with a piece of clear glass. This is only for the purpose of protecting the expensive filter glass. This protection is necessary because the operator must get close enough to the welding operation to see what he is doing. Flying sparks of white-hot metal will strike his helmet and the cover glass. These would ruin the filter glass very rapidly. Replacement of the clear glass with any piece of glass satisfactory for good vision is permissible. However, glass with flaws which tend to distort vision should be avoided.

Protective clothing and gloves always should be worn by the operator. Bare forearms, open shirt collars, or bare hands are an invitation to severe burns. Burning can take place through lightweight clothing if it 's exposed to the arc for any length of time. In making a two-minute ʒeld, there would be no problem. There is danger, however, if the operation continues for a half hour or more.

Although the operator receives the greatest amount of exposure because he is closest to the work, protection for a helper or another person working in the area is important. Many times another person will help the operator by holding a piece in alignment. There is usually more risk of injury to the eyes than to the operator's because the helper rarely wears a helmet. Instead, he will usually depend on turning his head or closing his eyes as the operator strikes the arc. It is much better for the helper to wear a helmet also. Better yet, the work should be set up so that the services of a helper are not required.

If arc welding is done in a special area, some kind of screen should be set up so that other persons in or passing through the area will not be forced to look at the light of the arc. This is particularly important in an area where persons not familiar with welding will be exposed to it.

There is little risk of arc burn on the skin for persons who are not actually doing the welding. Under most conditions, such exposure is too short to be of any particular consequence.

There is always a certain element of fire hazard with any welding operation. In general, this risk is about the same for arc and oxyacetylene welding when highly flammable materials are in the area. Under such conditions, welding should be avoided, or the materials removed before welding starts. However, around less flammable materials, particularly wood, there is much less fire hazard with arc welding because the arc does not release the blast of superheated gas which is released by the torch flame. It is not completely safe around any flammable materials, however, because it will throw sparks for considerable distance. The operator may not notice a fire started by sparks because he is blinded by the helmet.

The risk of serious injury through electrical shock is always present with any electrical machine. There is much less such risk from the current in the welding cables than from the current in the power lead to the machine. This is particularly true when a portable machine is used with a long plug-in cable. Worn insulation can cause short circuits. If the insulation happens to be in contact with the metal being welded or with a damp floor on which the operator may be standing, he can be injured seriously.

ARC-SPOT WELDING GUN

An arc-spot welding gun is shown in Fig. 147. This gun, used with the proper current supply unit, produces a weld spot to join two pieces of overlapped metal. It is for use in any position and on any seam which has been welded originally with resistance spot welds. The weld it produces is not the same as the resistance spot, because filler metal is added to it from the electrode, usually leaving a slight bump projecting from the surface. Typical arc-spot welds are shown in Fig. 148.

The chief advantages of the arc-spot gun are that it creates very little or no heat distortion, and it does not require an electrode to reach both sides of the seam. Both of these are important. Use of the oxyacetylene torch in many such spots will cause heat distortion requiring hours to work out. The use of a resistance-type spot welder is not practical for many panel replacement operations, because other panels prevent access of the electrodes to both sides of the seam.

The arc-spot welding gun makes an arc weld, but it requires conditions that are slightly different from those of manual arc welding. The differences lie in the use of a lower voltage welding current and a special electrode which will start the arc instantly on contact. The combination provides a means of control so that the exact amount of filler metal needed to make the weld can be fed into the puddle. Only two adjust-

Fig. 147 Arc-spot welding outfit.

Fig. 148 Typical arc-spot welds.

ments are required: the gun cable can be plugged into different outlets to provide more or less current for different metal thicknesses; and the knob on the side of the gun sets a cam which determines the length of electrode to be fed into the puddle.

Loading the gun consists of two steps: the electrode is inserted through the opening in the brass tip on the guide, and the guide is then extended until the end of the brass tip is flush with the end of the electrode.

The gun is used by placing the end of the brass tip against the spot to be welded and pushing inward on the handle. The arc starts instantly when the electrode touches the metal and continues as long as additional electrode is fed by pushing the gun inward on the guide rods. The arc is extinguished instantly when the inward movement of the gun body on the guide rods reaches the limit permitted by the setting of the adjustment knob.

To understand the operating principle of the arc-spot welding gun, it is essential to understand the relationship between welding current voltage and arc length. The length of arc which can be maintained is related directly to current voltage. Higher voltage will make a longer arc, which is easier to maintain. Normal voltages for manual arc welding will vary for different machines and different circumstances over a range from 60 to 80. This voltage is necessary because it is not humanly possible for the operator to maintain the arc at an exact length with no variations. Also, in manual arc welding, the arc can be extinguished at will by simply removing the electrode from the puddle.

The arc must be extinguished instantly when the arc-spot welding gun stops feeding the electrode into the puddle. The lower welding current voltage provides the extinguishing action automatically, because it will not maintain the arc after the electrode burns away from contact. The result is a much closer control of the welding process than can be obtained by hand operation.

The arc-spot welding gun has disadvantages as well as advantages. The surfaces to be welded must be clean, and particular care must be taken that no foreign material (such as paint or sealer) is sandwiched between the surfaces. This rules out the possibility of using a weld-through type of sealer between the surfaces, which can be done with electric resistance spot welding.

The arc-spot weld is much rougher in appearance than a resistance-type weld, but much smoother than a gas weld. Any surface which will not be hidden requires some type of finishing to make it as smooth as would be expected on an undamaged automobile. If space is left between the surfaces, it is apt to leave holes either in the center of the weld or on one side. Holes in the center usually go all the way through both pieces; a hole on one side of the weld usually only goes through the top piece. In either case, the result is a faulty weld.

The advantages of the arc-spot weld will more than outweigh the disadvantages, however. The time needed to clean the surfaces and fit them properly is far less in many cases than the time it would take to work out the heat distortion which results from the use of the torch.

WELDING SAFETY

Although the need for proper clothing and eye protection has been discussed previously, it is restated here for emphasis. The arc or the gas torch *never* should be used without proper eye shields, nor should any part of the body be exposed to the light from the arc because it will cause severe burns.

Eye protection and proper clothing are equally important for a welder's helper. In most cases, the helper holds parts in position for welding. This will place him in such a position that he will be subjected to about as much light as the welder. He is probably in greater danger of eye injury than the operator, if he does not wear a face mask, because he may attempt to watch the work.

The risk of fire is always present when any welding is done, particularly if flammable materials are present. A fire hazard often unnoticed until too late is that created when welding an automobile frame close to the gasoline line. A ruptured line can pour out several gallons of gasoline into a fire which can do almost any amount of damage.

Fire can be caused by sparks flying from the weld into any flammable material nearby, either on the automobile or in the area. Such fires are at first quite likely to escape the notice of the operator, because his vision is restricted by the mask and dark glass.

QUESTIONS ON WELDING

GENERAL WELDING

1. What is a weld?
2. What is necessary to make a weld?
3. What is a fusion weld?
4. What is a pressure weld?
5. What is the difference between fusion welding and brazing?
6. What welding methods are used the most in assembling an automobile body in the factory?
7. Why are most factory welding methods not suitable for use in repairing automobile sheet metal?
8. Why is heat distortion a problem in welding sheet metal?
9. What welding methods are best suited for use in repairing automobile sheet metal?

OXYACETYLENE WELDING

10. What is the pressure in a full oxygen cylinder?
11. What is the pressure in a full acetylene cylinder?

12. Why is an acetylene cylinder filled with porous material and liquid acetone?
13. In what position should an acetylene cylinder be when in use?
14. How many turns should the valve on an oxygen cylinder be opened?
15. How many turns should the valve on an acetylene cylinder be opened?
16. Should the oxygen and acetylene regulators be adjusted to the same gauge reading before lighting the torch? Why?
17. What sequence should be followed in hooking up a new oxyacetylene welding outfit?
18. Should the same sequence be followed in hooking up a used outfit which has been out of service for some time? Why?
19. What should be done to either a full oxygen or acetylene cylinder before attaching the regulator to it?
20. What is the sequence of lighting the oxyacetylene torch, starting with an outfit which has been shut off and drained?
21. Why should both regulator adjusting screws be released when the oxyacetylene outfit is shut off?
22. What causes the heavy black smoke when the acetylene is first lighted?
23. How can the heavy black smoke be avoided when lighting the torch?
24. What is a carburizing flame?
25. What is an oxidizing flame?
26. Why should the neutral flame be used when welding steel?
27. What is the result if an oxidizing flame is used to weld steel?
28. What is the result if a carburizing flame is used to weld steel?
29. What is the weld puddle?
30. What is the proper distance between the neutral flame tip and the weld puddle?
31. Under what conditions should the flame be moved forward in a straight line, and under what conditions should it be operated either with a weaving or a whirling motion?
32. Under what conditions should the filler rod be held directly in front of the flame, and under what conditions should it be held to one side or the other?
33. Where should the filler metal be placed to build up a high bead?
34. Where should the filler metal be placed to make a bead which is flush with the surface of the metal?
35. What is the cause of heat distortion?
36. Which will cause the least heat distortion: welding with a large tip adjusted to as large a flame as possible or welding with a relatively small tip and flame? Why?
37. Why is tack welding required on most seams?
38. In tack welding, how should the torch position vary from the normal position for welding a seam?
39. How far apart should the edges of a butt joint be spaced when welding metal of the thickness normally found in automobile body panels?
40. What is the effect of one edge of a butt joint being higher than the other?
41. In making a long seam, will welding without stopping make more or less heat distortion than only welding a short distance and waiting until the metal cools?
42. Why does heavier scale form on the underside of the metal than on the side on which the torch was used?
43. Why is tacking more important on a lap than on a butt joint?
44. Why should some means of holding the edge alignment be used when tack welding a long body seam?

45. Why is an inside corner weld more difficult to make than an outside corner?
46. What is a "buttonhole" weld?
47. What is the primary problem in making a buttonhole weld?

BRAZE WELDING AND BRAZING

48. How does braze welding differ from brazing?
49. Why is flux necessary in any brazing operation on steel?
50. What is the temperature range necessary for any brazing operation?
51. What force draws molten brazing material into an open joint?
52. What shape and size of joint is necessary to draw molten brazing material?
53. What temperature conditions are necessary to draw molten brazing material into an open joint?
54. Why is it difficult to obtain a true brazing action when making a lap joint with the torch?
55. What is the primary use of brazing in repairing automobile sheet metal?
56. Why will a lapped joint be stronger if brazing material is drawn between the surfaces than if the brazing material is only deposited over the edge of the overlap?
57. What is the primary advantage of brazing over fusion welding on a joint to which it is suited?
58. What color and general surface appearance should a good brazed joint have?
59. What color and general surface appearance will a burned brazed joint have?
60. Why does brazing an overhead or vertical seam require more care than fusion welding in similar positions?
61. What advantage is there in using flux-coated brazing rods?

RESISTANCE SPOT WELDING

62. How is the welding heat produced in resistance spot welding?
63. Where is the highest temperature produced in a spot weld?
64. Why are extra-heavy conductors required for spot welding?
65. Why does a relatively low-powered spot welder require a comparatively small contact area on the tips of the electrodes?
66. What is the principal advantage of resistance spot welding, as compared to torch welding?
67. Why is pressure on the electrodes necessary?
68. Why should the pressure on the electrodes be held briefly after the welding current is shut off?
69. What surface conditions of the metal to be welded are necessary for spot welding?
70. Why are long electrodes not as efficient as shorter ones?
71. How can a spot welded joint be sealed properly?
72. What conditions limit the use of a resistance spot welder in replacing damaged body panels?
73. What will be the result of attempting to press surfaces together which do not fit by using the electrodes as a clamp?
74. What is the result of leaving the welding current on too long?
75. What is the result of attempting to use a spot welder on a surface which has paint or other foreign material on it?

ARC WELDING

76. In repairing automobile sheet metal, why is arc welding not considered a complete substitute for the oxyacetylene method?
77. What type of joint in sheet metal is best suited to arc welding?
78. Why is a butt joint in sheet metal somewhat difficult to weld with the arc?
79. Where arc welding can be used, what are the primary advantages?
80. How is the arc started?
81. What is a DC welder?
82. What is an AC welder?
83. Can any electrode be used with either an AC or a DC machine? Why?
84. Are there sources of arc welding current other than the AC or DC machines?
85. What is direct and reverse polarity?
86. Why should the operator always wear the proper mask when arc welding?
87. Why should the slag from the flux always be removed before starting to weld a spot which has been previously arc welded?
88. Why does the arc-spot gun require lower voltage than normal arc welding?
89. What are the primary advantages of the arc-spot gun?
90. What are the conditions necessary to make a good arc-spot weld?
91. Why is it that the arc-spot gun cannot be used without special electrodes?
92. What are the disadvantages of the arc-spot welding gun?
93. What conditions are likely to cause holes beside the weld made by an arc-spot gun?

6

Filling

Filling has always been an important part of automobile body re-pair procedure. The original filling material was solder, often referred to as "lead" because of its high lead content. In recent years the use of plastic filling material has, to a large extent, replaced lead for several reasons. One of the more important reasons for the popularity of plastics is that relatively little skill is required in their application and no heat is required, avoiding the tendency to heat distortion. Other reasons would be the cost and weight of the material as compared to lead. There are disadvantages, which will be dealt with in a later section.

Any discussion of filling would not be complete without a warning about its excessive use. The term *lead artist* was often used to refer to the metal man who relied on the excessive use of lead to make up for his lack of skill in straightening metal. Similarly, the term *plastic artist,* or *sculptor,* is often applied to the excessive user of plastics. Although filling can save a tremendous amount of time on many jobs, we often find on jobs where an excessive amount has been used that it could have been done faster, better, and with less expense if only the repair man had developed the proper skills.

In the discussion which follows, both lead and plastic filling materials are considered. The viewpoint is strictly nontechnical. Information not necessary to the user in actual body repair work is not given.

In the discussion of the use of plastic fillers, emphasis has been placed on the proper metal procedures to keep the use of filler to practical limits. The techniques of application and finishing are discussed but not to the extent they are for lead. The beginner needs to know much more about the materials and techniques of working them to apply lead than he does to apply plastic.

Both lead and plastic are discussed because it is felt that the qualified body repair man should be able to use both. Even though plastic has largely replaced lead in general use, there are some advantages and disadvantages of both. A corner which may be subjected to rough usage would be less likely to break off if built up with lead than with plastic.

192

On the other hand, a large, relatively flat area of metal would be likely to suffer heat distortion if built up with lead but could be filled with plastic with no trouble at all.

PLASTIC FILLERS

Plastic fillers are available from a large number of manufacturers. A few have special features which make them different from the rest. Most of them, however, are quite similar in the way they are packaged, prepared for application, and finished. The following description applies to the majority of the materials which are similar, not to the exceptions.

In general, plastic materials are prepared by the manufacturer in two separate containers, the contents of which are mixed immediately before application. The mixing produces a chemical action which causes the material to harden, so that it can be finished smooth. The basic filler material usually has the consistency of caulking compound. This material is made up of a polyester resin to which various fibers and other materials which affect the working properties have been added. The second material, usually called the hardener, is commonly a cream type preparation packaged in a squeeze type, plastic tube. Liquid hardeners have been used also, but they seem to be losing favor in comparison to the cream type materials.

It is common practice to use a pigmented cream hardener which causes the color of the plastic to change as it is mixed. This provides a color key to the proportion of hardener used in mixing up the material for application. The more hardener used, the stronger the color of the batch.

A container, usually a quart or a gallon, of plastic and a tube of hardener are usually sold as a unit. In most cases, the material in a tube of hardener is enough for a gallon of plastic. Two points should be kept in mind when mixing these materials for application. One is that the proportion should be kept reasonably accurate. The other is that they should be mixed thoroughly.

The proportion of hardener to plastic is stated in terms of reasonable accuracy because almost all of the available brands of material permit a reasonably wide variation without serious ill results. The more hardener used, the faster the material will harden. The opposite is also true; the less hardener used, the slower the material will harden. If too much hardener is used, the material will set up so rapidly it cannot be worked. If not enough is used, the material may never harden. The desired mixture is somewhere between these points. It is best practice to always follow the manufacturer's recommendations.

Thorough mixing is of extreme importance because pockets of unmixed materials will not harden and may have to be dug out and replaced when

Fig. 149 Damaged door and quarter panel. Filling deep gouges will save considerable time.

the surface is finished. Illustrations showing the measuring and mixing will be found in the section dealing with the application of plastic to the body.

PLASTIC FILLING

The door and quarter panel shown in Fig. 149 are good examples of damage which can be repaired satisfactorily and quickly by proper use of plastic filling. In many cases, the outer panel of the door would have been replaced instead of repaired. However, when the cost of the replacement panel and the time to install it are considered, the saving involved more than justified the repair.

Another consideration which justifies the repair of a panel of this type is that the original factory welds and sealing are retained. A repair shop has no practical means of providing rust protection for the overlapped surfaces of the hem flange if the rewelding is to be done with the oxyacetylene torch. If the original sealing and welding are intact and the panel is repairable, the durability of the finished job will often be much better than if the panel was replaced.

It is felt that the quarter panel would be repaired by most shops. If replaced, however, there would be the same problem of rusting in the overlapped joint of the outer panel to the wheel housing on the lower edges.

In the discussion which follows, the metal straightening procedure is explained in much greater detail than that of the plastic application and finishing procedures. As stated previously, plastic fillers are relatively easy to apply. In most cases, the quality of the finished job is determined by how well the metal work was done before filling was started. If the metal work is right, excessive filling will be avoided automatically. Failure rarely occurs in a plastic fill which has been applied properly. When failure does occur, it will be where the material has been built up to great depth or applied over contaminated metal.

Metal Preparation. The damage shown in Fig. 149 was caused by a small, hard object being dragged across the door and quarter panel with considerable force. The owner reported that he turned too short and caught the end of the rear bumper of another automobile. All of the crushed or displaced metal above and below the line gouges has been carried in by the very small impact area, which in this case was moving.

There is considerable stretched metal in the deep gouges, and it is in areas where access to the underside is almost impractical. Filling is a very logical repair method for the gouges, but it is equally logical that as much of the displaced metal should be returned to its proper position before filling is started.

Starting with the door, the first repair setup is shown in Fig. 150. This is the application of tension. A much more thorough explanation of the use of tension is found in Chapter 7, and details of the three-step approach to any straightening job are found in Chapter 8. These basic ideas

Fig. 150 Jack and clamp set up on door.

Fig. 151 The pulling operation. Applying heat to the buckle while the jack is extended aids unrolling of the rolled buckle.

Fig. 152 Smoothing the rolled buckle area with the hammer and spoon dolly.

are not repeated here, and the student will do well to refer to these chapters if the outlined procedure is difficult for him to follow.

The purpose of the jack and clamps attached to the edges of the door is to pull the panel toward the original contour. As the impact carried the panel surface inward, the rear edge of the door was pulled forward. Note the wide space between the door and quarter panel edge in Fig. 149.

The start of the pulling operation is shown in Fig. 151. Note that the operator is applying heat to the sharp buckle as he operates the hydraulic jack. The purpose is to free the severely worked metal in the buckle so that it can roll out as it rolled in. (The use of heat to soften work-hardened steel is explained in Chapter 1, and rolled buckles are discussed in detail in Chapter 2.) Note that a small flame is used and is applied directly to the sharply creased area. When the jack was extended, the buckle started to roll downward. The torch flame was kept just ahead of the rolling action so that the resistance would be as little as possible.

In Fig. 152, most of the displaced metal has been pulled out, and the operator is inserting a spoon dolly to straighten the area of the rolled buckle. Access to this area is provided by the construction of the door, as can be seen in Fig. 153. Here, the operator is using a short pry rod to lift a spot of metal in the buckled area. Because this particular door has a very large opening at this point, it was practical to remove the door trim pad so that tools could be used in this manner.

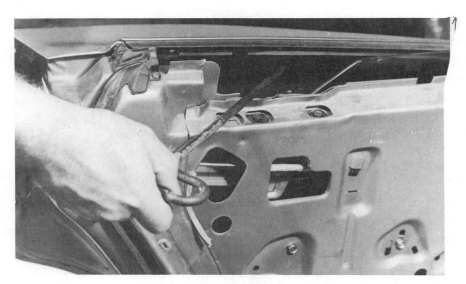

Fig. 153 View of upper inside of door with trim pad removed. Large opening provides access for tools.

Fig. 154 Prying out gouged area while tension is held on the panel.

In Fig. 154, the operator is shown using a pry rod to reduce the depth of the deep gouges in the lower section of the panel. The dent puller, shown in use in Fig. 163 on the quarter panel, could have been used here also. It was not, however, because there is easy access for the pry rod which provides better control of the movement of metal than the puller. Furthermore, it is felt desirable not to pierce holes in a panel where it can be avoided with satisfactory results.

Tension is being maintained on the panel while the prying is being done. Considerably more effort would be required, and the result would not be as satisfactory if the prying had been done without the tension.

The door is being held open for this operation by a block of wood, not visible, so that the operator has a solid base to pry against.

In Fig. 155, the jack and clamps have been removed, and heat is being applied to some of the high spots caused by the prying operation. They will be driven down to shrink the area partially as shown in Fig. 156. This shrinking operation would have been avoided by not lifting the spots so high, but it would have been necessary to make a much deeper fill. The time required to perform this operation is slight when it is done by an experienced man.

The metal preparation has been moved to the quarter panel in Fig. 157. The light duty body jack is shown set up to push out the lower edge of the wheel opening. This area was pushed in slightly by the impact. Although not showing, a short length of 1 x 2 wood was used under the

Fig. 155 Applying heat to partially shrink high spots.

Fig. 156 The partial shrinking operation. Operator moves pry rod to various low areas while driving down the high metal. (Practice enables right-handed operator to work left handed.)

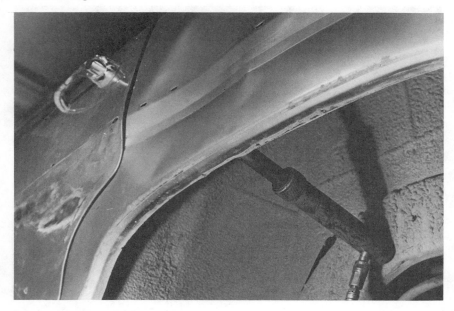

Fig. 157 Light duty body jack set up to push out lower edge of wheel opening.

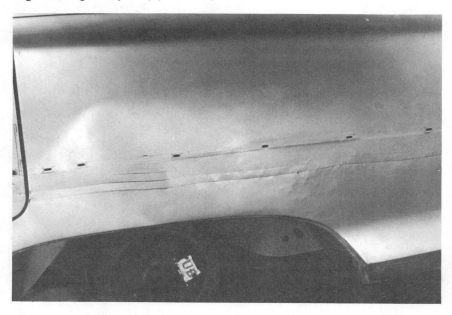

Fig. 158 The quarter panel after much of the rear end of the damage had been pried out. Prying was done from inside the trunk.

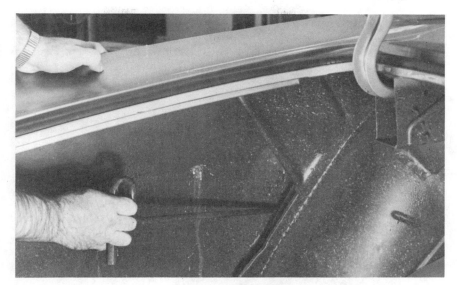

Fig. 159 View inside of trunk, showing how pry rod was inserted.

end of the jack to spread the force over a larger area of the inside of the wheel housing.

Considerable prying and metal straightening, with the hammer and heavy spoon, have been done on the rear end of the gouge, as it is shown in Fig. 158. Inside views of the pry rod and spoon applications are shown in Figs. 159 and 160. The purpose of these operations is to restore the general shape to the area as much as possible. Although the rear end of this gouge is relatively narrow, it has pulled a wide area of metal inward and below the proper contour. Bringing this back to rough shape reduces both the size and depth of the area to be filled. Being easily accessible, there is no need to use the dent puller.

The operator is shown using the hammer to work down a long ridge left after the gouge was lifted in Fig. 161. This ridge was much more apparent after the gouge was lifted out because of the outward movement of the surface below it. A flat bumping spoon could have been used for this operation. A beginner who has not yet developed good control of his hammer would be advised to use the bumping spoon on a ridge such as this because of probable damage from misdirected hammer blows.

A jack and tension plates are shown set up across the forward section of the gouge in Fig. 162. The jack is under just enough pressure to make the panel move outward as much as it will. After movement of the panel stopped, it would have been a serious mistake to have pumped the jack further. The purpose of the jack is to pull the surface as close to the

Fig. 160 View inside of trunk, showing how heavy spoon was used.

Fig. 161 Working down the long ridge at upper edge of dented area.

Fig. 162 Working down the high ridge after pulling the deep dent in forward end of panel. This operation relieved the high metal much better than would have been possible with the dent puller alone.

original shape as possible without causing additional damage. Thus, the tendency is to lift the metal under the jack, tending to pull the edge of the door opening back to position, and to pull the high ridge above the jack down. The operator is using the hammer on this ridge to free it for the maximum amount of movement.

This set up removed all of the high metal and lifted some of the low. The dent puller is shown in use on the worst of the gouge in Fig. 163. The jack is under pressure in this operation for the same reason that it was when the door was being pried out as shown in Fig. 154. Note that only a few holes were required.

The ground-off and partially metal-finished door panel and forward section of the quarter panel are shown in Fig. 164, and the complete quarter panel is shown in Fig. 165. In both views, note that the areas that could be finished easily have been finished so that they will not require filling at all. All of the surface of the door above the molding, except at the extreme rear edge, has been finished completely. Because of the straightening procedure used, this metal was smooth enough to make it easier to finish it without filling. The rear end of the gouged area and about two thirds of the metal above the molding line have been finished. All of the high metal was brought down to the proper level, and there were no deep holes that required excessive filling. Also, the space between the edge of the quarter panel and door was restored so that filling was

Fig. 163 Using the dent puller on the sharp gouge while tension is maintained on the area.

Fig. 164 The door and forward end of quarter panel after partial metal finishing. No filling will be needed above door molding line because it could be finished faster without it.

Fig. 165 The quarter panel, partially finished and ready for filling.

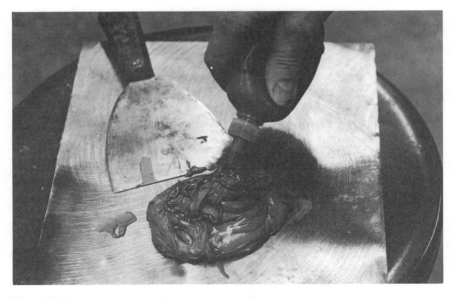

Fig. 166 Preparing plastic filler for application. Material has been dipped from container, and operator is adding cream type hardener to it.

Fig. 167 Mixing plastic filler and hardener. Kneading motion with broad bladed knife mixes in less air than a stirring motion would.

not required in the opening. Filling in a door opening with plastic is not recommended because of the probability of chipping off on the exposed corner. This or any other exposed corner should be built up with lead before the adjoining area is filled with plastic.

Plastic Mixing and Application. The preparation of plastic filler material is shown in Figs. 166 and 167. In Fig. 166, a quantity of material has been dipped out of the can onto a piece of sheet metal and the hardener is being squeezed out of the tube. As is common practice, the amount of hardener is being judged by eye. This presents no problem for, as stated previously, the exact amounts are not critical and the user soon learns to estimate the amount needed.

The mixing operation is complete when the hardener has been mixed uniformly with the plastic. The use of a pigmented hardener simplifies the problem because of the color change. When the color is uniform, the mixing is ready. However, care must be taken to eliminate air in the mixture, which will leave open pockets in the fill. A back-and-forth, kneading motion is much better than a stirring action. Note that the mixing is being done with a four-inch-wide knife. This knife will be used in applying the plastic to the panel. A knife six inches wide may be used in the final smoothing operation in some cases.

A precaution about the cleaning of the knives used to apply the material is needed. Fresh plastic material should never be dipped out of the

Fig. 168 Applying the first coat of plastic filler. The knife is being pressed hard against the surface to insure that no air pockets are left under the material.

container with a knife which has mixed material on it. This will carry hardener back into the fresh material, causing it, or some of it, to set up. This can damage the material remaining in the container.

The tools used in the mixing and application should be cleaned immediately after each use. If the material is allowed to set up on the blade of the knife, washing with lacquer thinner will remove it easily. Many shops keep a can of scrap thinner to put the application tools in immediately after each use. However, there are other, nonflammable solvents which will serve the purpose, and their use is recommended instead of thinner wherever possible.

The first step in the application is shown in Fig. 168. The operator is applying a thin coat to the surface, using stiff pressure on the knife blade. Note that the blade is flexed so that the edge is almost parallel to the panel. This is to eliminate the possibility of voids caused by air trapped in depressions in the metal surface. After coating the surface in this manner, additional material was built up to produce the surface which is shown being rough-finished in Fig. 169.

The rough-finishing operation is being done with a "cheese grater" type plane. It must be performed just as soon as the material has hardened enough to permit it. If hardening is allowed to progress too far, the plane will not cut it and finishing must be done by grinding or filing. Planing at this stage is much faster than grinding the hardened material, and it

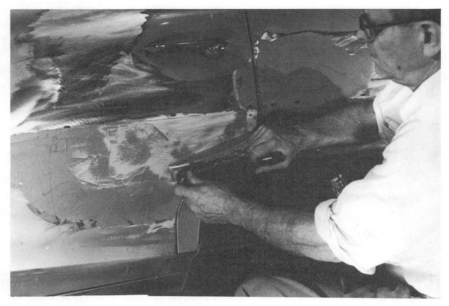

Fig. 169 The start of the rough finishing operation, using a "cheese grater" plane.

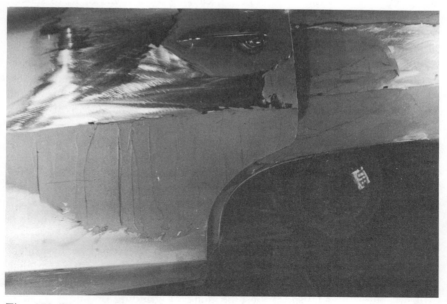

Fig. 170 The final coat of plastic, applied after the first was rough planed. This coat refilled the low spots showing in Fig. 169.

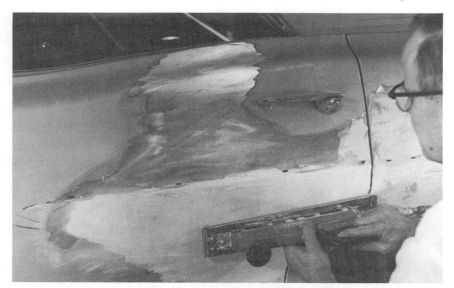

Fig. 171 Final finishing of the plastic, using a combination file-sander. Light planing preceded this operation.

is particularly effective in leveling high spots and showing up low spots. The plane has the disadvantage of leaving a rough, corrugated surface. This surface can either be refilled or sanded smooth if there are no low spots that need further filling.

In this case, the intention was to build up the surface almost to the desired level, plane off the high spots, and reapply a thin finish coat to the entire area. This final coat can be seen in Fig. 170.

There are several advantages to the use of a light final coat. The principal one is the almost complete elimination of pits and pinholes. If the first coat, or coats, of a deep fill has been made and planed down properly, the final coat will be almost uniform in thickness, making it very easy to apply.

The second coat was planed lightly and finished with an air-driven sanding machine, as shown in Fig. 171. Just enough planing was done to knock off the ridges left by the edge of the knife blade. The rest of the finishing operation was done by sanding. Sanding was started using 36-grit paper on the machine, and the final finishing was done using 80-grit paper. The same grits would be used if the sanding was done by hand.

The finished panels, ready for repainting and repainted, are shown in Figs. 172 and 173. The surfaces are smooth and have the proper contour because the metal has been straightened enough to return it to its proper

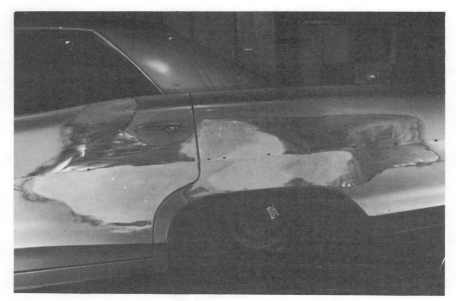

Fig. 172 The finished surface, ready for repainting.

Fig. 173 The finished job, ready for delivery.

general shape. The application procedure has eliminated the possibility of pits and pinholes. No telltale marks remain to reveal that these panels have been repaired after suffering relatively severe damage.

BODY SOLDER

The original body filling material used in both manufacturing and repairing was solder. It is still used in manufacture but only to a limited degree in repairing. There are several reasons for the waning use of body solder. Probably the most important are that relatively high skill is required in its use, that heat distortion is likely when applying it to flat areas, and that it is a relatively slow operation when filling large areas. Other, closely related reasons are the higher cost of material and that proper use of solder requires considerable attention to metal straightening operations before it is applied.

Advantages of solder are in its permanence and much greater resistance to rough usage. Properly applied, a solder fill will last as long as the metal on which it is used. Any corner subject to rough usage, such as a door opening, the edge of a fender adjoining a hood, or the edge of a trunk opening, should be built up with solder instead of plastic if the best quality of work is desired. Also, on small areas solder can be applied very rapidly, and there is no delay in hardening, as with plastic. The advantages of solder filling are strong enough to justify the beginner to learn to apply it, whether he makes extensive use of it or not. The effectiveness of soldered-on attachments, such as tension plates or other pieces of metal, to apply tension in the straightening of many damaged panels makes it desirable to have solder in the body shop, even though it is not used or used very little, for filling.

PROPERTIES OF BODY SOLDER

The reasons why body solder is suitable for use on automobile bodies are: it can be bonded permanently to the panel; it can be worked into any desired shape by means of a torch and paddle; it can be finished to a smooth surface; and paint will adhere to it as well as to sheet metal.

Solder will bond to steel, and many other metals, because it will tin the surface. Tinning is accomplished by heating the steel to the melting point of the solder, applying a flux to clean it, and applying the solder. When all conditions are right, the melted solder will form a coating on the surface with drops of residue from the burned flux floating on it. The metal man uses a cloth to wipe away the burned flux.

The fact that body solder can be worked into shape with the torch and paddle is due to its peculiar melting characteristics. Unlike the pure metals, solder does not melt from a solid to a liquid at a fixed point on the temperature scale. Instead, it begins to soften in the 360° to 370°F.

temperature range, and continues to become softer as it is heated until it finally melts to a liquid. The actual melting point is governed by the percentage of tin and lead; however, it will be below the melting point of lead, 620°F., and it can be below the melting point of tin, 455°F.

The higher the percentage of tin, the lower the melting point will be. For example: 30-70 (30% tin and 70% lead) solder melts just under 500°F. and 50-50 melts at about 420°F. Most of the solder used for body repair has 20% to 30% tin because it has a melting temperature high enough to provide a wide range of heat in which it is plastic enough to be worked. Solder of 50-50 composition is not practical for application by torch and paddle because the temperature range between first softening and final melting is too narrow to permit plastic working; but, 50-50 solder does have greater strength than body solder. It is used in radiator repair and most minor soldering jobs on the automobile.

Body solder should not be used for reinforcement or strength. If it is used to fill holes which are much larger than the metal thickness, the depth of the fill should be greater than the width of the hole. Holes larger than approximately ½ inch should not be filled without first welding or brazing shut. It is not uncommon for beginners to attempt to avoid welding a joint by soldering the edges together and covering them with a deep solder fill. Such joints will break with normal use of the automobile.

Paint will adhere to solder as well as to the sheet metal to which it is applied. However, the surface must be free of strong acids, oil, or other foreign material which may be imbedded in the solder if the work is done carelessly. A primary source of acid in solder is from raw muriatic acid which is used sometimes to remove weld scale or from muriatic acid cut with zinc, which is used sometimes as flux. A rotary wire brush mounted on the disc sander will clean the surface much faster than acid and leave it uncontaminated. There are many acid-free fluxes on the market, making it unnecessary to use anything which would contaminate the surface. Other foreign matter in the solder can be avoided by good work habits.

Preparing for Solder Filling

Filling may be used any place where it alone will restore the proper surface level. In most places where filling is used, it is necessary to do some straightening to prepare the area because some of the area will have been pushed above the proper level. Remember that filling must be restricted to surface areas which are below the proper level; low spots can be filled up, but high spots cannot be filled down. Straightening must be continued until all high spots are relieved.

Sometimes an attempt is made simply to drive a high spot down without paying any attention to the adjoining low metal. This procedure is unsatisfactory, because the adjoining low metal is serving as a prop to hold the high metal up—the high and low spots have what may be considered a cause-and-effect relationship. It is much better to remove the cause, by raising the low spot, before attempting to remove effect, by driving the high spot down. This is just the application of the basic principles of straightening as explained in Chapter 4.

The gouge-type dents in the two door lower panels, Fig. 174, are typical damage which may be repaired by filling after minor straightening is done. The step-by-step procedure of the straightening and filling necessary to repair the doors is used here to illustrate good solder filling practice. The use of a slide hammer to straighten the narrow strip between

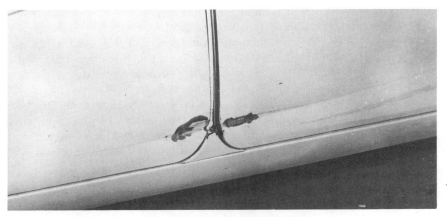

Fig. 174 Gouge-type dents on which filling will simplify the repair operations.

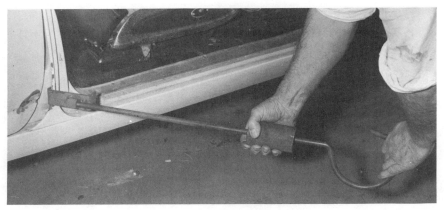

Fig. 175 Using the slide hammer to straighten the filler strip between the doors.

the two doors is shown in Fig. 175. The edges of the doors and this strip must be restored to the proper level and alignment before starting any filling operation.

The two steps shown in Figs. 176 and 177 were required on the front door. On the rear door, it was only necessary to drive the damaged corner out to level with a hammer and a block of wood (this operation is not shown). In Fig. 176 the hammer and dolly block are being used to relieve the sharp crease along the lower edge. In this operation, the dolly is tilted slightly outward at the bottom so that it will bring the extreme lower edge outward as the hammer flattens the crease line above it. This is a typical kind of damage on doors and should always be worked in this manner because it will cause some of the depressed metal above it to spring back toward the proper level. In this case, it will reduce the depth of the area to be filled, saving both material and time.

Prying to reduce some of the dent in the less severely gouged area is shown in Fig. 177. A blunt-pointed scratch awl is being used as the pry tool. Here the scratch awl has been inserted through a drain hole, but it is common practice to make holes where needed by driving the awl through the lower facing outside the weather strip.

These two operations, which required only a very short time, prepared the panels for solder filling and reduced the amount of solder required to make the fill. The rest of the work is simply a matter of building up enough solder so that the surface can be finished smooth to blend with the surrounding panel.

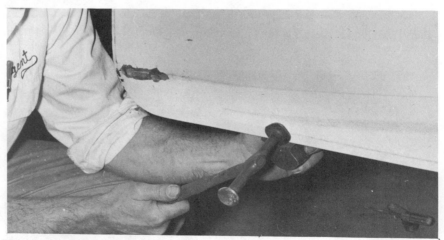

Fig. 176 Using the hammer and dolly block to relieve the strain on the ridge along the lower edge. The dolly block should be tipped outward slightly at the bottom.

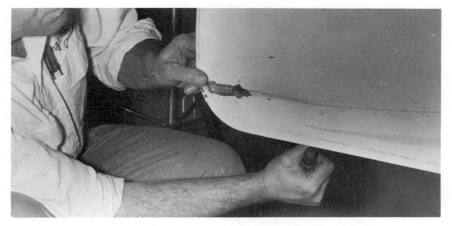

Fig. 177 Reducing the size of the dent by prying with a scratch awl inserted through the drain hole.

BODY SOLDER APPLICATION

There are four basic steps in applying body solder: (1) cleaning, (2) tinning, (3) filling and shaping, and (4) metal finishing.

The procedure for applying solder is essentially the same for any surface condition for which it is a suitable means of repair. The greatest problem for the beginner is to learn to use the torch flame on relatively flat metal so that heat distortion is avoided. For that reason, it is best for him to practice on higher crowned surfaces until he has developed some skill before he attempts to apply solder on the more difficult areas.

Cleaning. Any material must be removed that will prevent the solder from adhering to the surface to which it is to be applied. The materials which, under normal conditions, will be on the surface to be soldered are: (1) paint, (2) weld scale, and (3) rust.

Occasionally, body sealers, cements, or other foreign matter which has found its way onto the surface by accident also must be cleaned off. The same cleaning methods will be satisfactory for the removal of all types of material.

The clean, bright metal surface left by the disc sander is ideal for solder application. (See Fig. 178.) Wherever possible, use the sander to remove paint, rust, or weld scale. However, body solder is used as a finishing material over surfaces that are entirely too rough to be cleaned with the sanding disc; rough welds are an excellent example. Such surfaces are difficult to clean with the sander because it cannot get into sharp depressions and pits. Turning the sander up on edge to get into the bottom of such spots can cause it to cut away enough metal to weaken the panel but

Fig. 178 Removing paint with the disc sander.

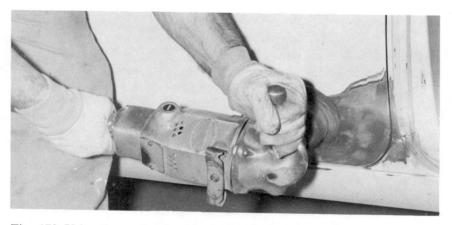

Fig. 179 Using the saucer-shaped wire brush on the disc sander to clean paint out of a deep gouge.

still not clean the surface properly. Other methods of cleaning are needed.

The saucer-shaped wire brush mounted on a disc sander, shown in use in Fig. 179, is an excellent tool for cleaning rough spots that cannot be reached with the edge of the sanding disc. Although not satisfactory for removing large areas of paint, it will clean out either paint or weld scale from sharp depressions very rapidly and without contamination. It is best, however, to avoid its use on any surface where cements or sealers are present, because it will smear such materials instead of removing them. Such materials may be removed much more easily by heating them and scraping.

Metal can be cleaned by chemical means for soldering, but in most cases it is best to avoid them. Muriatic acid sometimes is used to remove weld scale and rust; other chemicals are available which will remove both scale and paint. Such materials do the intended job very well, but there is a risk that traces of the strong acids will remain in the solder and cause paint failure and rusting after the job has been completed and the automobile delivered to the owner. Such risks will be avoided, if chemical cleaning of all kinds is avoided. In almost every case it is easier to do it mechanically, so there is no reason to risk contamination.

Tinning. Tinning is the operation of coating with melted solder the surface to be soldered. Any additional solder used is then built up on this coat. Tinning is essential in any soldering operation, whether it is an electrical joint, a radiator, or a sheet metal surface to be filled with body solder. The body solder operation differs from most other soldering operations in that the tinned surface must be wiped clean before the additional solder is applied. The reason for this is in the nature of the materials used for flux.

Flux of some sort is essential for soldering on almost all metals, but particularly so on steel. The flux serves as a chemical cleaner. Melted solder in contact with clean steel will join to it securely if a suitable flux is present to perform the cleaning action. In the process, the flux is burned, leaving a residue on the surface. This residue creates no problem if tinning and the adding of solder can be done at the same time, such as would be the case with a wire joint. When applying body solder with the torch and paddle, the flux residue must be wiped off before the filling material is added.

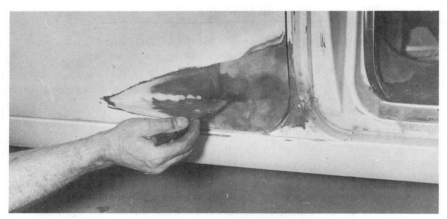

Fig. 180 Brushing flux on hot metal. Steam indicates proper temperature.

The procedure for tinning varies according to the type of flux used and the way that the solder for tinning is applied. Practically all of the fluxes used for body soldering are liquid; resin paste flux, used widely in electrical work, is generally unsatisfactory for use with the torch. Many liquid fluxes, which are very satisfactory for use on automobile sheet metal, are available from automotive jobbers.

Tinning compounds, composed of flux mixed with powdered solder, are also available. Many of these are very good, and they offer the advantage of being able to apply the tinning solder with the flux instead of afterward.

The tinning procedure with liquid flux is as follows:

1. Heat the surface to be tinned and brush on the flux.

2. Heat the fluxed surface until it is hot enough so that the solder will begin to run when the bar is rubbed against it. Apply solder in this manner to various spots of the area to be tinned. Approximately one-third of the area should be covered.

3. Heat the area until the solder begins to melt, then wipe it across the surface, using a clean cotton cloth.

With some fluxes the first heating operation can be omitted, but in most instances a better job will be done if it is not. The chemical action of the flux is increased on the heated surface so that the tinning action will be easier. This action is shown in Fig. 180.

Fig. 181 shows the application of tinning solder. Note that about one-third of the surface actually is covered. Some metal men prefer to cover the entire area with solder in this manner, but it is unnecessary. If care is taken to avoid burning the flux, it is possible to tin by covering less of the area than shown here.

The wiping operation is shown in Fig. 182. This is done by playing the flame over the area until the solder and metal are both of the temperature at which the solder is fluid. A cloth or wadded paper is used to spread the melted solder over the heated surface and to wipe away the flux residue. Care in the wiping operation is very important. Generally, the wiping action always should be in the same direction, and very light pressure should be applied. Heavy pressure will wipe the solder off instead of spreading it. If too much is wiped off, the surface should be refluxed and retinned.

When tinning a large area, it is best to heat and wipe alternately. After each wiping stroke, the torch should be played over several square inches of unwiped area, then removed, and the wiping cloth used to extend the wiped area across the spot. Working in this manner, the operator can carry the wiping across a large area, from one side to another.

It is desirable, but not an absolute necessity, to avoid reheating and

Fig. 181 Applying small quantity of solder for tinning. Note torch flame adjustment and distance from panel.

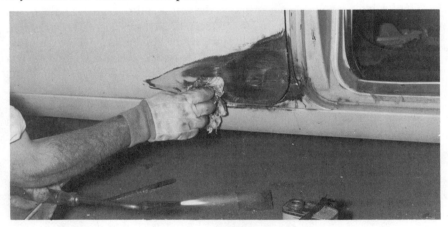

Fig. 182 Wiping melted solder over the surface to complete the tinning operation.

wiping an area that has been covered already. When this must be done, it is evidence that that spot was not clean originally, that it was overheated, or that it was rubbed too hard in wiping.

The tinning procedure with most of the tinning compounds differs from the preceding in that the compound is wiped onto the heated surface with a piece of steel wool. This one operation applies both the flux and the solder for tinning, leaving the surface tinned and ready for the application of filling solder. A large area can be tinned and wiped by heating and wiping alternately in the same manner as described for the liquid flux.

Filling and Shaping. Filling and shaping is the operation of adding solder to the tinned surface and shaping it to the proper contour so that it can be finished smooth. When done properly, the finishing operation should be quite simple. Excessively built-up or low spots should be avoided.

The most frequently used method for adding solder is to heat to the plastic state about an inch of the end of the bar and apply it directly to the tinned surface. (See Fig. 183.) The temperature of the tinned surface must be kept in the range which will permit the added solder to join the tinning coat. The addition of any quantity of solder by this method will take enough time so that the tinned surface will have to be reheated several times. This usually is done by heating the bar and then turning the flame on the surface as the softened metal is deposited. The operation can be repeated until enough solder has been deposited for the particular job. Learning to judge the right amount comes with experience gained from practice.

The beginner should learn to judge the temperature of the solder by its appearance. As solder begins to soften, its surface begins to brighten; when it is fully melted, it has a bright, shiny appearance. The temperature range in which it is plastic enough to work is somewhere between these two extremes. The ability to determine temperature from the appearance must be developed by observation.

When enough solder has been added to make the needed fill, it should be worked into shape by playing the flame over it until it is plastic enough to paddle. The paddle should be clean and preferably pretreated with oil. A light film of oil can be applied to the working face by rubbing the

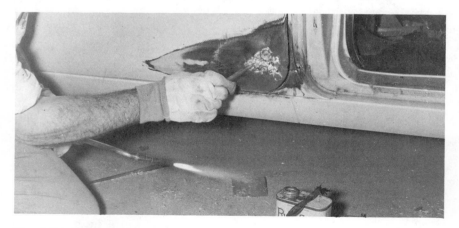

Fig. 183 Applying solder for filling. The torch flame has been used to soften the bar and keep the tinned surface in the plastic temperature range.

Fig. 184 Padding the solder into shape.

paddle on an oil pad or rag. Paddling (Fig. 184) is simply a matter of molding the softened solder into shape. For the beginner, this is usually not as simple as it sounds. However, it is fairly easy to master, if he watches the surface for the temperature and learns to manipulate the paddle properly.

The beginner usually has difficulty with the use of the solder paddle until he has developed confidence in his use of the torch flame. The first attempt invariably results in melted solder which either runs off or separates into lumps of tin and lead. Once the solder separates, the plastic working properties are lost and further paddling is impossible. It is only natural to attempt to avoid such trouble by not heating too much. Also, it is easy to forget to reheat while shaping a particular area. The result is a futile attempt to shape cold solder. Paddle soldering will not be easy until the torch manipulation becomes automatic.

Maintaining the proper temperature is easy if the operator does the following: (1) plays the flame over the whole area until the solder softens; or if the area being soldered is too large to be paddled all at once, plays the flame over as much of it as can be worked; and (2) reheats every few seconds.

This is not as difficult as it may seem because, once the solder has been softened, a flick of the flame will keep it in that condition, providing it has not cooled too much. The procedure is to make a stroke or two with the paddle, then pass the flame across the hot solder quickly and repeat the paddle operation. When done properly, applying the flame takes very little time.

The grain structure of solder will become coarse if it is kept heated for any length of time. This makes it very difficult to paddle, and very likely there will be pit holes in the finished job. Unless the torch is manipulated so that the paddling can be done quickly, a good job is very difficult to do.

With the solder properly heated, manipulating the paddle is very much like using a trowel to smooth plaster. Note in the illustrations that the solder was applied in the approximate center of the tinned area. As it was softened with the flame, the paddle was used to flatten and smooth it. The actual stroke of the paddle may be a downward pressure, to flatten, or it may be drawn across the surface to drag solder from one point to another. A very common beginner's mistake is to turn the paddle on edge to scrape solder from one point to another. This should never be done because the narrow edge of the paddle will cut into the soft surface, leaving it rough and irregular.

Rapid cooling, by quenching water, should always be done where there is any suggestion of heat distortion (Fig. 185). This means that all flat surfaces should be quenched by dashing water on them while the solder is still in the temperature range to permit paddling. On a vertical surface, the water can be thrown with a soaking-wet sponge or rag. Note the steam and water drops in the illustration. After the temperature has dropped enough to cool the solder, the wet sponge can be rubbed on the surface. This should not be done while the solder is at higher temperatures, because it will dig solder out of the smoothed surface and ruin it. On the other hand, waiting until the solder has cooled enough to solidify will, in many cases, cause some of the heat distortion to remain in the panel after it has cooled to normal temperature.

Fig. 185 Quenching the hot solder.

Metal Finishing Solder. The metal finishing operation on solder is very similar to that on sheet metal, except that care must be exercised to avoid cutting it away too fast. Since solder is soft, a body file will bite deep into it with very little effort as compared to that required to make the file bite into steel; it is very easy to cut well below the proper surface level, if the work is done carelessly.

Best results will be obtained if filing is started by blending the edges of the soldered area into the surrounding metal surface. As the work progresses, the center area is filed to blend it into the edges. When this procedure is followed on a fairly large area, it has the effect of progressively reducing the unfiled area from the edges toward the center. This

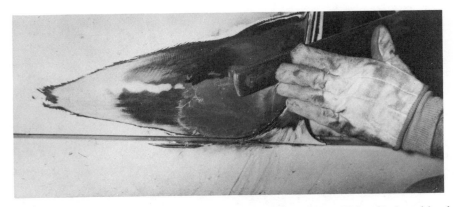

Fig. 186 First step in metal finishing solder. The edges will be filed to blend into the contour of the surrounding metal surface.

Fig. 187 Finishing the lower edge. The center area will be filed to blend it into the finished outer edges.

basic procedure was followed in the filing shown in Figs. 186 and 187. In Fig. 186, the upper edge has been blended with the panel surface above it. In Fig. 187, the blending operation has been started in the lower edge and will be carried forward. The finished areas will be joined across the forward edge, and the center finished last. A few vertical strokes will be used to finish the rear edge, which may be uneven because some of the lengthwise strokes probably cut deeper than others.

Final finishing of the filed surface is done with sandpaper. Note the sheet wrapped around the file in Fig. 188. This particular sheet is 50-grit production paper, which should be available in any body shop. Its use is almost essential if the surface is to be made smooth enough so

Fig. 188 Smoothing the surface with sandpaper wrapped around the file.

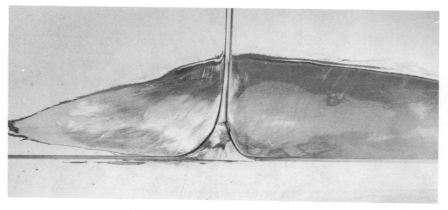

Fig. 189 Both door panels, metal finished and ready for repainting.

that it can be painted without excessive filling with paint materials. The file leaves deeper scratches and coarser marks in solder than in steel. Sandpaper is the best way to smooth these scratches and marks so that they will not be a problem in the painting operation.

The finished job, ready for repainting, is shown in Fig. 189. Filling was the only practical way to repair these panels; it eliminated disassembly and required far less time than would be needed to straighten and shrink the gouged areas.

Either of these dents would have presented a different situation if they had been located in an area where some of the adjoining metal had been pushed above the surface level. In that case solder would have been effective only if time could be saved without loss of quality by partially straightening and filling the rest of the dent.

Use of the Disc Sander on Solder. The disc sander is used on solder sometimes, but it is not recommended because of the health hazard involved. Dust from grinding lead can be absorbed through the skin as well as breathed into the lungs. Once lead enters the human body, there are no natural means by which it can be eliminated. Enough lead, obtained in any manner over any period of time, will cause lead poisoning. In almost every case of lead poisoning, the lead was picked up a little at a time over a long period. Inasmuch as lead poisoning is often fatal, it is only logical to avoid any practice which may lead to it.

If the disc sander must be used on solder, the operator should have a respirator, and he should wash the lead dust from the skin as soon as possible.

The Solder Mush Pot

The mush pot is a pot or pan (even an old hubcap will do) in which a large quantity of solder may be heated to the plastic state. A clean paddle is used to pick up the softened solder and to spread it on the tinned surface in much the same manner as a knife is used to spread butter. (See Fig. 190.) When a large quantity of solder is needed, the mush pot method is faster than applying it directly from the bar.

There are two advantages in using the mush pot: one is that it takes much less time than heating the bar and applying individual dabs, as shown in Fig. 183, the other is that when a large quantity is put on at the right temperature, it can be spread into shape without cold spots developing.

The mush pot has advantages only if the beginner has acquired enough skill with the torch and paddle and can shape solder rapidly. He first should practice flame manipulation (to maintain uniform temperature), and paddle manipulation (to develop the proper touch), on smaller

Fig. 190 Dipping softened solder from a mush pot.

quantities of solder. When this is mastered, it will be easy to handle the mush pot and larger quantities.

Use of the mush pot changes none of the procedure in solder filling, except the actual application of the solder to the tinned surface. There should be no difference in the quality of the finished job produced by either method.

QUESTIONS ON FILLING

1. On what type of surface conditions can the use of filling material save time?
2. What surface contour conditions are necessary before any filling material can be applied?
3. Why is it objectionable to have high spots of metal projecting through a plastic fill?
4. Why must the surface be free of paint or other foreign material before plastic is applied?
5. Where should the mixing directions for any plastic material be obtained?
6. Why should a long, flat block such as the sandpaper "file" be used in finishing a plastic fill?
7. Why should the flux be applied to hot metal?
8. At what temperature should the surface be when solder for tinning is applied?
9. What is the purpose of wiping?
10. Why should the application of the flame and the wiping cloth be alternated?
11. How much pressure should be applied to the wiping cloth?

12. What should the temperature of the surface be when solder is applied to it for filling?
13. How can the proper amount of solder be determined?
14. Should the paddle be turned on edge when it is necessary to move solder from one place to another? Why?
15. What is the purpose of quenching?
16. At what temperature should the solder be when it is quenched?
17. Why should the solder fill be filed around the edges before filing down the center area?
18. Why should the metal finishing operation be completed by using sandpaper?
19. What are the advantages of the solder mush pot?
20. What properties of body solder permit it to be molded into shape by means of a lubricated wooden paddle?
21. Is the melting point of lead higher or lower than the melting point of solder composed of lead and tin?
22. Does a higher percentage of tin make a solder which has a higher or a lower melting point?
23. Why is acid flux not recommended?
24. What is the purpose of flux?
25. How should the solder for tinning be applied?
26. What will be the result of wiping too hard?
27. What is the purpose of the rotary wire brush, driven by the disc sander?

7

Basic Straightening Procedures and Equipment

In the preceding chapters, the metal man's job was broken up into separate components dealing with fundamental information and basic operations. This was done for the purpose of study. In beginning the study of straightening operations on actual damaged panels, the viewpoint must be somewhat different. The purpose of this chapter is to show the application of fundamental information and the basic skills in repairing actual damage; therefore, the separate topics must be considered together.

This approach is made necessary by the trend toward more complex construction of the automobile. There was a time when all the metal man had to do was to drive a dent out from the underside, smooth the surface with his hammer and dolly block, and file it smooth. Such methods are still an integral part of sheet metal repair procedure, and probably will continue to be as long as sheet metal is used in automobile bodies. However, the long-term trend of automobile design has been away from the higher crowned surfaces for which such simple methods are adequate. The lower crowns, the sometimes nearly dead flat surfaces, which have been the result of this styling trend, have demanded the development of newer methods of straightening. Thus, the repair of the newer styles requires the old and new to be interwoven into better procedures.

Having taken the metal man's job apart in the previous chapters, it is necessary to put it together again. The first part of this chapter deals with the methods of applying force to the various types of damage conditions so that straightening will be accomplished with the least possible distortion. A discussion of the essential equipment also is included. The second part of this chapter is the how-to-do-it section. It is a discussion and explanation of the procedures followed on the repair of typical damaged panels.

THE PHASES OF STRAIGHTENING

In starting this study of actual repairs, remember that the operations of straightening any damaged panel can be separated into three or sometimes four groups. Regardless of the procedure followed, these three groups (or *phases*) are always required: (1) roughing, (2) bumping, and (3) metal finishing.

The fourth phase is aligning. It is sometimes considered separately and sometimes as a part of the roughing phase.

Each of these phases has been discussed previously. The more detailed coverage which follows deals with the reasons governing the selection of the proper repair method for the various types of damaged conditions.

ROUGHING AND ALIGNING

Roughing is the most important phase of the total straightening operation because mistakes, if made, will complicate all of the following operations. When done properly, roughing restores the over-all contour to the damaged area of the panel. If the damage includes misaligned reinforcing members, such as pillars, window frames, etc., these must be realigned as the roughing phase progresses.

Aligning often is considered as a separte phase in jobs where reinforcing members must be straightened so that they fit to adjoining panels or assemblies. This is particularly true when the damaged panel is to be cut off and replaced with a new one; the reinforcing members to which it attaches must be in alignment before the new panel can be welded to them.

Recognition of the separate aligning operation or phase is of much greater importance in doing major wreck jobs on which several panels are involved than on smaller jobs involving only one panel. The aligning phase often is entered as a separate item in writing an estimate of a major job, because it provides a means of placing a value on such work when needed. The listing of such operations in estimating follows the basic idea that an itemized estimate is more accurate than one based on a general opinion.

The exact conditions of a misalignment can vary widely. One example of misalignment could be a roof panel damage in which the roof rail has been driven down, causing misalignment of both the door and the windshield opening. Another could be a misaligned door opening resulting from a rear end impact. In this latter situation, often there are no dents or buckles in the metal surrounding the door opening. In both examples, however, the necessary alignment will be restored when the roughing has been completed properly. Because aligning and roughing are so closely related, there is little or no benefit to be gained in discussing them separately. Therefore, in the coverage that follows, they are considered together.

ROUGHING

Roughing is the application of force so that it will undo most of the effect of the damaging force. In one sense, roughing can be considered as a practical compromise, because, if the ideal could be obtained, none of the effect of the damaging force would be left. If such were true, no further bumping and metal finishing would be required because the panel would be restored to shape. The ideal, however, is very difficult to obtain, so it is necessary to follow procedures that will be practical.

In roughing a damage out of any panel, it should be realized that the repair force is such that it could add further damage if it is not used properly. The metal man must never forget that he is working with a relatively soft material which can be made to yield readily as force is applied on it. If, in yielding, dimensions are distorted, damage may have been increased instead of reduced. Such situations result in panels which may be back to almost normal shape, but the fact that they have been poorly repaired is evident even to the casual observer.

There are three basic methods of applying force to rough out a damaged panel:

1. To drive the metal back into place, using a heavy hammer, a dolly block, or other striking tool.

2. To push the metal back into place, using a jack on the underside.

3. To pull the metal back into place, using a jack as the power source and some means of attachment to apply tension lengthwise of the panel surface.

Each of these methods has advantages for certain types of damage conditions. Each also has limitations. In many cases, the damage on a particular panel will require a combination of two or all three of these methods. For the purpose of study, however, it is desirable to consider them separately.

Fig. 191 Pop-out type of dent.

DRIVING OUT DENTS

Driving out dents with a heavy hammer, a dolly block, or other tool must be limited to relatively simple damage. Whenever the shape of a dent is such that it offers considerable resistance to a driving force, serious upsets will result if it is driven out from the underside. The less force needed to drive the surface back to proper position, the more suited the damage is to being roughed out by that method.

Two simple, pop-out-type dents are shown in Figs. 191 and 192. Even though these two dents are different in size, shape, and over-all contour, they are alike in these respects:

1. They are relatively shallow dents with very little sharply folded metal.

2. The denting action has taken place in an area where the inward movement of the surface has not been resisted by adjoining, heavier construction.

On such surfaces, it is only necessary to apply light force on the underside to start outward movement. Some of the area affected has been under only an elastic strain which will snap back into place when the stronger, fully formed bends are relieved.

On a more severe dent, such as shown in Fig. 193, a driving force on the underside will cause trouble because the surface against which the blow would be struck is too rigid. The effect of any force on such a surface would be similar to the condition shown in Fig. 194. This is a piece of flat sheet metal which has been folded over to a full 180° bend and folded

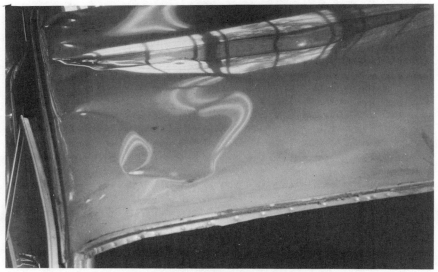

Fig. 192 Damaged roof panel with a large area ready to pop out when strains in the edges are relieved.

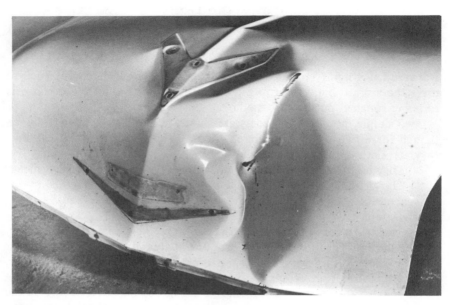

Fig. 193 A typical small dent which represents much more severe damage than the types shown in Figs. 191 and 192.

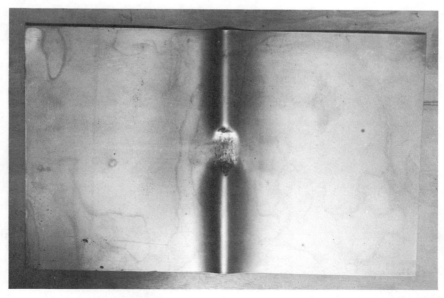

Fig. 194 A severe upset made by hammering down a crease in an unsupported piece of bent metal.

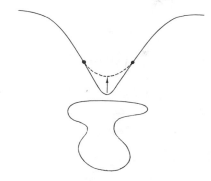

Fig. 195 Showing the upsetting effect of a sharp blow on a rigid buckle. Dotted line represents the upset.

back, leaving the typical buckle where work hardening resisted straightening. Several hammer blows were struck on the center area of the buckle to flatten it. This flattened section is severely upset.

Any blow struck on the underside of a sharp buckle will have some upsetting effect similar to that shown in the illustration. The extent of this problem depends on the conditions of the job. Inertia of the metal will cause some of this upset when any hard blow is struck with a hard object such as a dolly block or a hammer. The drawing in Fig. 195 shows a gross exaggeration of the effect of a blow with a dolly block on the underside of a sharp buckle.

The inertia effect can be completely disregarded when driving out what has been called pop-out dents because the total force involved in bringing them out is not enough to make trouble.

The drawing in Fig. 196 is a typical cross section of a dented door panel. The arrows indicate the point of impact, and the dotted lines the position of the panel in the damaged condition. Fig. 197 shows the flow of force through the surface of the panel when force is applied to it from the underside to lift it. The vertical arrow represents the lifting force, and the arrows parallel to the surface represent the flow of force pushing outward through the panel surface from the point of force application. Any resistance offered to this flow of force would be added to the inertia effect of the panel so that it is likely that a condition would be created similar to that shown in Fig. 194.

The two related drawings in Figs 198 and 199 show this effect as it applies to any panel. In Fig. 198, line *AB* represents a section of the surface of any low-crowned panel, and the lower line represents the effect of an impact on this surface. In Fig. 199, line *AB* represents the original contour, and the line below it represents the effect of driving a buckle out

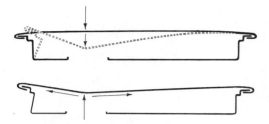

Fig. 196 *(Top)* Cross sectional sketch of a typical door panel showing facing pulled out of place by dented outer panel.

Fig. 197 *(Bottom)* Cross sectional sketch of a typical door panel showing the flow of force through the surface as the dent is either driven or pushed out.

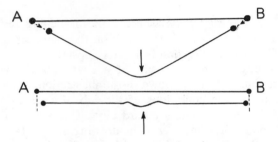

Fig. 198 *(Top)* Showing movement of any panel surface under impact. Line *AB* represents the original surface; the line below represents position after damaging impact.

Fig. 199 *(Bottom)* Showing the buckling effect of either driving or pushing out a dent. Line *AB* represents the original surface; the lower line represents the buckled, shortened panel.

against a strong resistance. The point of force application is shown rough, and the over-all length is too short.

The examples used here are exaggerated for the purpose of illustration. It would be a badly abused panel which was shortened as much as shown in Fig. 199. However, when working panels that are nearly flat, it is necessary to restore lengths to a very small fraction of an inch. The length demonstration illustrated in Chapter 1, Fig. 16, showed that only a 0.005-inch restriction on the length of the strip of metal 18 inches long would cause it to bulge approximately ³⁄₁₆ inch. Such a bulge, either inward or outward, would be entirely unacceptable in a finished panel which should be flat. Applying this reasoning to the condition illustrated by Fig. 199, it can be seen that only a few thousandths of an inch of upset in an area where force has been applied to drive out a buckle will cause trouble. Such an upset will have a gathering effect on the adjoining metal surface similar to that on the center of a sheet of paper when a sharp pleat-type fold is made in the edge.

All of the foregoing explanation has been related to low-crowned or flat panels. The nearer to flat the panel surface is, the more important it is that only the least severe dents be driven out. This does not apply on true high crowns, however. Most true high-crown dents should be driven or pushed out. The trend of automobile body design is such, however, that the metal man has few if any high-crowned panels to work on unless he is specializing in sports cars.

PUSHING OUT DENTS WITH A JACK

This procedure is similar to driving dents out, but it does offer some advantages. The primary advantage is that the steady push of the jack produces less of the effect shown in Fig. 194 and Fig. 199. At first this may seem to be a major advantage, but it is actually less than may be expected in most cases.

The chief disadvantage of pushing out dents stems from the resistance to unfolding offered by any piece of sheet metal. The basic flow of force from the point of application to the edges of the panel was shown in Fig. 197. Whether the primary force comes as a blow struck on the underside, or a slow, steady push, the metal of the panel must transmit it as a pushing force to the edge. Flat, or nearly flat sheet metal is simply a very poor material on which to apply a pushing force because it tends to buckle under the load. Usually the worst buckling will occur at the point of force application, as shown in Fig. 199. While this effect may be less when a jack is used to push out the dent instead of driving it out by striking it, there will still be enough buckling to cause a serious problem.

There is a further complication in the fact that, in most cases, the jack is used only because the particular area is too stiff to drive out. The up-setting effect on a severe damage caused by jacking it out may be much more than the upset caused by driving out a minor damage. This leads to the conclusion that if the dent is too stiff to drive out, care should be exercised in pushing it out, or the panel may be damaged by the repair procedure more severely than it was by the impact. It is very easy to restore a panel to general contour, but in the process to cause so much upsetting that it is almost impossible to make it look right. The operator may discover, also, that more time was spent doing the job wrong than would have been to do it correctly. Instead of driving or pushing such dents out, better results will be obtained with the use of tension.

Fig. 200 A typical setup in which a jack and tension plates are used to pull a dent out of a roof panel.

TENSION

The use of tension offers many advantages over either driving or pushing out dents, particularly in panels which may be classified as low-crowned. The main advantage is that the tendency toward upsetting is avoided, because force is transmitted through the panel surface in tension instead of pressure. It is a matter of lifting a dent out by pulling on each side of it, instead of pushing or striking it on the underside. A typical pulling setup is shown in Fig. 200.

The trend toward low-crowned, nearly flat panels has tremendously increased the importance of tension in roughing out major damages. As pointed out earlier, the effect of an impact on a low-crowned panel is to pull inward the metal adjoining the impact area. If the impact is strong enough, adjoining reinforcements will be drawn inward also. The use of tension to pull such damaged metal back to place simply means that force is applied to the already damaged metal in such a way that the least additional damage will be made by the repair procedure.

The difference in the effect of force acting through the surface of a piece of sheet metal in tension and under pressure was discussed in Chapter 2. It was shown that the length of a flat piece of metal makes no difference in the resistance to tension, but it can make a tremendous difference in the resistance to pressure. The limit of tension that can be used is the force required to cause the metal to actually yield. When tension is used properly,

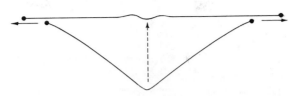

Fig. 201 Showing the basic principle of the use of tension to straighten dents. The lower line represents a cross section of a panel being pulled; the upper line represents the result.

however, the yield point never is reached. Almost all damages can be pulled into place with far less force than is necessary to cause yielding, because tension strains the entire area uniformly. The only qualification to this is that the point of attachment used to apply the tension must be wide enough, at least 2 inches or more, to avoid. stretching the metal. Another error to avoid is the tendency to use too much tension.

Tension also can be used to very good advantage where heat is used to reduce the yield point. This will be discussed in more detail in the descriptions of actual jobs.

In comparison to using tension, pushing or driving a dent out tends to concentrate force on relatively small areas, which upset easily. The panel never can be restored to proper contour unless these upsets are relieved. In addition to being a fast method, tension avoids these upsets.

The basic principle of the use of tension, the tendency to produce a straight line, is illustrated in Fig. 201. The lower line in this sketch represents a cross section through a typical dent. The upper line represents the same cross section after it has been pulled out. Note particularly that some of the original bend, which in most cases would be the valley section of a rolled buckle, remains in the upper sketch. Even though pulling will restore the contour of a dented flat panel to the roughed-out state better than any other method, it is necessary to do some straightening on sharp bends. Pulling will reduce sharp bends so that they are much easier to straighten, but it will never straighten them completely.

The need for some straightening is illustrated in Figs. 202 and 203. In Fig. 202, a strip of metal with a sharp bend in it is shown set up so that it can be pulled by means of a jack and two parallel jaw clamps. The bend was made by folding the metal over double and then opening it enough by hand to reach the clamp jaws. In this condition it represents a typical cross section through a typical dent which should be straightened under tension.

In Fig. 203, the strip has been stretched until it has almost broken. Note the narrow spot in the right end. Also note that the bent area has retained almost its original width, but the rest of the strip has narrowed enough to

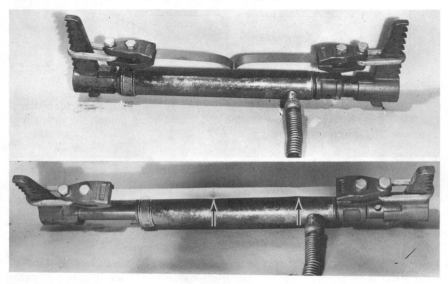

Fig. 202 *(Top)* Jack and clamp setup on bent metal strip to show the limits of straightening by tension alone.

Fig. 203 *(Bottom)* Jack and clamp setup after stretching strip almost to the breaking point. Center arrow points to trace of the original buckle remaining in strip. Arrow at right points to narrow section which is breaking.

make this wide point noticeable. Work hardening, resulting from the bending, has strengthened this bent area enough to cause almost all of the yielding to take place elsewhere. Also, a slight trace of the original bend remains. If the intention had been to straighten this strip, instead of using it as an example of what not to do, it only should have been pulled tight, and the buckle worked with the hammer and dolly block.

Factors Governing the Use of Tension

The procedure for straightening any damaged panel must be determined by examining the conditions existing on it. Such an examination will determine whether the damaged area should be driven, pushed, or pulled out. On panels where the use of tension is indicated, it is necessary to determine the exact points of attachment to use in applying tension, how hard to pull, and to form a general idea of the step-by-step procedure. This problem is not as complicated as it may seem at first, if the factors governing the use of tension are understood. Such an examination then becomes an intelligent analysis which will result in a practical answer to the problem.

Of the basic factors which must be considered in using tension to pull dents out of low-crowned panels, the most important are: (1) leverage angle, (2) lift reaction, (3) work hardening of the buckled area, (4) variations of surface crown, and (5) alignment with the crown of the panel.

These factors are discussed and explained separately.

Leverage Angle. The leverage angle is the most important factor in determining the effectiveness of any pull on any panel. This is illustrated in Figs. 204-207. In these four sketches, the metal on each side of the sharp buckle is considered as two levers. When tension is applied to them, they open in much the same manner as the handles of a pair of tongs. The leverage angle is the angle made by two lines connecting the two points of tension application to the lowest part of the dent. The lines which form this angle will become a straight line when the panel has been straightened.

In Fig. 204, the two lines forming the leverage angle are in a 180° fold. It is rare in any panel repair that a full bend such as this is encountered. However, such a bend will provide the maximum leverage angle.

In Fig. 205, the outward movement of the two surfaces has started to open the bend and draw it closer to a straight line. As the angle between the two surfaces becomes wider, the leverage they can exert against the stiffened bend decreases proportionally. A leverage angle as small as this, however, is larger than is commonly encountered in most repair work.

In Fig. 206, the outward movement of the two surfaces has increased

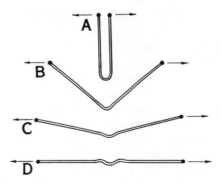

Fig. 204 *(A)* First of four sketches showing the loss of leverage as a bend is straightened. A full 180° bend has the maximum leverage.

Fig. 205 *(B)* Showing the loss of leverage as a bend is straightened.

Fig. 206 *(C)* Showing the progressive loss of leverage as a bend is straightened. Note the indications of outward bends beside the original inward bend.

Fig. 207 *(D)* Showing the loss of leverage as a bend is straightened. Slight buckles remain, but all leverage has been lost.

the angle and made a further decrease in the leverage as the depth of the dent has been reduced. Note that typical outward bends are shown on each side of the original inward bend. These outward bends usually form because the original bend is stiffer, due to work hardening, than the adjoining metal. If the dent were being driven out from the underside, these bends would form in exactly the same manner, except that they would be sharper because of the resistance to movement of the adjoining metal.

The position shown in Fig. 206 is more nearly typical of a cross section through a dent suitable for straightening under tension than the conditions shown in the previous sketches. The remaining leverage is much less than with a smaller angle, but there is still enough left to be very effective.

In Fig. 207, the metal on each side of the original bend has been drawn almost to a straight line. Note that the sketch shows some of the original bend, and some of the outward bends formed in straightening. Further tension will not pull these out, because there is no leverage on them, and they are the strongest metal between the two points of tension application. Whatever remains of the original bend will require straightening by the use of hand tools.

In the discussion of leverage angle so far no consideration has been given to the size of the dent and the over-all length of the panel. It is not uncommon to have a condition such as represented by the cross sectional sketch in Fig. 208. This represents a small, fairly sharp dent in a relatively long panel. The dotted lines connecting points *AA* and *BB* represent the leverage angles which could be used. Pulling from points *BB* would provide a more effective angle than pulling from points *AA,* because the angle is sharper. The sharper angle provides greater leverage.

Another factor, lift reaction, must be considered before deciding whether the attachment to pull out a dent should be made close to the damage, as in Fig. 208, points *BB,* or at the extreme ends.

Lift Reaction. An understanding of the term *lift reaction* requires knowledge of one of the basic laws of physics. This rule is: for every action there must be an equal and opposite reaction. This can be demonstrated in many ways. If explained in terms of lifting an object off of the ground, it means that when enough force is applied to lift it up, there also will be an equal amount of force exerted against the ground. If explained in terms of applying force to straighten a panel, it means that when enough force is applied

Fig. 208 Showing the different leverages to be obtained by pulling from points close to or at a distance from a shallow dent in a long panel.

to raise the dent, there also must be an equal amount of force applied in the opposite direction somewhere on the panel surface to support the lift.

Sometimes a person who has not made a study of the basic sciences has difficulty in understanding this law, because he is accustomed to thinking of a force application as involving motion. This is not necessarily true; force can be applied without motion. A table standing on a floor is exerting a downward force, and, likewise, the floor is exerting an upward force. The fact that there is no motion simply indicates that the forces are in balance, so the objects involved, the table and the floor, remain at rest. However, if enough weight is added to the table, its downward force may be increased until it is greater than the floor can resist. In that case, the table would push its way into the floor, bending or breaking it.

Applying this reasoning to the problem of lifting a dent is simple if the directions of force application are recognized. An upward force under the dent is required to raise it. It is still an upward force whether it is applied directly to the underside, or indirectly by pulling on the metal on opposite sides of the dent. For this force to act, there must be an equal force acting in the opposite direction. If the dent is being pushed out, the opposite force would act on whatever supports the panel. If the dent is being pulled out, it will act on the points to which tension is applied. This is the *lift reaction*.

The points to which tension is being applied are referred to hereafter as the *attaching points*. In the following discussions, lift reaction on the attaching points is considered as a downward force because it is the opposite of the lifting action.

Lift reaction is illustrated in Fig. 209. Arrows pointing outward at each end of the curved line indicate tension being applied to lift the dent. The arrow pointing upward in the center indicates the lifting action on the dent. The arrows pointing downward at each end indicate the lift reaction. The combined lift reaction on both attaching points must always be equal to the force required to lift the dent.

This sketch and the discussion which accompanies it should make it clear that the force exerted outward to pull, or lift, the dent is not the same as the force exerted downward by lift reaction. When the dent has been pulled up to the proper level, lift reaction will drop to nothing. However,

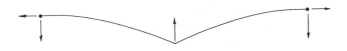

Fig. 209 Showing lift reaction. End points will be subjected to down thrust equal to the resistance to lifting offered by low point in center.

any amount of force, even enough to tear the panel, could continue to be applied in tension on the already lifted surface.

The importance of lift reaction is in the fact that it must be considered in selecting the points of attachment to which the tension will be applied. If these points are not rigid enough to resist the reaction to the lift, they will collapse instead of lifting the dent.

Thus in repairing any panel, attaching points should be selected which are rigid enough to support the load. Many times there is no problem. For example: in pulling a dent in a door panel, simply attach clamps to the edges. The edges, being rigidly supported by the facings, provide far more support than is needed to lift the load. In other cases, there is a real problem, because one or both of the desirable attaching points will not provide sufficient support to lift the dent. It then is necessary to do one of two things: (1) compromise by shifting to a more rigid though less desirable point, or (2) provide extra temporary support for the point.

It would be impossible to detail all of the conditions under which each of these alternate methods would be employed. Common sense will dictate when they should be applied.

An example of shifting to a stronger though less desirable attaching point will be found in most damaged door panels on which the dented area is close to one edge. On many such panels, a large part of the surface will not be forced out of position by the damage. The ideal attaching points would be one edge, using a clamp, and the center area of the panel, using a tension plate. However, the practical methods would be to use two clamps, one attached to each edge of the panel. This would increase the length of the pull and leverage angle, and slightly decrease the effective leverage; but, the loss would be offset by the simpler hookup and the much greater support under the edges.

Temporary support should be provided only when the problem cannot be solved by shifting to a stronger point. Usually such conditions will be found on deep dents in long panels, such as roofs and quarters. One means of temporary support is to set a jack under the attaching point; this works particularly well with roof panels because the underside usually is open. Another method suited to quarter panels is to extend the jack tube to some rigid point and block up under it.

The important point is to prevent the collapse of the attaching point because it only complicates the damage. There will be no difficulty if the basic law of physics is understood and applied to the job at hand.

Work Hardened Metal. Work hardened metal in the buckled area is the direct result of the working which occurred as the panel folded under impact. Such hardening cannot occur without some changes in the dimensions of the affected area. Most such changes are upsets instead of stretches. The repair problem is to rework this metal back to the original dimensions.

Except in cases where heat will be used, reworking will add to the already slightly hardened condition. This is normal; if it does not prevent the panel from being restored to original contour, there is no reason to be concerned if an area of metal is slightly harder than the adjoining metal.

The need to rework the hardened metal to proper shape accounts for most of the work of final smoothing and metal finishing of a damaged area after it has been pulled. It is the metal man's problem to determine how to do this so that the dimensions are restored. When they are restored, the panel surface will be restored also. If there is access to the underside so that the dolly block can be used, the hammer and dolly block will be the best means of working the area. When they cannot be used, it is necessary to resort to spoons, pry tools, or any other means available.

Regardless of the method used to rework an upset area in a panel which has been pulled, as much of the area as possible should be reworked before the tension is released. The reason for this is simple: the work done on any upset area should tend to stretch it back to full length. If it is under tension while this work is being done, the tendency to return to full length will be much greater. This is illustrated in Fig. 210. The arrows at each end indicate that tension is acting on the metal represented by the line. The wavy section of the line in the center represents the remaining part of the original bend, which in most cases would have been a rolled buckle. The rougher this wavy part of the surface is, the more it will tend to shorten the panel, causing loose, springy bulges in the adjoining surface which often are mistaken for stretched metal. By holding the entire area under tension, whatever length is lost in the curved sections will be regained when they are straightened.

Holding tension on the panel during as much of the final straightening operation as possible also removes any springback tendency caused by adjoining reinforcements. A common example of this often is found on a door panel which has been pushed in so far that the facing has been pulled

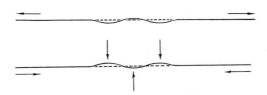

Fig. 210 *(Top)* Showing the desirability of straightening the remaining buckles under tension.

Fig. 211 *(Bottom)* Showing how pressure from an adjoining area can resist straightening of remaining buckles.

far out of line. Pulling the panel back to shape also will pull the facing with it; but, when the tension is released, the facing will tend to spring back toward its position when bent. This springback action is illustrated in Fig. 211. Note the arrows at each end pointing inward. Pressure acting inward on a section of metal that is not finally straightened will tend to resist the flattening action when hand tools are used on the remaining buckles. Such an area will tend to rise in a bulge instead of blending with the level of the adjoining metal. In some cases, the springy action of such an area will be enough to be noticed by an experienced metal man.

In considering work hardened metal as a factor in determining the procedure in the use of tension, it must be recognized that each individual job differs. On some it will be so minor that it may be ignored; there is no problem with work hardened metal on a panel which pops back into shape when about half pulled. On others, it is a major problem, and, if ignored, excessive labor may be necessary to work it out.

Sometimes the metal may be work hardened so severely that heat must be used to relieve it. Examples of this are given in the repair procedure section. Heat is used when the work hardened area has been upset so much that it is causing a serious bulge in the adjoining surface. The heat softens the metal so that it can be stretched back to, or close to, the original length.

As with the other factors, good judgment will determine whether allowances must be made for the effect of work hardened metal. Releasing the tension before the panel has been restored to final smoothness may cause a springback action which will make final straightening very difficult. Or, on another panel it may not.

Variations of Surface Crown. This factor must be considered when analyzing any damaged panel to determine where tension should be applied. The crown of almost every automobile panel varies to some degree. Many of them vary from a relatively flat crown over a large part of the surface area to combination high and low or reverse crowns along the edges; others may include every possible kind of crown on the various areas of the surface.

The variations in the details of the damage which can be found on different panels are almost without limit. Regardless of the details, however, all damage can be reduced to five basic conditions: (1) simple displacement, (2) simple bends, (3) rolled buckles, (4) stretches, and (5) upsets.

These basic conditions were covered in detail in Chapter 3, so they will not be discussed here except to point out that these conditions will be relieved when damage is repaired properly. To repair any panel, force must be applied so that it does the most good. This means relieving the bends and rolled buckles so that the simple displacements can snap back into place, and the upsets and stretches can be worked out with minimum effort.

Fig. 212 Folded-over door edge which should be straightened under tension and heated to relieve the upset.

The best results will be obtained from the use of tension when it is applied where it has the greatest effect, and that is on conditions which tend to shorten flat crowns. These include practically all rolled buckles and any other damage in which adjoining areas tend to be drawn together. An excellent example of the latter condition is the folded-over door lower edge shown in Fig. 212; this is similar to a rolled buckle, even though it is actually only a combination of simple bends in the outer panel and the facing.

Rolled buckles are found most frequently extending into a combination high- and low-crown area adjoining a relatively flat area. The severity of the rolled buckle is determined by the amount of break-over path that it has formed. When break-over paths have been formed, they usually will extend well into the high-crowned area. The more severe the break-over path, the more important it is that tension be applied close enough to it that it will be subjected to as much of the pulling force as possible. This, then, is the first rule: if there are severe upsets in the high-crown area, tension should be applied to it as close as possible.

The ideal approach to unrolling many rolled buckles would be to make the first pull just below the highest point. As the high point rolled down to the line of tension, the attaching points would be dropped and another pull made. In this way, it would be necessary to make several attachments to unroll a single buckle. This is the ideal procedure, but a more practical solution usually demands compromise; a single pull made at the point where the high and low crowns blend is often almost as effective as though several pulls had been made by starting much farther into the high crown and working progressively back to this position.

When working a damaged area such as the folded-over door edge shown in Fig. 212, tension should be applied directly to the edge. Here this would mean applying the greatest amount of force to the strongest part of the damage. The flanged door edge welded to the facing is much stronger than the panel adjoining it. Furthermore, if upsets are left in the door edge, they will have a gathering effect on the adjoining flat metal. In many cases such as this, it is desirable to use heat on the buckles while they are under tension to restore full length. Only a few thousandths of an inch of upset in this edge will cause severe gathering of the adjoining metal; this would be the condition called false stretch in Chapter 3.

Alignment with the crown of the panel must be correct if the desired results are to be obtained from the use of tension. The problem of determining proper alignment of the pulling setup with the crown of the panel is simple; the answer is based on the fact that tension tends to produce a straight line. Therefore, the tension setup must be aligned with the flattest surface line of the panel. If this rule is followed, there should be no problems arising due to improper alignment of the pulling force with the panel surface.

Many a beginner has not been taught the importance of this rule, and he may be tempted to use a diagonal pull on a panel which has considerable crown in one direction. However, a diagonal line across the surface of such a panel would describe a curve instead of a straight line. Applying tension diagonally across such a panel would flatten or distort it by tending to make a flat surface where it should be crowned.

There are exceptions to this basic rule, but they never apply except where only a limited amount of force is needed. An example is minor damage of the pop-out type which probably would not be severe enough to warrant the use of tension.

SHOP EQUIPMENT

Straightening badly damaged body panels is nothing more than using force properly. To do so, requires considerably more equipment than the metal man's hand tools. Whether owned by the shop or the metal man, such equipment normally is thought of as *shop equipment*. There are many basic shop equipment items available from more than one manufacturer; there are also many special items made by a single manufacturer but not widely distributed. There is no need to list every piece of equipment available, and for that reason, this discussion has been limited to those items which are felt to be basic to the job. If these are well understood, the special equipment will be, too.

The tools which will be discussed and explained are: (1) body jacks, (2) clamps, (3) solder-on tension plates, (4) external pull jacks, (5) portable frame machines, and (6) frame tram and center-line gauges.

Body Jacks

The important feature of any body jack is that it is fitted with screw-threaded ends to which extension tubes can be attached. Such threads also permit the attachment of special fittings or ends which have been designed to apply force to various sections of the automobile sheet metal with the least amount of damage.

Most of the body jacks available for use on sheet metal are hydraulically operated although a few of the friction type are quite popular. The hydraulic type is available in two basic sizes: light duty, usually equipped to be used with ¾-inch inside diameter extension tubes; and heavy duty, usually equipped to be used with 1¼-inch inside diameter tubes.

The capacity of jacks made by different manufacturers varies. Most light-duty jacks are rated from 3 to 4 tons, and most heavy-duty jacks are rated from 7 to 10 tons. For working sheet metal, however, the selection

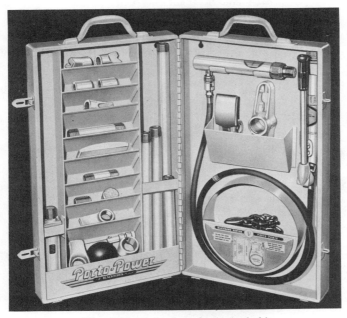

Fig. 213 Light-duty body jack kit.

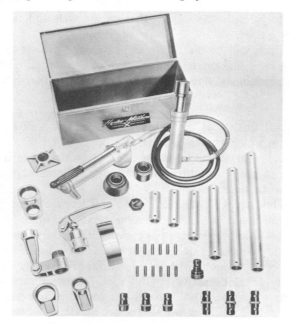

Fig. 214 Another light-duty body jack kit.

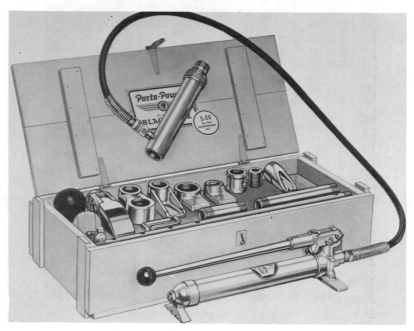

Fig. 215 Heavy-duty body jack kit.

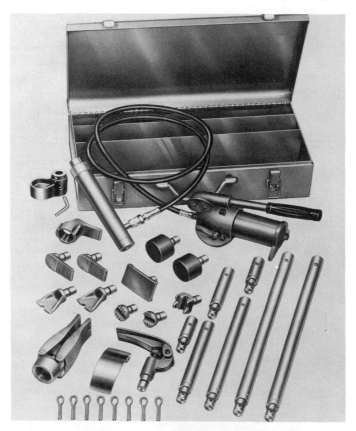

Fig. 216 Another heavy-duty body jack kit.

of the jack is determined mostly by the rigidity required of the tubes rather than the capacity. Where the jack must be used with offset loads, there is a tendency for the jack and tubes to bend; therefore the jack and tubes must be rigid enough to withstand this. Because of this, the heavy-duty jack often must be used, even though the load is well within the capacity of the lighter one.

The body jack is also an important tool in straightening frames. Such work is practically limited to the heavy-duty jack. Two typical light-duty body jack outfits are shown in Figs. 213 and 214. Two typical heavy-duty body jack outfits are shown in Figs. 215 and 216.

CLAMPS

Four types of clamps are shown in Figs. 217-220. The standard body clamp, Fig. 217, is equipped with a swivel-mounted tubular bracket which

Fig. 217 Standard body clamp.

Fig. 218 Heavy-duty "C" clamp.

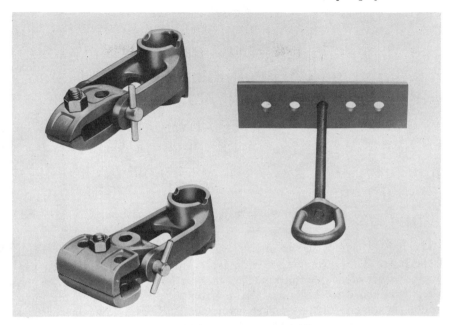

Fig. 219 Special body clamps and eye bolt assembly.

may be attached to the heavy-duty jack tubes by means of pins inserted through the holes in the sides. This feature makes it possible to attach the clamps and set the jack in place with the least amount of effort.

Other features of this camp are:

1. The swivel bracket may be mounted in three positions—on the flat upper jaw, on the bottom of the curved jaw, or on the back of the curved jaw.

2. Gripping surfaces 4 inches long distribute the load over an area wide enough to prevent stretching the panel at the point of attachment.

3. The clamp may be used alone by removing the tubular bracket.

This type of clamp can be attached to any panel which has suitable edges. This includes practically all doors and any part of the body where suitable flanges are provided by the construction.

The heavy-duty "C" clamp, Fig. 218, is intended primarily for use with the external pulling machine, described later, but it has many other uses. Its deep frame permits it to be attached over wide flanges or other construction. It is particularly suitable for pulling fenders, gravel shields, quarter panels, etc., back into place. This clamp has the disadvantage of requiring space both above and below the surface to which it is attached because of the heavy frame and screw.

Fig. 220 Adjustable grip, parallel jaw clamp.

The pair of clamps shown in Fig. 219 are similar except for the width of the jaws. These clamps are equipped with a special fitting which can serve as either a clevis or an attaching bracket for a body jack. When the clamp is attached to the body jack, the tube is passed through the large opening in the end of the bracket. Note that the pin holding the bracket to the clamp may be removed and inserted through the open holes in the rear edge of the clamp jaws. The eye bolt and bar shown in the same illustration may be used in areas where a clamp cannot be attached. The eye bolt either is inserted through an existing hole in the panel, or a hole is made and later welded shut.

The parallel jaw clamp shown in Fig. 220 may be adjusted to any thickness of metal because of the design of the two bolts. The rear end bolt serves as a spreader, and the center bolt provides the clamping action. It is very easy to attach a chain or ring to this clamp because of the open section of the rear bolt.

In addition to the clamps shown here, there are many others which are excellent tools.

Solder-On Tension Plates

The solder-on tension plate, Fig. 221, provides a means of using tension where there are no suitable edges or flanges to which clamps may be attached. The development of tension plates has been a significant contribution to sheet metal repair technique because they make it possible to use tension on panels which otherwise could not be repaired in that manner.

The general use of tension plates is essentially the same as that of clamps; however, there are special problems in their use, and in the technique of attaching them, which must be understood to obtain the best results.

The effectiveness of a solder joint as a means of applying force often is

Fig. 221 Solder-on tension plates.

questioned. This attitude is natural because the strength of any lead base alloy is relatively low. It is effective, though, because of the nature of the joint and the way that tension is applied to it. The joint is made between two flat surfaces—the tension plate and the panel—and tension must be applied so that it either tends to move the plate parallel to the surface of the panel, or tends to force it against the panel. (See Figs. 222 and 223.) If tension is applied so that it tends to lift the plate away from the panel, it will strip it from the solder joint with very little force. (See Fig. 224.)

When the conditions in Figs. 222 and 223 are analyzed, it may be seen that the plate holds because the parallel surfaces distribute the load over the entire area of the joint. Thus, the total strength of the joint is in direct proportion to the total area of solder.

The effectiveness of the solder joint is illustrated in Figs. 225 and 226. These are before and after views of a tensile test of a joint made by soldering two strips together so that they have a 2-inch overlap. The procedure used to make the joint will be described in the next section. These strips are both 1 inch wide and 0.037 inch thick, and are from stock similar to the strip shown in Figs. 3-7, Chapter 1.

In Fig. 225, the soldered strips have been drawn tight but not stretched, then the two marks 10 inches apart were made. In Fig. 226, the two strips have been stretched until the same marks measure 12½ inches apart, but the solder joint is still holding. Note that the strip has narrowed except in

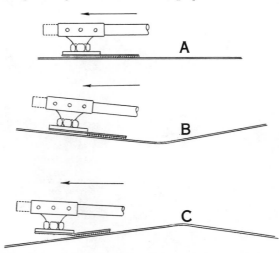

Fig. 222 *(A)* Showing the uniform load on the solder joint when force is applied to the tension plate parallel to the surface to which it is attached.

Fig. 223 *(B)* Showing that the load on the solder joint also will be uniform when force applied to the tension plate pushes it toward the panel surface.

Fig. 224 *(C)* Showing that the load on the solder joint will be uneven, causing it to strip, when force is applied to the tension plate away from the panel surface.

the solder joint, and at one point, to the left of the solder joint, it has narrowed sharply because it is almost ready to break. In fact, one more stroke of the jack pump did break it.

This test shows that a properly made solder joint is stronger than the metal to which it is attached when force is applied to it to pull lengthwise of its surfaces.

*Attaching Solder Tension Plates.** More skill is required to attach a solder tension plate than to attach a clamp, but the procedure is easily mastered. It is easier to learn than solder filling. Any metal man who has learned to paddle solder should have no difficulty in making a tension plate hold. The key to the operation is in proper timing; the tinned surface of the plate and the hot solder on the panel surface must be brought together at the right temperature and quenched without delay.

The steps in attaching the solder tension plate, using liquid flux, are as follows:

1. Remove the paint from the spot where the plate is to be attached.
2. If the surface of the plate is rusted or scaled, sand it bright.

*Procedure courtesy of Blair Equipment Co.

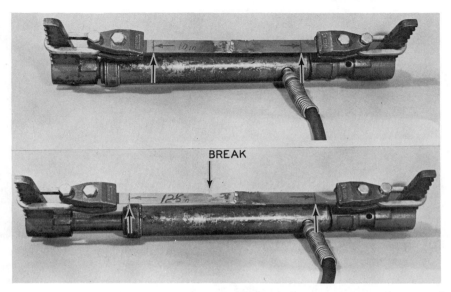

Fig. 225 *(Top)* First view of the jack and clamp setup used to test the strength of the solder joint. The joint was overlapped 2 inches. Marks 10 inches apart were made on the strip before testing.

Fig. 226 *(Bottom)* Second view of the jack and clamp setup to test the solder joint. The strip is breaking after stretching 2½ inches without breaking the solder joint.

3. Apply flux to the panel surface and to the plate.
4. Tin the plate, but do not wipe.
5. Tin the panel, but do not wipe.
6. Build up the solder pad on the panel.
7. Heat the solder and the plate to the temperature at which the solder is quite soft.
8. Working fast, shut off the torch or hand it to your helper; pick up the sponge; press the plate into the hot solder pad; quench instantly.

This procedure can be varied. Powdered flux can be used instead of the liquid material listed. In using powdered flux, the application and tinning operations would be combined. Also, once the basic technique has been mastered, it is easy to learn to perform the last step without the aid of a helper. The complete procedure, with and without a helper, is explained and illustrated on the following pages.

In some cases it may be desirable to remove the paint without leaving the scars made by the disc sander. Sanding it off by hand is laborious and usually not justified. Acrylic lacquers can be removed with lacquer remov-

Fig. 227 Metal surface sanded smooth for tinning.

ing solvent, leaving the prime coat to be hand sanded. Any paint, lacquer or synthetic enamel, can be removed by scorching it with an oxidizing flame and wire brushing the burnt paint off. When this is done, it is important to remove the phosphate coating under the primer as well as the paint. The best procedure is to rebrush the surface vigorously after starting the tinning operation. The result will be much better adhesion.

When removing paint with the sander, care should be taken to avoid making deep scratches, or, if the surface is particularly rough, to avoid cutting through high spots. A smooth surface, such as shown in Fig. 227, is the desired result.

It is equally important for the surface of the tension plate to be clean so that it will tin properly. If it is not clean, it usually will be because of one of two conditions: scale on the surface due to being overheated as it was removed from a previous attachment; or rust due to lack of use. Either must be removed before the plate can be tinned so that a secure bond can be made to it. This can be done with the disc sander, but it should not be done too often because it will thin the plate, causing it to break under load. Coarse sandpaper may be used safely, if the plate is heated and wiped clean of solder first.

Flux is applied in just about the same way as for solder filling. Be certain that sufficient flux is applied to tin the spot properly. With liquid flux, best results will be obtained if the surface is heated first. This operation is shown in Fig. 228.

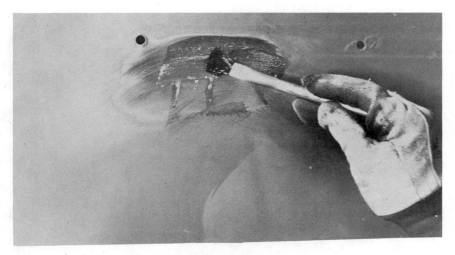

Fig. 228 Applying flux to a heated surface.

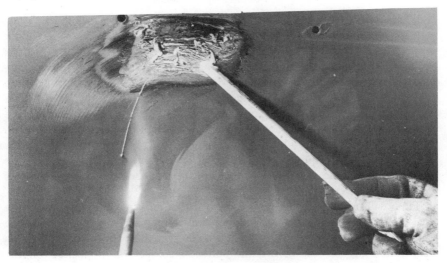

Fig. 229 Tinning by rubbing the solder bar on a heated surface.

Tinning the surface is essentially the same as for solder filling, except that there should be no wiping. If the surface has been cleaned and fluxed properly, solder can be spread over it very easily by rubbing the end of the bar of solder on it while the flame is played over it. Note the positions of the flame and the solder bar in Fig. 229. The same procedure should be followed on the plate.

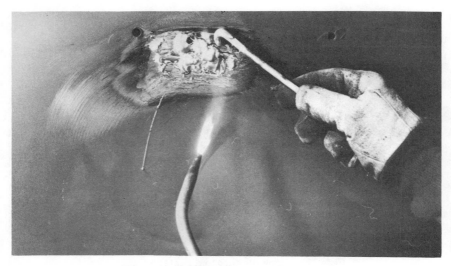

Fig. 230 Building up the solder pad.

It is sometimes difficult to convince metal men experienced in solder filling that a good joint can be made without wiping. Making this joint is different from making a solder fill. Strength is important here, not appearance. Wiping may remove solder from the tops of the tiny ridges between the sanding grit marks, leaving the bond weakened over the entire area. The only thing accomplished by wiping is to remove the residue of the burned flux so that it will not cause pits. The loss of strength in the area of a few pits is not nearly so much as can be lost by wiping the entire area. The only strength required of a solder fill is to hold itself to the panel; the solder used to hold a tension plate in place may be strained as much as 1,000 pounds per square inch.

Time will be saved if the plate is tinned first and laid aside before doing the spot on the panel. As soon as the panel is tinned, the solder pad can be built up, Fig. 230. Note the softened solder on the end of the bar. This action was caught just before the softened solder was deposited on the surface.

The amount of solder needed will vary to some extent with the nature of the job to be pulled. The harder the pull, the more solder should be used. In most cases, it will be desirable to use at least one-quarter of a half-pound bar, and on a hard pull this may have to be doubled. Extra solder should not be used to build up a high pad; instead, it should be used to cover more area. The amount of solder shown being applied in Fig. 230 made a pad approximately ⅛ inch thick over about two-thirds of the plate surface. (See Fig. 238.)

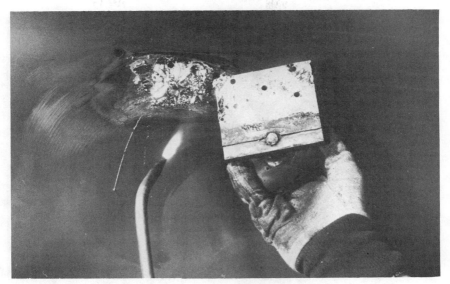

Fig. 231 Heating the solder pad and the tinned surface of the plate.

Maintaining the temperature of the solder pad and rewarming the tinned plate requires good timing. By holding the plate close to the solder pad, as shown in Fig. 231, it is easy to play the flame over both of them as needed. The trick is to bring them both to the proper temperature at the same time. This temperature can be judged quite accurately by appearance. When it is right, the surface of the plate will glisten, and the solder will begin to settle. If too much heat is used, it will cause the tinned surface of the plate to darken, and the solder will begin to run. As heating progresses, it may be desirable to use the edge of the plate to shape the solder into a better pad. Also, a little hot solder may be picked up on the surface of the plate to aid in checking its temperature. If this is done, the plate should be heated just enough to cause the solder to begin to run.

When the temperatures of the solder and the plate are right, it is necessary to dispose of the torch and pick up the wet rag or sponge. If the operator is working alone, the torch should be shut off before laying it down, unless a safe hook or other means of holding it is provided. Most torch users train themselves to operate the valves with the thumb and first finger of the hand holding it; thus no time will be lost in shutting it off. Handing the torch to a helper will eliminate this step, but he should shut it off immediately to avoid the possibility of damage or bodily injury. The beginner should practice doing the job by himself so that he will not require a helper.

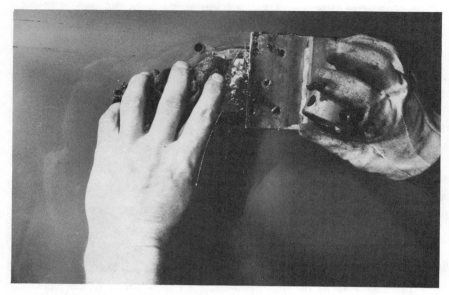

Fig. 232 Position of the hands before setting the heated plate into the hot solder. The gloved hand will press the plate into the solder; the bare hand will press the wet cloth against the back of the plate to quench it.

Fig. 233 The quenching action.

The procedure after disposing of the torch is shown in Figs. 232 and 233. In Fig. 232 the right hand is placing the plate on the solder pad, and the left hand is ready with a wet cloth with which to quench the solder as soon as the plate is pressed into place. Fig. 233 shows the steam rising from the quenching. This is where timing is critical; only a few seconds should be required to lay aside the torch, pick up the wet cloth, set the plate into the solder, and quench it. When this is done right, the plate will sink into the soft solder, spreading it, but it should not sink far enough to contact the panel. The quenching action stops the movement of the solder at the right time if the wet cloth is applied soon enough.

The time lost in laying the torch down and picking up the sponge can be avoided by learning to hold them both in one hand at the same time. When this is done, it is important that the torch flame be directed into an area where it will do no harm while the quenching operation is performed. This technique is shown in Fig. 235 and Fig. 236. Note in Fig. 235 that the torch is being held so that the flame is directed just exactly opposite to normal, making it necessary for the operator to twist his wrist to bring it onto the job. Also, a wet shop towel, which serves as well as a sponge, is held between the thumb and fingers on the back side of the torch handle. This brings the flame into a safe position when the wet rag is placed on the back of the tension plate, as shown in Fig. 236.

The beginner should not attempt holding his torch and sponge or wet shop towel at the same time until he has mastered the operation with the

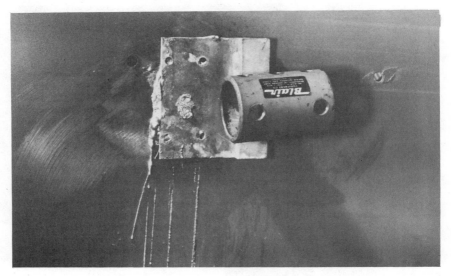

Fig. 234 The solder tension plate attached to the surface.

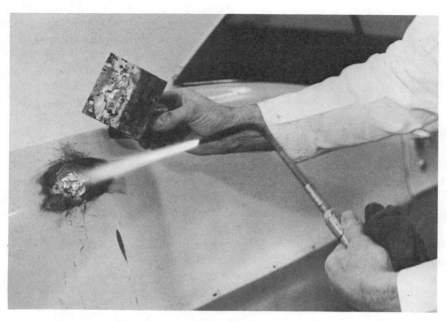

Fig. 235 The proper hand position for holding the torch and wet rag. The torch is turned exactly opposite to the normal position in the hand and the wet rag is held on the back side of the torch handle. Twisting the wrist brings the flame onto the solder.

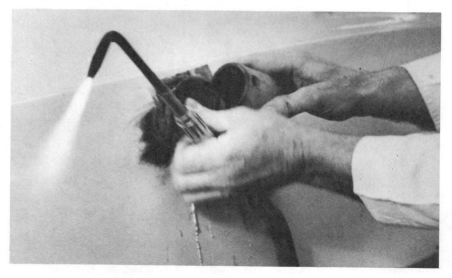

Fig. 236 The position of the hand while quenching. The flame is turned away from the work and the operator is placing the wet rag on the tension plate.

help of an assistant standing ready to take the torch and hand him the wet sponge. There is too much risk of a mix-up in which he could be burned severely or the body damaged. However, as soon as he has learned to do it with the aid of an assistant, he should start practicing doing it without the assistant because it is both faster and easier, once the technique is mastered.

The attached plate is shown in Fig. 234. Note that the solder has pushed out from under the edge and through the holes in the plate. Also, solder can be seen through the outer holes, indicating that it has spread to this width. This plate was subjected to a strong pull after this picture was taken. If the proper procedure is followed, a plate coming off under load should be a rare occurrence.

Attaching Other Pieces of Metal. The same procedure can be used to attach any piece of metal to a panel for special hookups. There are several cases where this practice will be more satisfactory than the use of the tension plate. Two of the most common are: (1) where the tension force will be applied by means of a chain instead of a jack and (2) where the attaching surface must swing through a wide angle as it is pulled out.

When a piece of metal is selected instead of a tension plate, a clamp usually is used to complete the hookup. If a chain is used, it is because the pulling will be done from some point away from the dent instead of from two points on each side of it. In such cases, the tension plate should not be used because it is not adapted to work with a chain.

Where the attaching surface must swing through a wide angle as it is pulled out, the piece of metal used to make the hookup must bend as the panel straightens. It is much better to use a scrap of light body metal than to attempt to use the tension plate, because the metal in it is much heavier. If the plate is used, it may be damaged by the bending, and also its stiffer metal will resist the proper movement of the panel to which it is attached.

Use of a piece of metal with a clamp is only practical in jobs where the end of the piece can extend over the edge of the panel to provide clearance for the clamp.

Removing Solder Tension Plates. Following proper procedure in removing solder tension plates is just as important as it is for attaching them. The worst problems result when they are overheated. Overheating will burn the tinned surface of the plate and cause heat distortion of the panel surface. If the tinned surface of the plate is burned, it will be difficult to make it hold the next time it is used unless it is ground or sanded bright again. Failures from such causes are unnecessary and can be avoided. If the panel surface is distorted by overheating, extra labor will be required to work it out again. Sometimes such spots are very difficult to work out to their original shape.

Overheating can be avoided by applying heat slowly to loosen the plate. The torch flame should be adjusted as for solder filling and held so that it

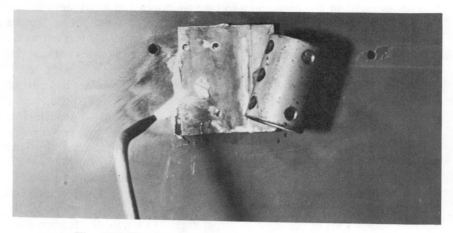

Fig. 237 Heating the solder tension plate to remove it.

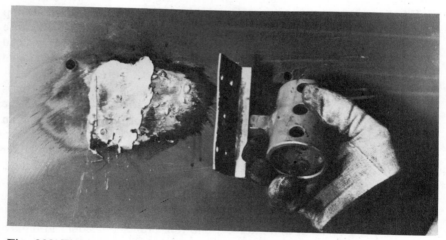

Fig. 238 The solder tension plate removed from the solder pad. The solder has not melted.

does not actually touch the plate. Note the position of the flame in Fig. 237. If the solder pad is smaller than the plate, which is usually the case, the flame should be kept away from the overhanging edges to avoid overheating them.

Slow application of heat permits time for it to flow through the steel of the plate into the solder pad. When the solder in contact with the plate reaches the temperature at which it begins to soften (slightly above 360° F.), it loses enough strength so that the plate can be lifted off. This

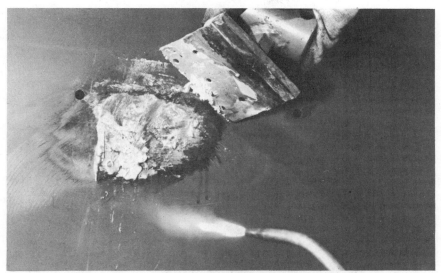

Fig. 239 Using the solder tension plate to chip off the solder pad.

point is easy to determine by trying to lift it off as the flame is played on it. After a few tries, the plate should snap off, leaving a smooth, unmelted solder pad, as shown in Fig. 238.

The solder pad should be removed without melting it. This can be done by holding the flame well away from it and waiting long enough for the heat to penetrate to the surface of the metal below. When the proper temperature has been reached (slightly above 360° F.), the edge of the plate can be used to knock off the solder in chunks, as shown in Fig. 239. The remaining bits of solder around the edges can then be removed, using the torch and a dry cloth, unless there is too much danger of heat distortion. After wiping, the surface should be quenched, as shown in Fig. 240. If the possibility of heat distortion is too great, quenching should be done immediately after the large chunks of solder have been knocked off. The remaining solder then would be cut off, using either the body file or the disc sander.

The worst mistake one can make in removing a solder tension plate is to put the torch flame on it and wait until the solder melts. It is true that this procedure will remove the plate from the panel, but the tinned surface of the plate will be burned as the solder runs away from it, and the panel will be overheated in small spots. By taking more time and breaking the solder bond at the lowest possible temperature, the highest temperature reached may be kept as much as a hundred degrees lower than if the solder is melted rapidly. The difference in time will not be more than a minute,

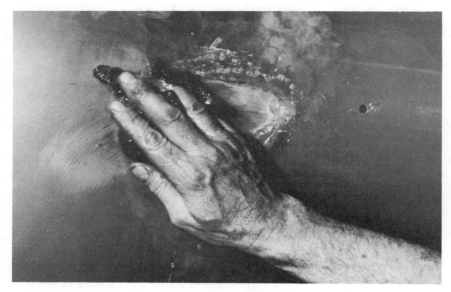

Fig. 240 Quenching the heated surface after removal of the solder.

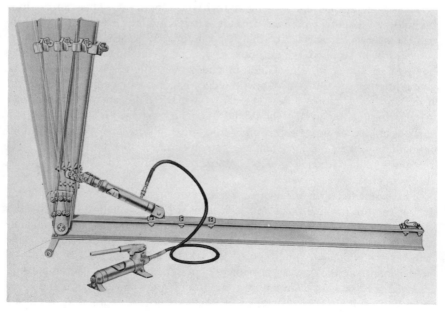

Fig. 241 External pull jack.

probably less; the difference in the results can be the cause of many minutes of lost time in trying to make a burned plate hold the next time it is used, or in working out an unnecessary heat distortion.

EXTERNAL PULL JACKS

The term *external pull jack* is used to identify a basic type of body-pulling machine which has come into wide use in recent years. There are several such machines available from different manufacturers. These machines vary in design details, but they all operate on the same principle: to provide a rigid point outside of the body from which tension can be applied. This requires some kind of long, rigid member, one end of which is provided with an upright from which the tension force is applied, and the other extends under the automobile and anchors against some point of the understructure. Two typical machines are shown in Figs. 241 and 242.

Although the force exerted by the external pull jack is in tension, it differs from the tension applied by means of a conventional body jack and two clamps or tension plates in the way the reaction force is applied. In using two clamps or tension plates, one is mounted on each side of a dent, and the jack is mounted between them. Thus the action of one end of the jack meets a reaction from the other acting along a direct path in the panel surface. In using the external pull jack, which anchors against some point under the automobile, the reaction must follow an indirect path through the structure to the anchor point.

On some jobs, the use of the external pull jack is almost a necessity, but on others it is a matter of choice. In the use of any such machine, it is important to remember that the effect of tension acts in a straight line between the points of attachment. In almost every case, these machines will be hooked up so that the anchor point is well below the point on the panel being pulled. The result is that the machine tends to align itself with the angle of the line between the two points of attachment. On some jobs,

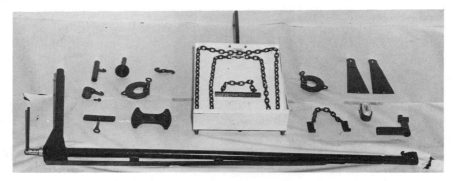

Fig. 242 Another type of external pull jack and attachments.

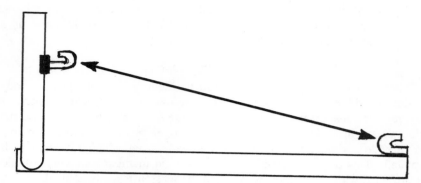

Fig. 243 Showing the angle of pulling of any external pull jack.

where there is sufficient rigidity to resist the lifting effect this creates, this is no problem. On others, the machine must be blocked in some manner to prevent this lift, or the job will be damaged. The angle of lift is shown in Fig. 243.

PORTABLE FRAME MACHINES

The portable frame machine is somewhat of a heavy-duty version of the external pull jack. It was developed originally for straightening the conventional automobile frame, and in the hands of a capable operator it is a very effective tool.

Although originally intended as a frame tool only, the portable frame machine has found wide use on bodies as well. The design of most automobiles is such that some means of making an overall pull is required to straighten the effect of many collisions, particularly rear end impacts. The portable frame machine is ideally suited to this type of body repair work, although its name implies that it is intended for frame work only.

Two examples of portable frame machines are shown in Figs. 244 and 245. A pair of anchor clamps, which permit these machines to be used on the so-called unitized body, are shown in Fig. 246.

The chief difference between the portable frame machine and the external pull jack is in size and capacity. The portable frame machines vary in length and other features because they are products of different manufacturers. The machine in Fig. 244 can be adjusted over a wide range of length, and the machine in Fig. 245 can have the pulling and anchor upright beams adjusted to any position on the horizontal beam. Both are desirable features.

The effectiveness of the portable frame machine is due to the fact that almost all frame damage, on either conventional or unitized construction, is a crumpled condition due to a crushing impact. If the damage is severe,

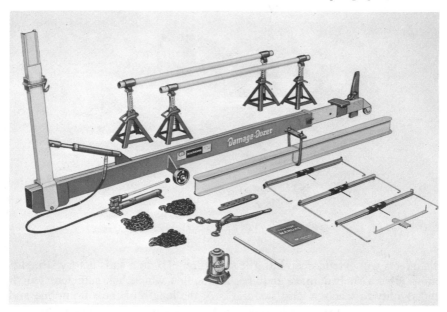

Fig. 244 Portable frame machine and accessories.

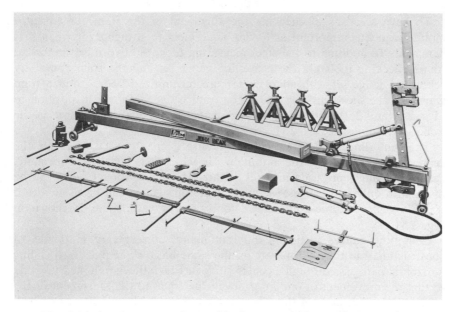

Fig. 245 Another type of portable frame machine and accessories.

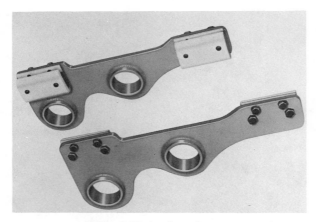

Fig. 246 Anchor clamps.

the effects will extend deep into the structure. To do a satisfactory straightening job on such damage requires a machine which has sufficient length and rigidity to reach at least two-thirds of the length of the automobile and withstand the thrust of a heavy-duty jack. It must also be able to pull effectively at any angle as well as lengthwise and sidewise.

Frame Gauges and Their Use

To have a means of checking the alignment of the frame of an automobile is just as important as having equipment to straighten it when it is damaged. In addition to the steel measuring tape, the two most important frame checking tools are the centerline gauge set and the tram gauge. A centerline gauge set with adapters for use on unitized bodies, and a tram gauge set are shown in Fig. 247. The tram gauge is shown in position in Figs. 249 and 250, and the centerline gauges are shown in position on the same automobile in Fig. 251.

The centerline gauge is so called because it can be used to locate the centerline of the part of the automobile in which it is installed. Normally, centerline gauges are used in a set of three; however, some checks can be made with only two gauges. A single centerline gauge can be used with a tram to make a three-point check for raises or sags. This is shown in Fig. 251.

Centerline gauges made by different manufacturers vary in details of construction, but they all operate on the same basic principle. Two sliding horizontal bars pass through a center guide in which they are linked together so that the movement of one must always be equal to the movement of the other. The outer ends of these bars are equipped with upright arms which have right-angle hooks or pins on the upper ends; these hooks may be

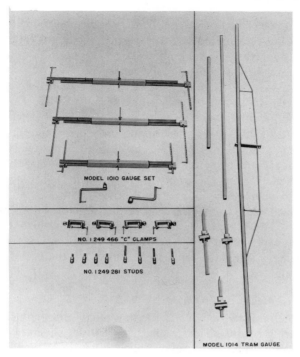

MODEL 1010 GAUGE SET

NO. 1 249 466 "C" CLAMPS

NO. 1 249 281 STUDS

MODEL 1014 TRAM GAUGE

Fig. 247 Frame centerline gauges with accessories, and tram gauges.

placed over a flange or through a hole to attach the gauge to the frame. An upright pointer on the center guide serves to mark the centerline, because it always will be equidistant from the upright arms.

The centerline gauges shown in Figs. 247 and 251 are equipped with upright arms which may be adjusted to any required length. This feature permits the gauges to be set up so that all of the horizontal bars are on the same level when the length of the upright arms are set to the specifications for datum line given by the automobile manufacturer. More details on the use of these gauges will be given in a later section which follows the explanation of the centerline and datum line and their use in frame checking.

The tram gauge provides a means of taking measurements between two points even though the direct line between them is blocked by other parts. It also can be used to measure the horizontal distance between points which are not on the same level. It is sometimes used with three pointers to check the height of one point against the height of two others.

Tram gauges made by different manufacturers vary in detail, but they all consist of some kind of long, light bar to which upright pointers are attached. For most measurements, two pointers are used; however, three may be used in checking for raised or sagged conditions. The pointers are designed so that they may be moved to any position on the bar and extended to any height above it.

Measuring with the tram may be done in either of two methods. The tram pointers may be set to points on the automobile, and the distance between them measured; or, the pointers may be set to a measured distance and then held against the proper points on the automobile. When three pointers are used to measure the height of one point against the height of two others, it is done by setting all three pointers to fit to the points to be measured, then checking the fit of the tram to corresponding points on the other side or on another automobile. However, frame centerline gauges, if they are available, provide a better means of making such checks.

More details on the use of the tram gauge will be given in the section following the explanation of the centerline and datum line and their use in frame checking. This is the same section in which the use of the centerline gauges is explained.

THE FUNDAMENTALS OF FRAME AND BODY LAYOUT

In straightening any body or frame, the repairman must remember he is simply restoring it to the measurements which the engineer specified when it was designed. The purpose of this section is to explain how these dimensions are established originally and to show how the repairman can use them as a guide in his work. Once these basic ideas are understood, the use of the gauges to check alignment of the frame or body is easy to learn. For that reason, this explanation of basic frame layout has been placed before the section on the use of the gauges to check it.

The original layout of any automobile is made from two bases: the centerline and the datum line. In checking the alignment of the frame or the body, the repairman is determining whether or not the various parts of the damaged area are the same distances from these bases that they were originally.

To make the checking easy, the manufacturers of automobiles furnish in their shop manuals the dimensions of the frame, or the frame section of unitized bodies. An example of the method by which this information is supplied is shown in Fig. 248. This shows a bottom and a side view of the structural members of the frame. Note that in the bottom view, dimension lines, marked with capital letters, are shown between various points. Also note that in the side view, dimension lines, marked with small letters, are shown extending from the datum line to the frame. The points on the frame from which these dimensions are taken are called *reference points*. A reference point is always something which can be identified easily, such as a bolthead, a rivethead, or a hole. In the shop manual, the

**UNDERBODY ALIGNMENT
REFERENCE DIMENSIONS**

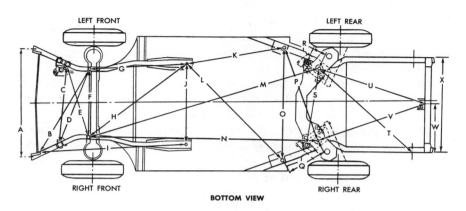

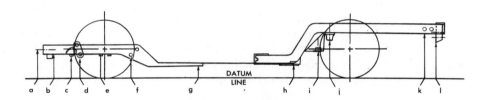

Fig. 248 A typical frame layout furnished in a shop manual.

exact distance between reference points is given in a separate list. Sometimes these lists contain information for two or more series or models of automobiles by the same manufacturer. In using information from such lists, it is essential to determine the series or model of the automobile for which it is needed. All checking of actual jobs should be done by using information which applies to the automobile being repaired.

The bottom view of this frame layout has been drawn as though the observer were looking up at it from the underside. To avoid confusion when using a drawing such as this, the book should be turned so that the outside edge of the page faces the reader. This will put the left side of the drawing to the reader's left.

A centerline will be found running lengthwise through the bottom view. The importance of both the centerline and datum line is explained in the following pages.

CENTERLINE

In making the layout for the frame and the body, the engineer must work from the centerline because the automobile is essentially a symmetrical object. Corresponding parts on opposite sides must be equidistant from the centerline. Of course, there are some exceptions to this rule, but not many. Where corresponding parts are not equidistant from the centerline, the fact will be noted, and the proper information given in the manufacturer's shop manual.

Although the term centerline is used, it is actually a center plane which extends vertically through the length of the automobile. A good way to visualize this is to imagine the automobile as having been sawed in half lengthwise through the center. The right and left halves would correspond exactly except where the designing engineer may have been forced to make them different.

The use of the term centerline probably comes from the method of making mechanical drawings. In any mechanical drawing, a plane is represented by a single line. It is only natural to refer to this as a line instead of a plane.

The repairman rarely makes a direct measurement to the centerline. Instead, he either uses centerline gauges to establish its position in three points, or he measures across it diagonally. Diagonal measurements are made frequently when minor damage is suspected. The procedure is to first adjust the tram pointers to a pair of reference points on one diagonal, then change the tram to the corresponding reference points on the opposite diagonal; this procedure commonly is called "X" checking. Whether the measurement is made in this manner or made by the use of the centerline gauges, the basic symmetry of the automobile is used in checking it for frame damage.

DATUM LINE

The use and purpose of the datum line often is considered to be more difficult to understand than the use of the centerline. This is probably because the datum line is outside of the automobile, instead of in the center of it. There should be no problem, however, if the datum line is recognized as the base from which all vertical measurements are established.

It was pointed out in the previous section that the centerline is actually a plane. The same is true of the datum line. To understand this, imagine the automobile as being set up on a surface plate— a slab of iron which has been machined to an extremely flat surface. The automobile could be set up so that the measurement from the surface plate to the reference points shown in the side view, Fig. 248, would be the same as given in the table in the manual. If it was found that measurements to any particular section of the frame varied more than the stated tolerance from those found in the list, it would indicate that that section was bent out of alignment.

FRAME CHECKING PROCEDURE

The purpose of checking a frame is to determine if a misalignment exists. The common misalignments can be classified as:

1. Simple bends
2. Collapsed sections
3. Side swayed sections
4. Twisted sections
5. Diamonded conditions

All frame damage consists of one or a combination of two or more of these conditions. Some of these can be checked with a simple steel measuring tape. Others, because of more severe damage, may require the use of the tram or the centerline gauges.

The most important check made on any damaged frame is to look it over carefully, noting every bend or visible misalignment. The information gained from visual inspection indicates to the repairman what checks he should make to determine the exact condition of the frame. A suggested general procedure for making these checks follows.

Checking Length with the Tram. The tram may be used either to check the distance between two reference points and, with either a third point or a centerline gauge, to check for sags or raises. Either check can be made with the tram set to shop manual specifications, or they can be comparison checks. Comparison checks are made by setting the tram to reference points on one side of the automobile and transferring it to the corresponding points on the opposite side. Comparison checks are dependable and accurate when there is positive evidence that the section used for comparison is undamaged. For example, a frame could be hit on one side of the front or rear, shortening one side rail without any damage to the other. The repairman could check the accuracy of his straightening job by setting his tram to the undamaged side and transferring the measurement to the repaired side. This operation is not illustrated, but the procedure would be similar to that shown in Fig. 249, except that the reference points used would both be on the same side.

Cross, or "X," Checking. Cross, or "X," checking is one method of determining side sway. However, most repair men usually prefer to check side sway with the centerline gauges. An "X" check is shown in Fig. 249. This is a comparison check made to determine if a section of the frame has been moved off its centerline position. If the difference in distance between the points shown being measured and the corresponding opposite points exceeds the allowable tolerance, the frame needs correction. This is an accurate check if it has been determined that the side rails are both undamaged lengthwise. If one rail is shorter than the other, this check would be meaningless.

Fig. 249 Diagonal, or "X," checking a frame with the tram. The tram may be either set to opposite reference points or to shop manual specifications. Length on one side may be compared to the other in the same manner.

Fig. 250 Three point check, using centerline gauge as third point, to determine raise of sag. Tram has been set to opposite side. Arrows placed on frame and tram point indicate the amount of raise.

Checking Raises or Sags. Checking for raises or sags using the tram and one centerline gauge is shown in Fig. 250. This is a comparison check in which the tram has been previously set to the left side and transferred to the right. This check is accurate provided that it is made over a section of the frame long enough to minimize error. In the operation illustrated, it was suspected that the front end of the right side rail had been raised. This automobile had been rolled over completely, striking back against the earth on its right front corner. The condition of the right front fender and end of the bumper indicated the need for the check. Also, when viewed from the front, there was a definite list, or sag, on the right front corner.

To make the setup for the check, the centerline gauge was installed in the frame under the cowl section of the body and the tram adjusted to it on the left side. Adjusting the tram means that the length of the pointers was adjusted so that the horizontal bar was in light contact with the gauge when they contacted the frame.

To make the check, the tram was transferred to the right side with the rear point in contact with the rail and the horizontal bar in contact with the centerline gauge. As shown in the photograph in Fig. 250, the front point did not reach the frame, indicating that the end of the rail had been raised in striking back against the ground.

As stated previously, this is an accurate check, but it must be made carefully. The tram shown here is braced with a truss bar on the under-side to reduce flexing. However, not all trams used in this manner are braced. Even with a braced tram, there is a possibility that the operators will flex it slightly, causing error, unless they handle it carefully. Two men are required. They should not change ends when changing from one side to the other. The tram should be· held by the ends and grasped in exactly the same manner in making each check. When placing the points against the frame, the contact should be light. Any strain that will tend to flex the tram differently in one position than in the other will defeat the purpose of the check.

Selection of Reference Points. In measuring a frame with a tram, it is important that dependable reference points be used. The reference points from which shop-manual specifications are given are dependable. They have been selected by service engineers because they are in critical loca-tions. It is important, in using shop-manual specifications, to determine if the measurements are to be made point-to-point or on the datum line. Point-to-point means that the measurement specified is the straight line distance from one point to another, regardless of the difference in level of the two points. Datum line measurements means that they are to be taken on the datum line between vertical lines extended from the datum line to the reference point. Thus, datum line measurements between two points in the same plane would be the same as point-to-point measurements. If, however, the two points are on different levels above the datum line, this would not be true. In effect, the datum line measurement between these points would be the base of a right triangle. And, the point-to-point measurement between them would be the hypothenuse of the same triangle.

It is unfortunate that there is considerable difference in the method used to provide the specifications for frame measurements by the different automobile manufacturers and some other sources of information. Some manufacturers have simply reproduced engineering drawings in their shop manuals. This is difficult for the repair man to use because he lacks the elaborate checking equipment required by the engineer and the time to use it if he did have it. Others have made considerable effort to provide direct, or point-to-point measurements, which can be used easily. In many cases the repair shop can obtain frame specifications from outside sources that are more usable than the information in the manufacturer's shop manual.

In general, the frame should be considered as having three sections when selecting reference points. These sections are: the front, from the cowl forward; the center, the level section under the passenger compartment; and the rear, from the passenger compartment to the rear end. There are two reasons for this. One is that sags, raises, and side sways usually occur at the corners of these sections; the other is that diagonal checks show the maximum variation when made across square sections. These sections are not necessarily square, but they are close enough to make these checks reasonably accurate. A diagonal check over a long, narrow section, such as full length of the frame, would be almost meaningless because only major errors would be detected. Also, opposite errors in different sections could cancel each other out.

Checking with Centerline Gauges. Centerline gauges set up to show a raise on the right front corner of a frame are shown in Fig. 251. This is the same automobile on which the three-point check is shown in Fig. 250. (This is a telephoto picture taken with the camera placed far forward to make the automobile appear shorter than it actually is.) It is easy to see that the horizontal bar of the first gauge is not parallel to the second. Also, the second gauge is parallel to the third.

The repair man must interpret what he sees when he sights across a set of centerline gauges. This is a matter of relating the evidence obtained from the gauges to the rest of the evidence on the automobile. Without the evidence on the front bumper and front fenders on this automobile, it would be difficult to determine whether the right side rail had been raised too high or the left one had been lowered too much. However, both the bumper and front fenders show that they have been struck downward against the ground. Under these conditions, the right rail could be driven up, but the left rail would not be driven down.

Fig. 251 Centerline gauges set up to show raise on the right front end of frame. Note wedge shaped opening between first and second gauges and narrow, parallel sided opening between second and third gauges. Vertical bars supporting second gauge are hidden by stands supporting automobile.

Sighting across centerline gauges should be done from the center position. When sighting for parallelism, the eye level should be raised or lowered to permit looking over the top of one gauge and under the other. Thus, if the gauges are not parallel, a wedge shaped opening will be seen between them instead of parallel edges.

When sighting for centerline, the eye should be positioned in line with the two center pins in the center section of the frame. The position of the center pin in the end section should be determined in relation to that line. If the horizontal bars are parallel and the end center pin is out of line with the other two more than ¼ inch, it is evidence that the frame is off centerline. This statement is based on the assumption that the gauges have been checked for accuracy and the frame has the correct width at each gauge position.

Referring to Fig. 251, the center pin on the first gauge does not, and should not line up with the second and third. This pin is lifted up and to the right (left in the picture) by the position of the raised right rail. If the vertical arms of the gauge were extended farther, this condition would be exaggerated still more. The reason is that the pin has moved on a circular path around the attaching point on the left rail. When the right rail is lowered, the pin will move back to, or close to the centerline.

The centerline gauges are the easiest and most accurate means of determining twist. Twist is not illustrated, but it can be described by visualizing an additional wedge shaped opening between the second and third gauge similar to the one between the first and second in Fig. 251. This would indicate that the side rails were out of parallel through the full length of the front and center sections. This condition can be seen at a glance with the centerline gauges but is very difficult to detect with the tram.

The centerline gauges will not detect a diamonded condition. In a diamonded condition, one rail has been driven back in relation to the other so that a difference in diagonal measurements shows up in at least two of the three frame sections. When this is suspected, it is essential to check with the frame tram. In some cases, checking for a diamonded condition may have to be delayed until some of the other straightening has been done. This occurs when an essential reference point has been shifted inboard or outboard by other damage, making a check to it useless until it has been restored to its proper position.

QUESTIONS ON BASIC STRAIGHTENING PROCEDURES AND EQUIPMENT

1. What is meant by roughing, or roughing out?
2. What is meant by bumping?
3. What is meant by aligning?
4. Why is the roughing phase of the straightening job the most important?
5. What methods may be used to rough out a damaged panel?
6. How can the proper method of roughing out be determined for any panel?
7. What is the effect of driving out sharp dents with a hammer or a dolly block?
8. When is pushing a dent out of a jack a better procedure to follow than driving it out?
9. Why does the edge of a dented flat panel pull inward?
10. Why is it desirable to use tension when roughing out deep dents in relatively flat panels?
11. Can a bend in a piece of metal be pulled straight with tension alone? Explain.
12. Will tension be more effective on a deep dent or on a shallow one? Explain.
13. Why does the effectiveness of tension decrease as the panel surface is brought close to a straight line?
14. What is lift reaction?
15. How much downward thrust is applied on the points of attachment used to pull a dent out of a. panel?
16. On a shallow dent in a long panel, is it desirable to attach as close as possible to the dent or should the attachment be at the extreme edge? Explain.
17. Referring to question 16, how would lift reaction affect the selection of the attaching point?
18. How will work hardened metal affect the straightening operation?

19. Why is it desirable to do as much straightening as possible before releasing the tension on a panel which has been pulled to rough it out?
20. Why should the application of tension be aligned with the flattest line of the panel?
21. In attaching a solder tension plate, why should the hot solder be quenched?
22. In removing the solder tension plate, why should the solder not be melted?
23. In removing a solder tension plate, why should the tinned surface be quenched after it is cleaned of solder?
24. Why does an external pull jack tend to lift as it pulls unless it is blocked to prevent it?
25. What tools can be used to check a frame or a unitized body for sagged or raised conditions?
26. What is the purpose of a frame tram?
27. What is the datum line?
28. What is a side sway?
29. What is meant by "X" checking?
30. What is a reference point?

8

Repair Procedures

The actual repair jobs discussed here have been selected as good examples to which the fundamentals presented in the preceding chapters can be applied. Some of the damaged areas are more severe than others. Two panels, a fender and a hood, probably would not be attempted in most repair shops. The others represent a cross section of the work a skilled metal repair man might be called on to do in the normal course of his day-to-day work. The more simple jobs are presented first, followed by the more severe ones. However, the sequence of presentation is not intended to indicate that the last is necessarily the most difficult.

One frame straightening job has been included because it is felt that this work is as much a part of the metal man's job as work on sheet metal panels. Many body repair shops are equipped with portable body and frame machines so that they can do such work instead of sending it out to a specialty shop. Although there are differences in body and frame work, both are governed by the same principles.

It is felt that the procedures offered here are efficient and practical. Efficient and practical means that a skilled repair man working in a well equipped shop would be able to do a quality job in good time by following these procedures on similar jobs. It must be recognized, however, that an exact application of a procedure to another job in another place and time would be difficult. These jobs should be studied to recognize the basic ideas as they apply to the similar construction and shapes and the related damage patterns. The general idea can be carried to another job but rarely a specific procedure. An attempt to establish a procedure that can be applied to any panel of a particular make and model of automobile would be useless.

It is hoped that the beginner or the experienced metal man who is attempting to improve his techniques will recognize the basic approach. Both will be helped if they can see their work from a viewpoint broad enough to enable them to apply a lesson learned on one job to another.

THE THREE-STEP APPROACH

All of the procedures on actual damage in the following sections have been organized in a three-step approach. This approach is to:

1. Inspect the damaged area to determine the types of damage conditions present and the basic repair procedures suited to the conditions.

2. Determine the exact repair procedure to be followed.

3. Do the job.

This approach is recommended for any job and to any metal man, beginner or experienced. The amount of time spent in the first two steps no doubt will vary widely for the beginner and the experienced man, because the beginner may be forced to study to learn facts about a job which the experienced man can see at a glance. However, the amount of time spent in deciding how to do the job is not in itself an indication that the job will or will not be done properly. It is much more important that the correct procedure be followed than it is to get started in a hurry. A few more minutes spent in getting all of the facts so that the job is started right may avoid mistakes that will require hours to correct.

INSPECTION

In making the inspection, certain specific information must be learned about the damaged panel. This can be done best by forming the habit of following a definite pattern or sequence of examination. It is also essential to know what to look for. The following list of inspection steps includes the information needed; it is arranged in the sequence to be followed. In making an inspection, look for this information:

1. Location of the point, or points, of impact.

2. If two or more impacts are involved, determine:
   a. Are they equal, or should one be considered as the major and the others as of minor importance?
   b. The exact areas of secondary damage related to each one.
   c. Will the repair of the damage from one impact be related to the repair of the others, or are they independent?
   d. If they are related, which one should be started first so that it will reduce the severity of conditions in the other, or others?

3. The exact nature of the various damage conditions—upsets, stretches, rolled buckles, hinge buckles, displaced metal, etc.—which make up the total damage and determine which are the most severe.

4. Relate each of the damage conditions to the repair method best suited for roughing it out.

An inspection of the damage on an automobile will reveal many facts about the collision which caused it. The information that is of particular interest to the metal man has to do with the nature of the other object involved and the action which took place. Speed, size, rigidity, and direction of motion of the impact object all leave telltale marks which serve to reveal the exact nature of the damage.

DETERMINING REPAIR PROCEDURE

After the inspection has been completed, the next logical step is to determine how to proceed to straighten the damage. In some cases, this may be such a simple process that practically no thought at all is required; in others it may be so complicated that it is difficult to decide where to start. In either event, the only source of information to guide the metal man in applying his skill is what he reads from the panel surface. His problem is to visualize the folding action that took place as the damaging force was applied and to find the best way, or ways, to apply force to accomplish the opposite effect.

One of the worst mistakes that can be made is to start the job without any particular plan. This is even worse than to have analyzed the damage incorrectly and started with the wrong plan, because, with the wrong plan, it will soon be seen that the desired results are not being obtained. With no special plan, there is also no pattern of results to be expected.

An excellent way to plan the repair procedure is to find the answer to such questions as the following:

1. Where should the start be made?
2. Should it be made by driving, pushing, or pulling?
3. What will the shape of the damaged area be as the result of the first step?
4. If there is more than one impact area and related damage, should one be completed before the other, or, should both or all be worked together?
5. Where should the next step be taken after the starting and each of the following steps are completed?
6. What methods should be used as the work progresses through the various steps?

General questions such as these can be applied to any damaged panel. The answers, of course, will vary widely from one panel to another because the damages vary. The value in finding the answers is that intelligent thought is applied to the problem *before* starting to work. The ideal result of such thinking would be to change the repair of any damaged panel from a problem to a series of simple steps to be carried out in predetermind sequence.

DOING THE JOB

Doing the job is putting the planned procedure to work. If perfection could be obtained, this stage would be no more than just a specified amount of labor. This is rarely the case, however, because the almost infinite number of variables make it necessary to be on the alert for undesired results. This means that the metal man should be constantly inspecting and analyzing the results of his various steps so that he can modify his procedure as required.

Failure to observe that the desired results are not being obtained accounts for more wasted effort and substandard jobs than any other cause. The reason for this is easy to understand. The use of force is required in every step. The forces used must be enough to bend, upset, or stretch the affected metal in some way in each step. If the wrong results are being obtained and the repairman continues to work, the damage will be compounded.

The three-step approach outlined here is nothing more than the thought processes of a skilled metal man put into words. Such thinking is essential to analyze any job before it is started. As skill is developed, much of the thinking becomes automatic. Automatically or painfully slowly, however, the metal man must know what he is going to do before starting to do it.

DENTED FENDER

The fender dent shown in Fig. 252 is relatively minor damage. It has been selected for discussion because it is a typical example of a dent which can be straightened easily and quickly by proper use of the hand tools, even though access to the underside is partly blocked.

The question as to whether or not a job such as this should be filled should be answered. In this case, it is possible to use a dolly block and a pry rod on the underside of the metal, even though the access is limited. It would not be possible to finish the job with filling alone because of the high ridges above and below the impact point of the molding.

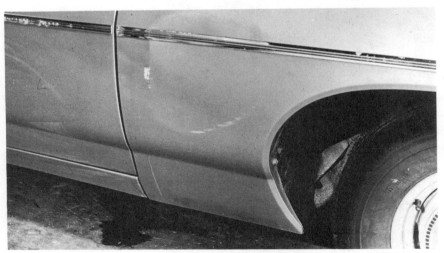

Fig. 252 Minor dent in the side of a fender. Note that there are no severe distortions.

These ridges must be lowered before the shape can be restored by filling. Just a little more care in the use of the hand tools in doing this necessary straightening will leave no place to fill. The extra time to do this straightening is minor, less than would be required to apply and finish the filler.

This same dent farther forward on the fender would probably require filling, unless a lot of extra time was used on it, because it would be much more difficult to reach the underside. In that case, the procedure would be considerably different from that discussed in the following pages. It would then be a matter of prying it out to rough shape and filling the rest.

INSPECTION

Inspection of this damage reveals the following information:

1. There are no severe distortions.

2. Most of the dented area is under only an elastic strain and should pop out when the buckles in the ridges are relieved, leaving only minor roughness.

3. Limited access to the underside is provided by the construction of the fender and cowl. In Fig. 253, it may be seen that the underside can be reached for limited use of the hammer and dolly block, and all of the area can be reached with a pry rod.

Fig. 253 View of the underside of the fender from the rear end with the door open.

4. The curved buckle above the molding is the most severe. Less severe buckles are at the lower edge, following the line of rub marks, and vertically at the rear edge where the metal has bent over the inner reinforcement.

5. A minor concave buckle can be expected under the crushed molding. In the undamaged condition, the upper edge of this molding follows a convex crease stamped in the side of the fender. This crease line will have to be restored as a part of the straightening procedure.

REPAIR PLAN

The repair of this damage should be planned to take the maximum advantage of the elastic condition in the center area. The more nearly that it can be made to pop out to shape, the less additional work will be required to finish the job. The upper ridge and the concave buckle under the molding are holding the area out of shape more so than the lower buckle. For that reason, the lower buckle will be left until the upper area has been worked out.

If space under the fender permitted, the concave buckle under the molding could be driven out by striking with the dolly block. As this is not practical, the dolly can be held against the under side, and stiff pressure exerted against it while the ridge is wcrked out with the hammer. Reaction to the hammer blows will cause the dolly to drive out much of the low metal.

Additional work with the dinging spoon and the hammer and dolly should smooth the area so that it can be metal-finished.

REPAIR PROCEDURE

It was necessary to remove the damaged molding before the repair procedure could start. Access to the clip bolts over the wheel—in order to remove the nuts—is difficult, so the molding was pried off and the bolts removed by drilling, as shown in Fig. 254. The clip head was pried up and held by the vise grip pliers while a ³⁄₁₆-inch drill was used to drill through the head. The bolt then popped out. It is possible to remove and replace these nuts, but to do so requires removal and replacement of the battery on the right hand side.

The first repair operation is shown in Fig. 255. The repair man is reaching through the door opening to the underside of the fender to hold the lip of a general purpose dolly block against the crushed crease line, indicated by the line of elongated oval marks. Stiff hand pressure is being applied to the dolly block while the hammer is used on the upper ridge, here indicated by a long line with short cross marks. This operation reduced most of the ridge and allowed much of the displaced metal to snap back to shape.

Fig. 254 Drilling out molding clip bolts. Vise grip pliers prevent bolt from turning with drill.

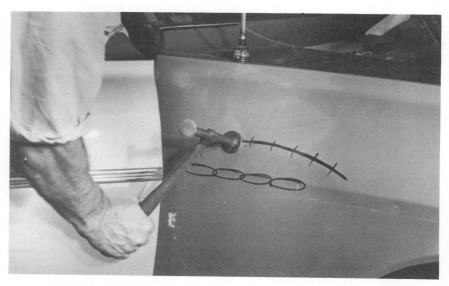

Fig. 255 Working out the dent with the hammer and dolly block. The lip of the dolly is being held under the area of the elongated oval marks and pushed outward with as much pressure as possible.

Fig. 256 Using the dinging spoon on what remains of the high ridge.

After most of the ridge had been removed with the hammer, the ding-ing spoon was used as shown in Fig. 256. This would not have been prac-tical for the first operation for two reasons: one, the original ridge was too sharply formed to work with the dinging spoon; and, two, the reac-tion of the dolly block on the underside would have been lost. After this operation was completed, additional work on the crease line was done with the hammer and dolly block.

In Fig. 257, the small head of the hammer is shown being used on the vertical crease. It was used also on the lower ridge. The small head was used because these ridges are both in areas which are springy, making it desirable to reduce the area of hammer contact as much as possible. Using the large head or the dinging spoon will not work in areas such as these as well as the small head.

The worked out area is shown in Fig. 258. The area is relatively smooth, and most of the original crease line above the molding has been restored.

The result of the first sanding operation is shown in Fig. 259. The sander has been stroked over the area in the back and forth motion used for finishing metal. Note that a few low spots are indicated by the black primer remaining in them, but the overall surface is in good condition. An overlay of dust from the sanding operation can be seen on the paint above and to the right of the area which has been sanded. This is normal.

The sanded area has been filed, showing up the remaining low spots in greater detail in Fig. 260. The file strokes are parallel to the flattest

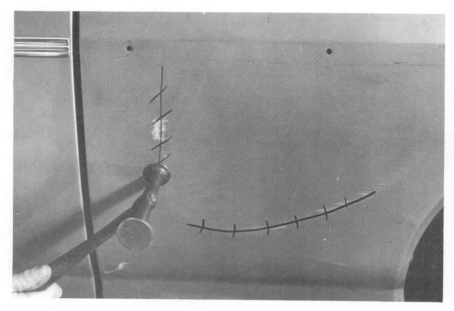

Fig. 257 Using the small head of the bumping hammer on the vertical ridge. The small head is more effective on springy metal than the large one.

Fig. 258 The straightened area, ready to start metal finishing.

Fig. 259 The result of the first sanding operation. A little paint remains in the low spots.

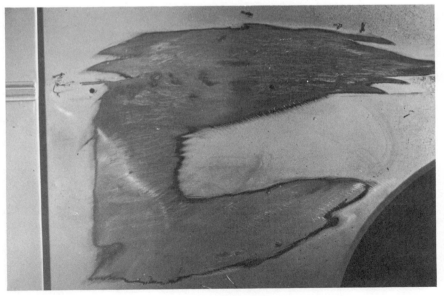

Fig. 260 The result of the first filing operation, showing the remaining low spots in much greater detail than they appeared in the ground surface.

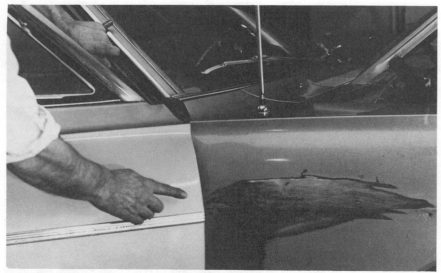

Fig. 261 Using a pry rod on the low spots through the rear end of the fender. Some doors do not swing out of the opening to permit this operation.

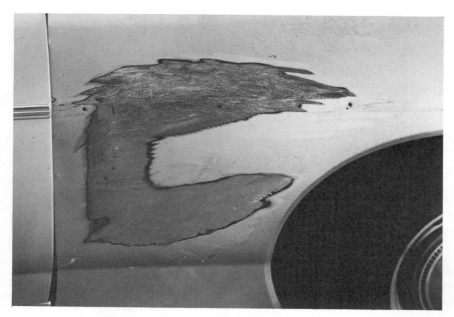

Fig. 262 The surface after filing off the pried-up spots. Low spot in molding line will be covered after molding is replaced.

crown of the fender, except at the lower edge where it was necessary to slant them downward to avoid interference with the reverse crown on the edge of the fender. No picking has been done on the filed area, but enough filing has been done to show sharp outlines of the low spots. This is the method of filing discussed in Chapter 3. In effect, it is in part a smoothing operation and in part an inspection operation. The overall area was near enough to final smoothness before the finishing operation was started so that the larger areas of smooth filed metal can be considered as finished. All that remains to do is lift the low spots slightly so that they can be filed to blend into the adjoining areas.

The repair man is shown in the process of prying up low spots in Fig. 261. The upper hinge is being used as a fulcrum for the pry rod as the point is shifted from one low spot to another. Note that the repair man is pointing with one finger toward the spot being lifted. This is not necessary, but many repair men find that this helps them to locate the spot they wish to pry. The principal caution to observe on an operation such as this is not to pry too hard. It is better to pry the same spot several times than to pry it once too hard.

The filed off panel, ready for final sanding, is shown in Fig. 262. The time for this filing operation was very short, only a few minutes—less time than would have been required to fill and finish the surface with either solder or plastic.

The result of the final sanding operation is shown in Fig. 263. This

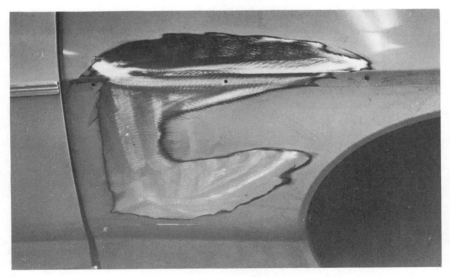

.g. 263 The finished surface after buffing, ready for repainting.

sanding was done with a buffing stroke, as described in Chapter 3. For this buffing operation, the sander pad was held so that the swirl marks run as near as possible to the lengthwise direction of the panel, and the machine was stroked up and down instead of back and forth. A worn 36-grit disc was used, and the pressure on it was very light because the intention was to buff, not cut.

Note that a little less attention was paid to the metal which would be covered by the molding than to that in the other areas. A slight low spot which will be covered, in this case by a molding, will not be a problem because it can not be seen after the automobile is reassembled.

The final, repainted fender is shown in Fig. 264. It is in excellent shape, and it was done very quickly. The repair man took advantage of the construction features of the automobile and the nature of the damage and made them work for him. Not all makes and models are so designed that easy access at the rear end of the fender is provided. On some automobiles, different procedures would be a necessity. The important point is that the construction features of the automobile must be considered when planning the repair procedure and the maximum advantage taken of those that simplify the job.

BUCKLED FENDER SIDE

Inspection of damage on the side of the front fender in Fig. 265 reveals the following facts about it.

1. It is a relatively minor buckle; there are no severe metal distortions.

2. The actual contact with the impact object was on the die cast molding around the fender opening.

3. The sharp buckle at the upper edge of the damage appears to be the result of a much more severe impact than the overall appearance indicates. This suggests that the impact area has been driven in much farther and snapped back to the position found here.

The important facts revealed by this inspection are simply the cause and effect relationship between the impact area on the molding and the buckled metal above it.

REPAIR PLAN

Recognizing the cause and effect relationship of the impact area on the molding and the buckled metal above it makes it simple to plan the repair. The impact area is the cause of the buckled metal and, therefore, it will have to be relieved before the buckles can be relieved. In this particular case, they will not have to be worked together because the total damage is not severe enough. The inner edge of the fender flange can be pushed back to its proper position and held while the buckles are worked out.

Fig. 264 The finished job.

Fig. 265 Buckled right front fender. The buckle was caused by a glancing impact on the heavy, die-cast molding around the wheel opening.

A construction feature of this automobile complicates the repair of this damage. The inside of this fender is protected by a wheel housing, which is not removable. This blocks access to the under side with a dolly block. Fortunately, the housing is installed so that it is simple to reach the underside of the fender with a pry rod and, at the upper edge, a spoon dolly.

REPAIR OPERATIONS

The first repair setup and its results can be seen in Fig. 266. The molding has been removed and a light-duty body jack set up between the inner edge of the fender flange and the frame to push it out. Note that a block of wood has been used between the pipe coupling on the end of the jack and the fender flange. This is to spread the force over enough of the flange to cause a wide area to move. If this was not done, the flange would probably buckle and cause additional damage.

Pushing out the flange has reduced the depth of the depressed area above it so that it will be simple to work out. There are no buckles remaining in the forward section on the right side of the jack, but a minor buckle remains at the extreme rear of the damaged area. See Fig. 265.

The second operation and the tools with which it was performed are shown in Fig. 267 and Fig. 268. In Fig. 267, the spoon dolly is being held above the area where it is being used in Fig. 268. There is just enough room between the inner edge of the fender and the wheel housing to permit the spoon dolly to be used in this manner. An inside view

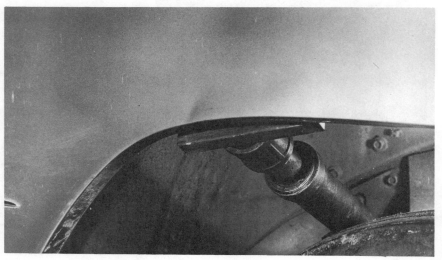

Fig. 266 A body jack and a block of wood set up to push the fender flange back to position.

Fig. 267 The hammer and spoon dolly, which will be used for most of the straightening.

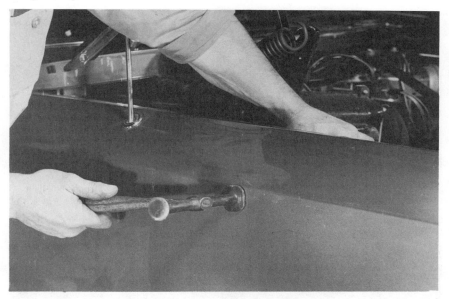

Fig. 268 Using the hammer and spoon dolly. An opening between inner fender flange and the wheel housing will admit the spoon dolly but is too small for the operator's arm holding a dolly block.

of the fender is not shown. The buckle was first punched out by pushing the end of the spoon dolly against it. The area was then smoothed with the hammer. Very light blows were used because the end of the spoon dolly contacts only a very small area on the under side.

The hammer and a flat bumping spoon are shown in use in the third operation in Fig. 269. Note that this is a ball peen hammer instead of the metal hammer. The metal hammer should never be used to drive any tool. Part of the high spot on this position was removed by the previous operations, but a part of it still remained. The spoon worked out this remaining high spot almost perfectly.

The hammer and a pry rod are shown in use in Fig. 270. The underside of the fender, showing how the pry rod was inserted, is shown in Fig. 271. (Some fenders and inner skirts are assembled so that the use of a pry rod in this manner is not practical.) Only light pressure was applied to the pry rod, and light hammer blows were struck beside the spot being pried out. The effect of the hammer is to set the bend in the area being lifted without prying it too high. Most of the hammer blows were struck against spots which had been lifted. Such spots were already slightly high, so the effect of the hammer was to reduce them slightly while the pry rod was raising another. Careful use of the hammer and pry rod in this manner can produce a surface which is surprisingly smooth.

Fig. 269 Spooning down high metal above the crease line after the buckle was popped out.

Fig. 270 Underside of fender, showing space between fender flange and wheel housing which permits easy entry for the pry bar.

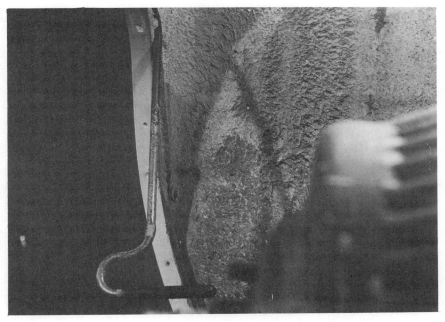

Fig. 271 Hammer and pry bar being used to smooth the buckled area.

In Fig. 272, the surface has been ground off, using a 24-grit sanding disc on a flexible, nine-inch pad. Note that the sander has been stroked back and forth so that the disc swirl marks make a crisscross pattern to show up the low spots. Each remaining patch of paint indicates a slight low spot which must be raised. Most of the raising will have to be done with the pry rod, just as was done in the straightening operations.

A different pry rod is shown in use on some of the low spots in Fig. 273. Note that the area has been reground after the first lifting operation was completed. The same crisscross motion was used.

In Fig. 274, a few file strokes have been made over the ground area to make a closer show-up of the low spots than made by the grinding operation. The surface left by the sander was close to the proper smoothness, but the file shows up a few more, identified by slight shading in the low spot. These low spots were lifted and refiled to complete the operation.

The prepared job, buffed off and ready to refinish, is shown in Fig. 275. For the buffing operation, the sander was stroked up and down, with the disc held so that the swirl marks run as near lengthwise of the flat crown as possible. Very light pressure was used to obtain the maximum buffing action, instead of digging into the metal. This is just the opposite of the action desired in the first sanding operations.

The refinished fender, ready for delivery to the owner, is shown in Fig. 276. No traces of the damage remain.

Fig. 272 The straightened area after the first disc-sanding operation.

Fig. 273 Lifting minor low spots before filing the ground surface.

Fig. 274 The filing operation almost completed.

Fig. 275 The damaged area, buffed and ready for refinishing.

Fig. 276 The refinished job, ready for delivery.

Fig. 277 Severe front end damage. Only the front fender and radiator core support were repaired. Arrow indicates sharp, accordion type fold. Windshield discoloration is frost.

CRUSHED FRONT FENDER

The automobile shown in Fig. 277 has suffered severe front end damage, probably by striking the bumper of another automobile. Most of the damage is above the bumper, indicating that this bumper slipped below the bumper of the automobile which it struck. Note the sharp accordion type folds at the headlight level, indicated by the arrow, where the shape of the other bumper is imprinted into this fender. The severity of the fender damage is even more evident in Fig. 278. There is damage to the core support also. In the discussion of repair procedure which follows, both the fender and core support will be considered, but the emphasis will be on the fender.

There is no question that this fender would be considered for replacement in most body shops. *However, it can be straightened.* It was selected for use here because it offers an excellent example of a difficult looking job, which can be done efficiently by proper use of tools and equipment. No doubt, some time could have been saved if only the minimum straightening had been done and extensive filling had been used. However, the time difference could not have been great because it was done in good time by the procedure shown.

The purpose of using this fender here is to explain practical procedure on metal which has been distorted severely. It is the type of damage

Fig. 278 View of front end of fender and core support. Arrows indicate bends in core support and fender flanges.

which is a test of the metal man's skill; it is also the type of damage which leads to the development of high skill for the metal man who is willing to attempt difficult jobs. The metal man who has learned to handle jobs such as this can race through the easy ones.

INSPECTION

Close inspection of the damage on this fender and core support reveals the following information, some of which has been mentioned in the preceding paragraphs:

1. Most of the damage was caused by a direct impact by the bumper of another automobile.

2. The impact has driven the fender back so that it overlaps the edge of the door (the overlap is not shown clearly in any of the photos).

3. The most severe distortion is found in the sharp folds in the impact area, indicated by the arrow on Fig. 277.

4. The crumpled and torn metal over the headlight area was caused by the folding action as the impact area collapsed.

5. The impact on the grille penetrated to the core support (a bend in it can be seen at the extreme left in Fig. 278) and buckled the inner flange of fender. Arrows indicate these conditions.

6. The welded-on bracket at the front of the fender, to which the headlight body attaches, was almost torn off.

REPAIR PLAN

To obtain a reverse effect on this fender, the buckled metal will have to be pulled forward. Inasmuch as both the fender and the core support have been driven back, it will be worthwhile to set up the body and frame machine to make the necessary pulls. Heating of the sharp buckles will be necessary; otherwise they will break and require welding.

The first operation will be to pull the folded-over, extreme front point of the fender around to approximate position. Then enough heat and tension must be applied to the sharp folds to restore the original length fore and aft. Considerable reworking of the buckled area will be required after the proper length has been restored because of the severe distortion. This is work to be done with the hammer and dolly and torch.

The buckle over the wheel opening will be reduced greatly when the shape of the front end of the fender is restored. It will not be touched until the other work is completed.

REPAIR PROCEDURE

The first pull setup is shown in Fig. 279. This being a light pull, the setup is simple. The hook on the pull chain on the upright beam is caught directly on the flange of the front end of the fender. The details of the anchor setup are shown in Fig. 280. The hook on this chain is caught in a conveniently placed hole in the lower frame flange. This

Fig. 279 Overall view of first pull setup. Note that rear end of fender has been driven under forward edge of door.

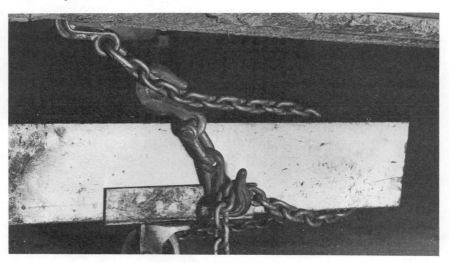

Fig. 280 Close-up view of another setup. The hook is caught in a hole in the frame, safe only for light pulls.

is safe here but on a hard pull it probably would cause damage to the flange.

Two conditions can be seen in Fig. 279. One is the overlap condition at the door edge. Note that the end of fender disappears under the door edge. The other is that the sharp buckle over the wheel opening has almost snapped out. The outward spread at the impact caused this buckle. This pull has reduced the outward spread enough to remove its effect on the buckle, permitting much of it to pop out. What is left may be worked out easily. This seemingly minor point is emphasized because a very common mistake in metal working is to attempt to work out buckles such as this before the cause has been relieved. The result of such effort is additional damage instead of repair.

A close-up view of the effect of the first pull is shown in Fig. 281. The front end of the fender has been brought around almost to its proper position, and the sharp folds have been partly opened up. Heat has been applied to these folded areas and the buckled area at the top of the fender. If these areas had not been heated, in this case to cherry red, the hook would have torn out the flange instead of moving the metal. Further pulling with this setup would have torn out the flange instead of doing more good. There are two reasons for this: one, the front end of the fender curves inward enough so that the hook is not in a straight line ahead of the buckles; and, two, the distorted metal in the buckled area is stronger, even though heated, than the flange. So, it is time to change the hookup.

Fig. 281 Close-up view of the effect of first pull. Note that chain is hooked to fender flange. The point of the fender has swung around, and the pleated area is opening.

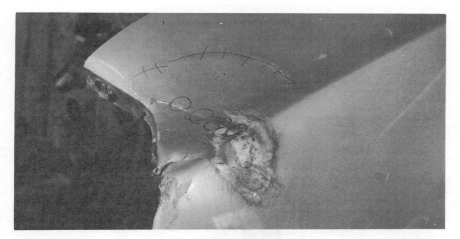

Fig. 282 View of top area of fender after the first pull and some hammer and dolly work. Cross-marked long lines were hammered. The dolly was used under the circled areas.

Before making another pull, the area at the top, Fig. 282, was worked into rough shape with the hammer and dolly block. The areas worked with the hammer are marked with long crayon lines crossed by several short lines. The areas worked with the dolly block are marked with rough circles. Referring to Fig. 278, the long lines are on what remains of a convex hinge buckle, and the circles are on what remains of a concave hinge buckle. The movement of the front end of the fender had set up the condition which tended to cause these buckles to unfold. The pull had caused some movement in these areas, but further movement was resisted by metal in the buckles which had been stiffened by work hardening. By working this area at this time, the effect of the hammer and dolly block was added to the tendency to movement. The skill involved is to gauge the proper force of the blows—so that the stiffness in the work-hardened areas is overcome, so that the metal moves—and not to beat the area excessively. The beginner is cautioned in a situation such as this not to overdo it. When moderate hammer blows on the outside or dolly blows on the inside do not cause further movement, even though the area still lacks much of being back to shape, *stop*. Something should be done to increase the tendency to movement. Further beating will cause damage.

Most of the work in this area was done with the hammer and dolly block separately. The area, as it appears in Fig. 282, is just about ready for final straightening by working off- and on-dolly. This work could have been completed at this time, but better procedure was to leave it until the distortion in the impact area was relieved.

In Fig. 283, the spot weld cutter is shown cutting the two remaining welds holding the headlight bracket to the flange of the fender. Removing it made it much easier to work the side of the fender.

The hookup for the final pull on the fender is shown in Fig. 284. The use of a clamp in this position is a compromise. Note that it has had to

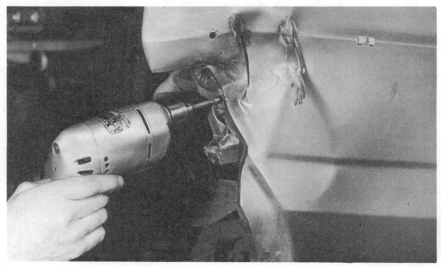

Fig. 283 Removing headlight bracket, using spot weld cutter. Only two welds remain unbroken.

Fig. 284 Close-up view of the second pull setup. Arrows indicate buckles which must be drawn out in addition to the sharp folds.

be set at an angle to the line of pull so that the metal it holds will be twisted as it is drawn forward. The need to compromise was dictated by the closeness of the severe distortion to the front edge of the fender and the slanted shape of the edge. A better hookup would be to solder a piece of metal above the clamp on the molding line, if it was not necessary to apply heat on the sharp distortions. The heat would be so close to the solder that the joint would be broken before the pull was completed.

It is important on any job such as this to understand exactly how much pulling is required. The answer to this question lies in the ridge indicated by the arrows and the alignment of the flange of the front edge. This ridge is the remains of the sharp buckle which formed around the impact point. The metal forward of it must move forward enough to permit it to be driven down level with the surrounding metal. Ideally, the area would be put under tension, heat applied to the sharpest part of the distortion, light hammer blows applied to the ridges, and the area would settle into shape. Practically, there is usually more work than that to be done because the heat and force cannot be concentrated as much as they should be.

The final pull was stopped when the condition shown in Fig. 285 was reached. Because of the angle of the clamp, a section of metal was partially broken out, but most of the buckles have been reduced so that they can be worked out with the hammer and dolly block, except in the areas

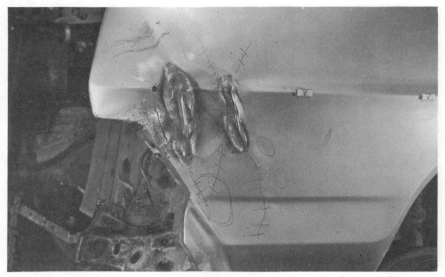

Fig. 285 Close-up view of the result of the second pull. Crossed lines and circles indicate areas requiring further hammer and dolly work. Twisting of the clamp has broken the attaching point.

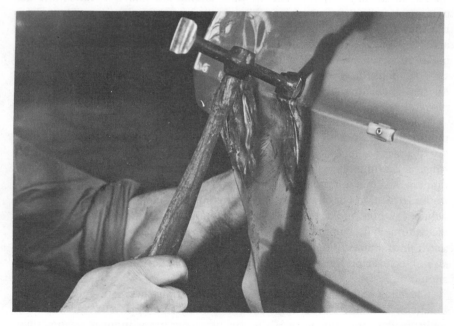

Fig. 286 Reshaping reverse curve, using radius-faced hammer and lip of dolly block.

of sharp distortion. These sharp folds remain because, even though heated to cherry red, the yield to tension takes place in adjoining areas. It would be very difficult to concentrate force on them so that they would unfold exactly as they folded under the impact.

If the clamp had not broken the flange as it did, it would have been worthwhile to carry the pulling operation a little farther. Also, this pulling was done with the body and frame machine from a single point of attachment. This was desirable because the fender had been driven back into an overlap under the edge of the door. Pulling on the front end of the fender would tend to move it forward into alignment. It did not move all of the way, however, until the hookup shown in Fig. 291 was made. If additional pulling had been done, it would have been best procedure to make a tension plate attachment on the other side of the buckles, right side in Fig. 285, and concentrate force on them from both sides. This was not done because the result obtained with the hookups shown accomplished almost all that was needed.

The operation of reshaping the bead section of the fender is shown in Fig. 286. The lip edge of the dolly block is being held in the crease, while the radius hammer is used to work the metal into shape. In Fig. 287, the work marked out on the surface in Fig. 285 has been completed. There are some bulged areas in this which are not marked but may be seen after shrinking was performed on them in Fig. 288.

Before starting the metal finishing operation, the headlight bracket was welded in place and the final alignment of the fender to the door was

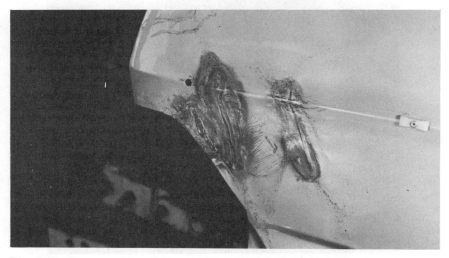

Fig. 287 Close-up view of damaged area after work indicated in Fig. 285 was completed.

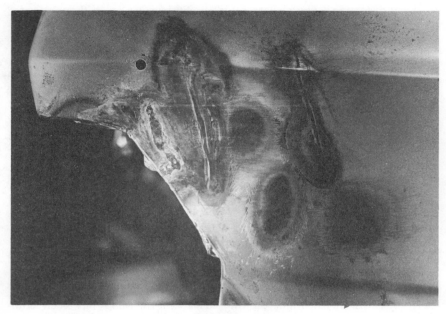

Fig. 288 Close-up view of damaged area, ready to be metal-finished. Black spots below and between folds were shrunk, using low heat.

Fig. 289 The headlight bracket, straightened and ready to be welded back in place.

Fig. 290 Pull setup on radiator core support. Chain has been passed through existing hole and around heavy bar. Arrow indicates straightened flange on core support.

made. The headlight bracket is shown being held in place in Fig. 289. It has been straightened so that it will fit to the flange of the fender and will be clamped into place. Aligning it is simply a matter of making sure that the weld marks fit into their original places. No welding details are shown.

The first pull on the core support is shown in Fig. 290. The chain has been passed through an existing hole in the front baffle and around a heavy bar of steel. As this was pulled forward, the oblong hole in the upper flange, indicated by the arrow, was straightened. It was found later, after installing a new hood panel, that the center of the core support was driven back too far for the hood latch to engage. The hood was not available for fitting when this work was done, and there was no other automobile of the same make and model to measure, so this was not taken care of at this time. It would have been desirable, but not a necessity, to have fitted the hood latch to the hood before the next operation was performed.

The hookup shown in Fig. 291 was used to pull the fender into alignment with the door and reduce the buckle in the flange at the core support. A chain hook has been bolted to the flange by removing the original bolt and replacing it with a longer one. The bolt in this position threads into a lug nut permanently attached to the flange of the core support, so it is

Fig. 291 Setup to pull fender forward. Note bolted-on hook on fender flange.

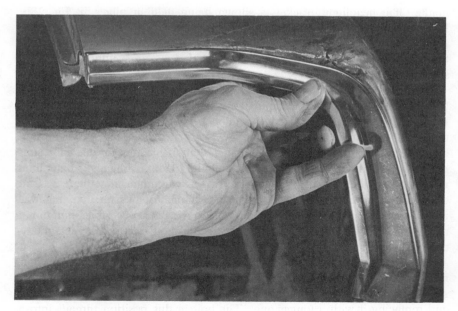

Fig. 292 Using the molding to check the shape of the front end of the fender before welding the break in the top edge.

only necessary to change bolts and draw the new one down securely to hold the hook. The fender was subjected to a hard pull without loosening the bolts holding it to the upper part of the cowl. This was to straighten any twists which were in the attaching brackets. Then, the upper bolts were loosened and the fender pulled enough to make it stand in proper alignment to the door without being held. The bolts were then retightened.

It is important to establish the free alignment of a panel in conditions such as these. If this fender had simply been drawn forward until the proper space was established and the bolts retightened, there would have been a locked-up tendency for it to slip back. It is quite probable that it would have been necessary to realign the fender and door in a short time to satisfy a customer complaint. By drawing it forward far enough so that it will spring back to the proper position, future complaints are avoided.

Checking the alignment of the front end of the fender to the new front end molding is shown in Fig. 292. The flange has been straightened, but the welding of the torn area has been left until this fitting operation was complete. Note that the corner is a little too high at the area of torn metal. This was dropped to level, only a hand push outward at the lower edge was needed, and the area welded.

Fig. 293 View of damaged area after the first grinding operation. Some picking and regrinding have been done but no filing.

The first grinding operation on the side of the fender is shown in Fig. 293. A few low spots have been picked and reground, and the area is ready to finish with the body file.

In Fig. 294, filing has been started in the beaded area, using a shell file. It is always best procedure to file beads or other areas which are reinforced by shape before filing the adjoining, relatively flat metal. Picking or other straightening necessary to complete the filing operation in such areas will tend to pull or displace areas in the adjoining, relatively flat metal. If the beaded area was left until last, it could have been necessary to rework some of the adjoining area after finishing it once.

The fender after filing was completed, and the welded areas had been filled with body solder, is shown in Fig. 295. Much of the unground surface is covered with dust from the grinding operation. Fig. 296 shows the fender after final buffing, using a 50-grit disc on the disc sander, and ready for repainting. Note that the edges of the door and fender are in alignment. The repainted and rebuilt automobile is shown in Fig. 297. Note that the hood, grille, and headlight are all in alignment to the fender.

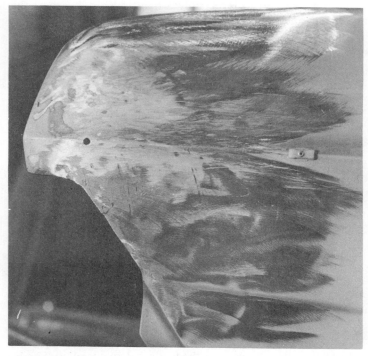

Fig. 294 The start of the filing operation on the beaded area.

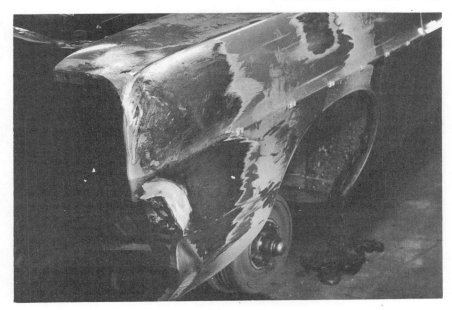

Fig. 295 Overall view of fender. Filing was completed and welded areas solder-filled.

Fig. 296 Final view ot completed repair job on fender. The hood has been fitted and removed for painting.

Fig. 297 Side view of finished fender.

Without quoting exact figures, the value of the time to do this job would compare favorably to the cost of replacement. Even though circumstances prevented use of the ideal hookup, Fig. 284, proper procedure and skill made its repair a relatively simple matter. Repeating what has been stated on previous pages, the beginner should be assigned to do some jobs involving severe distortion such as this. It is from such experience that high skill is developed.

DAMAGED HOOD PANEL

The hood which is a part of the damaged front end sheet metal on the automobile in Fig. 298 is in bad condition. It is doubtful whether it would be straightened in most repair shops. The fact that it has been repaired and the procedure recorded and explained here is not to be construed as a recommendation that such panels should be repaired. It has been used here because it provides a source of illustrations of most of the repair techniques which apply to hoods which have solid inner panel construction.

Many hoods having similar but less severe damage can and should be repaired. Such damage would not involve all of the problems encountered with this particular panel. For example, instead of being damaged across the entire front, the damage could be confined to only one front corner. Some of the techniques illustrated and discussed here would apply to it,

Fig. 298 Hood and front end sheet metal which has suffered severe front end damage. Only the hood was repaired. Arrows point to severe distortions.

but the time and effort would be less. The lesser damage could be repaired satisfactorily and profitably.

This repair job has been made more time consuming by metal finishing the top surface instead of using plastic filler. This was done to show that such areas can be worked if the repair man will develop the necessary skill. It is hoped that some of the beginners who study this repair operation will be influenced toward the development and appreciation of skill.

As with most other panels, the primary problem with this hood is metal collapsed under pressure. There are six points where collapse has caused severe distortion. Arrows on the top panel point to four of them. The other two are on the inner panel. The arrow in Fig. 299 points to one; the other distortion is in the corresponding position on the other side. An understanding of the causes and corrections of these conditions is essential to understanding the repair of any severe sheet metal damage. Conditions such as these are found on nearly every panel on which the damage is more than a simple dent. The repair man who understands the cause of these conditions and is willing to exercise his ingenuity in setting up a means of relieving them is well on his way to handling any problem.

The problems on this hood are doubled in that they are duplicated on each side. In the discussion which follows, attention is given to the problems and procedures on one side only to avoid needless repetition.

The most severe distortions on this panel are the sharp ridge buckles indicated by the downward pointing arrows on the outer edges in Fig. 298. If the fundamentals explained in Chapters 1 and 2 are understood, it should be clear that length must be fully restored to these buckled areas if the adjoining low crown metal is to be restored to its proper level and appearance. If these buckles are not restored to full length, the low crown metal will be bulged upward and springy. This latter is the condition referred to in Chapter 2 as *false stretch*.

The upward pointing arrows at the front edge of the panel indicate additional upsets. These are not as severe as the outer ones, but they affect the same area, making them a strong complication of an already severe condition.

The buckle on the inner panel, Fig. 299, is the normal result of bending any box member. The reinforcements pressed into this inner panel are deep enough to provide considerable rigidity. When this inner panel is welded into the outer, the result is a box member. Box members bend by collapsing on the inside of the bend. It also happens that the point of the greatest concentration of bending force falls where the change of shape provides a natural yield point. The result is a sharp collapse, as seen here. Almost identical buckles will be found on many damaged hoods.

There would be some buckling at the outer edges of this hood top, even if there was no inner panel. These buckles are in an offset section

Fig. 299 Inside view of left front corner of hood inner panel. Arrow points to severe fold-over buckle.

below the level of the rest of the upper panel. As the panel bends downward, the metal at the lower level is on the inside of the bend and subjected to a compressive force. The compressive force is opposed by the tension on the metal on the outer level. To bend, one must yield. Yielding is almost always in the metal under the compressive force. The result is a buckle. However, without an inner panel, the buckle would not be as severe as these are because the reverse crown which makes the offset would spread sideways to relieve some of the pressure.

INSPECTION

Most of the conditions of this hood panel have been mentioned in the preceding discussion. These may be summarized as follows:

1. The primary problem is in the six sharp buckles in the inner and outer panels.

2. Straightening and metal finishing the metal outside of these buckles will be relatively simple if they can be fully relieved. If not fully relieved, a condition of *false stretch* will affect the areas.

3. Buckling of the inner panel has forced it upward so that it is pressed against the outer panel.

4. Other than the downward bend at the front, there are no twists or other misalignments.

5. The inner panel blocks access to the outer panel for tool use.

6. There is no damage except on the extreme front end of the panel.

REPAIR PLAN

In planning the repair of this hood, it is necessary to consider two problems often encountered in repairing box section hoods. When an attempt is made to jack out the complete assembly, the inner panel tends to pull away from the outer in the center area. And, the outer panel tends to bulge in the buckled area. The first condition can usually be relieved by proper heating of the inner panel buckles as they are jacked out. The second condition is difficult to avoid because it is necessary to force the inner panel past the point of correction to allow for spring back. In doing so, the outer panel is often damaged, adding to the already existing buckled condition.

These conditions can be avoided by cutting the welds to separate the inner panel from the outer across the front end. In cases of lesser damage, this permits straightening of each panel separately. In this case, it will be necessary to straighten the inner panel partially to remove the interference with the outer panel under the edge buckles. The center area can be left open to provide tool access until the upper panel has been straightened and metal finished.

With these conditions in mind, the repair plan would be as follows:

Fig. 300 First repair operation, relieving inner panel buckle just enough to pull it away from outer panel.

1. Separate the inner and outer panels by cutting the spot welds across the front.

2. Straighten the buckles on each side of the inner panel just enough to relieve interference with the outer panel.

3. Straighten the outer panel, starting with the severe buckles on the sides. The general contour of the top should be restored next. The next operation will be to relieve the buckles in the front edge.

4. Straighten the inner panel and reweld the cut spot welds to complete the job. The shape of the front end can be checked off the car by using the new header panel which will be installed in front of the hood. If it fits off of the car, it will fit on the car.

Repair Operations

The first repair setup is shown in Fig. 300. A light-duty body jack has been set up to push out some of the buckle in the inner panel while heat is being applied. The use of the adjustable spoon makes it easy to push forward on the front flange. In this view, the hood is lying upside down on a bench, but the bracket which will later attach it to the repair rack has been installed to provide a base for the jack. This bracket is *home made*. It consists of a length of angle iron and a short section of steel pipe of the proper diameter to pass over the arms of the repair rack. More detail can be seen in Fig. 303 and Fig. 313.

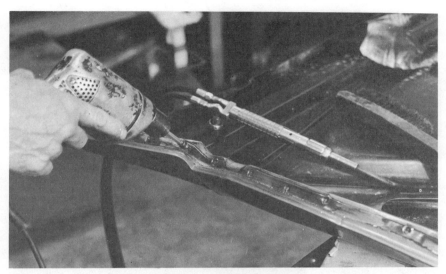

Fig. 301 Cutting spot welds across front of hood.

The spot weld cutting operation is shown in Fig. 301. The paint was removed from the welds before the cutting operation by scorching it with an oxidizing flame and wire brushing. Removing the paint is desirable because these welds will later be rewelded by brazing. The clean metal will braze much easier than if the paint were left on.

Notice that the operator's other hand is not in sight. The spot weld cutter will sometimes jump out of the cut and spin across the adjacent surface. If the operator is holding the panel close to the cut, the cutter may spin into it. The result may be a badly cut hand. *Do not hold any panel close to the cutter.*

In Fig. 302, the repair man has separated the panels and is forcing the upper panel away from the inner. The amount of force which can be applied in this manner will not damage the panel, and it will provide access for the next operation.

The setup to apply tension to the buckle in the upper panel is shown in Fig. 303. The flange of the inner panel has been pulled back enough to permit inserting the adjustable spoon into the offset end of the outer panel. This operation was performed on the repair rack. Note the details of the special bracket which permits the hood to be raised and lowered as needed. (Brackets such as these and a length of pipe mounted between two benches will serve the same purpose.)

The pulling and heating operation is shown in Fig. 304. Note the end of the adjustable spoon under the front edge. Before the torch was ap-

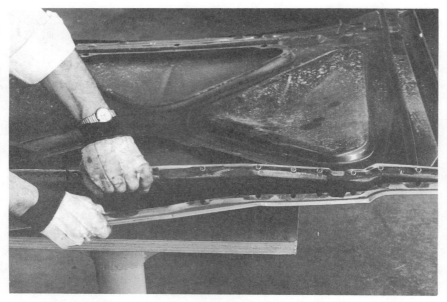

Fig. 302 Separating inner and outer panel after cutting welds.

plied, the jack was extended until further operation did not cause additional movement in the panel. After the heat application, the jack was extended carefully as the hammer was used on the remaining buckles outside of the heated area. No hammering was done on the heated metal until after it had cooled. Light hammering has been done on all of the ridge from the outside edge to the center of the panel.

A further reshaping operation is shown in Fig. 305. The center of the upper panel is propped up on wood blocks, and the jack is being used as a temporary prop under the edge close to the offset. The repair man is applying pressure downward with his left hand while he reworks the reverse crown with a radius-faced hammer. Most of the buckle has been eliminated.

The hammer has been used on the ridge across the top, and some smoothing work has been done along the front edge. Similar operations have been performed on the opposite side.

In Fig. 306, the hammer and a heavy spoon are being used to smooth the area adjacent to the reverse curve. By leaving the panels separated, this operation is easy. There is no other access to this area without cutting a hole in the inner panel. The latter is impractical because of the problems of replacing the cutout section.

In Fig. 307, the spoon dolly is being used in the same manner as the

Fig. 303 Applying tension to outer panel. Inner panel flange has been bent back to admit adjustable spoon into flange of outer panel.

spoon in Fig. 306. This tool is more satisfactory than the spoon but, being thicker, cannot be used where the space between the panels is too narrow.

A pull operation setup is shown in Fig. 308. This is the sharp buckle indicated by the upward arrow on the right front edge (left in the picture) in Fig. 298. The purpose of this setup is to stretch the front corner enough to permit the buckles in the panel to blend into the adjacent area. Actual stretching is required because, in buckling, the edge has upset. An attempt to drive this down instead of stretching the edge would spread it but leave a bulged area. Nor is shrinking practical because it would be an attempt to blend the panel surface to a shortened edge

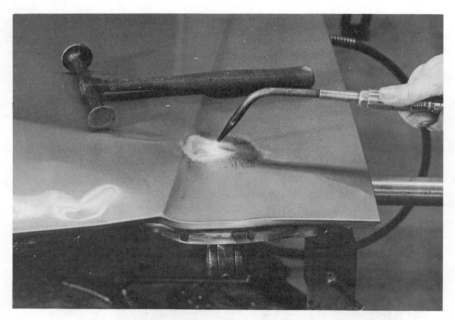

Fig. 304 Applying heat to buckle in outer panel while it is under tension. Note end of adjustable spoon under flange.

Fig. 305 Reshaping reverse crown area and lifting front end by forcing it against prop.

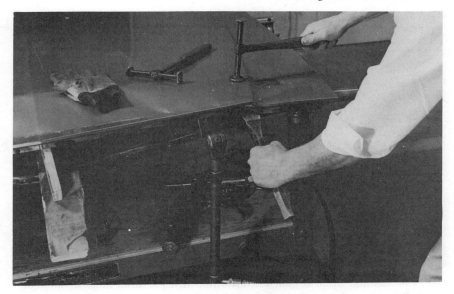

Fig. 306 Using heavy body spoon and hammer to smooth buckled area.

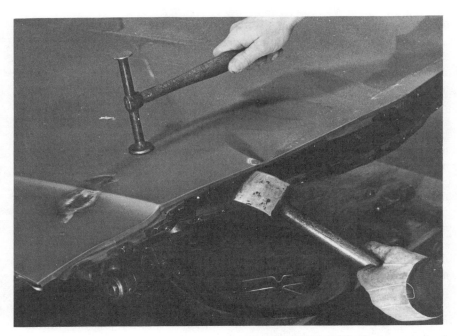

Fig. 307 Using spoon dolly and hammer to smooth buckled area.

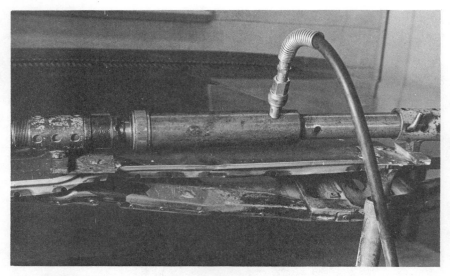

Fig. 308 Tension setup to pull out distortion in right front edge of hood top panel. Paint has been removed from buckled area by scorching and wire brushing.

which is reinforced by its shape.

A close-up view of the heating operation on the edge is shown in Fig. 309. The heat is being confined to the reinforced edge. As the edge was heated and stretched, the adjacent buckle began to flatten. Good judgment is essential to determine just how much tension to apply. Some work has to be done on the buckle to make it drop all of the way to a flat surface. In some cases on a job such as this, the edge should be heated and pulled and the jack removed to permit hand work on the buckle. The jack can then be replaced and additional heat applied as needed. This was done here.

The straightened panel, ready to metal-finish, is shown in Fig. 310. Essentially the same operations have been performed on both sides. The front edge of the panel has approximately the right shape, and the top is relatively smooth.

At this point, the procedure would be different if the intent was to finish the surface by use of plastic filler. The inner panel would have been straightened and rewelded to the outer and the hood fitted to the automobile before the application of the filler. However, because the surface was to be metal finished, the inner panel was left open to provide access for the tools. Fig. 311 shows an in-between view of the partially finished job. Fig. 312 shows the finished panel.

Fig. 309 Applying heat to buckle to permit actual stretching of edge.

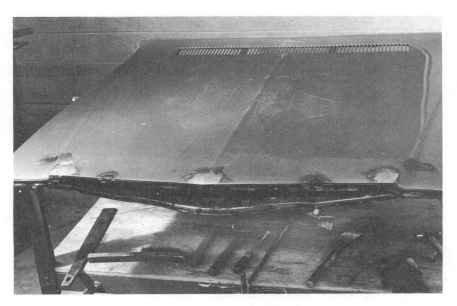

Fig. 310 The straightened top panel, ready to metal-finish.

Fig. 311 The damaged area, partly metal-finished.

Fig. 312 The metal-finished top panel.

Fig. 313 The straightening operation on the inner panel. Two light-duty jacks are in use. The stretch and heat operation was repeated on the opposite side.

The straightening operation on the inner panel is shown in Fig. 313. The light jack has been replaced under the inner edge, close to the inner panel buckle, and heat is being applied to it. At the same time, a lift under the center of the inner panel is being made using straps, a chain, and another light jack. The base of the jack is supported by the chain which is hooked into the straps. The lower end of the jack tubing is resting against the frame of the repair rack to prevent it from swinging to the rear. A prop from the jack tube to the rear end of the hood would perform the same function. The jack and heat being used on the right side (left in the picture) were transferred to the left, and the operation repeated. Some work was done on the center area of the inner panel with a block of wood and a heavy hammer. This operation is not shown.

The overall shape of the front end was checked with the header, as shown in Fig. 317, before the welding operation was started. Two steps in the welding operation are shown in Fig. 314 and Fig. 315. In Fig. 314, a welding clamp has been put on the edge, and the back of the inner panel flange is being preheated. The purpose of preheating is to reduce the time required to raise the temperature of the old weld button to welding heat. If heating is done from the outside, there will be a tendency

Fig. 314 Preheating the inner panel in preparation for braze rewelding of the old slot welds.

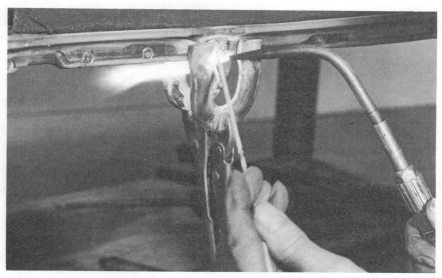

Fig. 315 Braze welding the old spot welds. Folded wet shop towel on top panel prevents heat distortion.

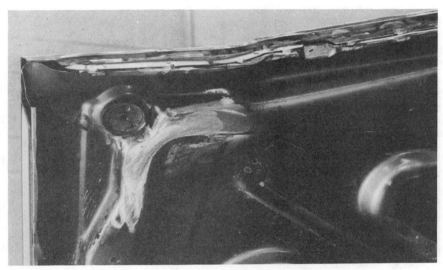

Fig. 316 View of inner panel buckle after straightening and finishing with body solder.

to overheat the edges while heating the weld button. The result will be an unsatisfactory weld, particularly if braze welding is to be used, as was done here.

The actual braze welding operation is shown in Fig. 315. The torch has been transferred to the front side, and metal from the flux coated brazing rod is being deposited on the surface.

The folded cloth lying on the front edge of the top panel is saturated with water. Its purpose is to prevent heat distortion by keeping the surface cool as the welding is done. If it is available, a paste made of ground asbestos and water will serve this purpose better. The wet cloth is satisfactory in most cases, particularly on a horizontal surface. If the work must be done on a vertical surface, it may be difficult to keep the cloth in place.

A view of the welded front edge and the finished surface of one buckle in the inner panel is shown in Fig. 316. The braze welds were ground smooth with a disc sander. The buckled surface was filled with body solder and ground. No attempt was made to finish the solder to a perfect surface because, being an inner panel, its appearance is secondary as compared to the outer panels.

A final check with the header panel is shown in Fig. 317. As stated previously, this check was made several times in straightening the upper panel and fitting the upper and inner panel together before the welding operation.

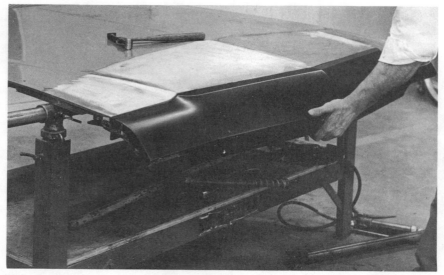

Fig. 317 Checking shape of front edge with new header panel.

The repaired hood, installed on an automobile and latched, is shown in Fig. 318. This is not the original automobile from which the hood was taken but is one of the same make and model. The repaired hood fits as well as the undamaged hood which was removed so that this one could be installed.

DOOR LOWER PANEL

The discussion of procedure for this damaged lower door panel, Fig. 319, has been retained from the first edition because it is a typical example of the day-to-day work which the metal man does. Although this is a relatively simple repair job, it is an excellent example of one which can be ruined by following the wrong procedure.

INSPECTION

An inspection of this panel reveals the following facts which should be considered in planning its repair procedure:

1. It is the result of a single impact by a small, rigid object which has been dragged along the surface for a distance of about 7 inches, leaving a typical gouge which is stretched severely.

2. The sharp gouge is the only severe condition in the damaged area. The sharp folds in the front and lower edges, where the panel has bent over the facing, and the partly formed rolled buckle above the molding are

Fig. 318 The straightened hood, fitted to an automobile.

Fig. 319 Door lower panel with a typical gouged dent.

not as severe as the gouge, but they prevent the broad, smooth dent from snapping back into place.

3. The wide gap in the space between the door edge and the fender indicates some bend in the facing. This also would tend to prevent the smooth dent from snapping back into place.

4. The two minor rolled buckles in the lower corner will be no problem, except that they are rough and will require some additional metal finishing.

5. The molding is perfectly straight; the panel has only pulled away from it.

REPAIR PLAN

The repair operations on this panel must be planned to take advantage of as much as possible of the snap-out tendency indicated by the smooth, hollow area. To do this, it will be necessary to relieve the bend in the front facing, the sharp ridges in the front and lower edges, and the rolled buckle above the molding. All of these conditions indicate the need for the use of tension, particularly the bend in the facing.

A typical condition found on almost all damaged door panels, on which the dented area extends to the edge, exists in the front and lower facing. The outer panel has been pushed in much farther at the instant of impact than it is now. The bends on the front and lower edges offered considerable resistance to the snap-out tendency of the panel at that instant and are still under a strain. This strain should be relieved before the application of tension so that there will be the least possible resistance to the lifting action.

This job can be done without removing the door from the body, or removing the trim panel from the door, a considerable saving in time. It should be possible to leave the molding in place because the metal under it shows no evidence of sharp bends. Because there won't be any disassembly, one of the drain holes in the lower edge will have to be enlarged to permit the entry of a pry tool. This hole should be closed after the job is finished.

Whether the panel is repaired on or off the body, the deep gouge still is in a position where it is difficult to reach for shrinking. Solder filling will make a satisfactory repair for this area after the large, smooth dent has been brought out to the proper level. There are no high spots to be worked down before solder can be used.

REPAIR OPERATIONS

The first step in repairing this door panel is shown in Fig. 320. A series of hammer blows along this sharp bend will straighten it partially and reduce the strain it exerts on the adjoining metal. The same operation will be repeated on the bend on the lower edge. It is difficult to catch

Fig. 320 First repair operation—relieving strain in the ridge along the edge.

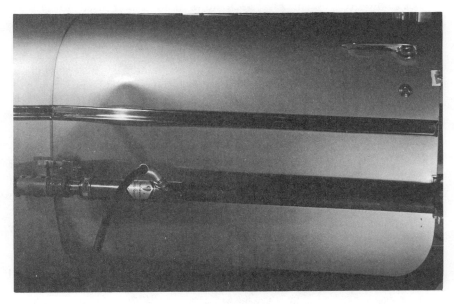

Fig. 321 Body jack, clamp, and tension plate setup used to pull out the dent without removing the door from the body.

the full effect of this operation in an illustration so it can only be described; it caused a definite lifting effect which extended at least 2 inches into the panel.

In working a ridge such as this it is important to start at its beginning, in this case at the upper end. This will have the maximum relief effect on the adjoining metal because it tends to reduce the damaged area. If the work had begun at the position of the hammer, each blow would have had more of a tendency to upset the metal in the sharp bend. Use of a dolly block to back up the outer edge would have been even more beneficial, but this could not be done unless the door were removed from the body.

The next step is shown in Fig. 321. The door is being held in a partly open position by a special clamp-on bracket. Tension is being applied by means of the jack, one clamp, and one tension plate. The tension plate had to be used because the door was not removed. This is no handicap, however, because the plate can be soldered in place almost as fast as the clamp can be installed. The plate and the clamp were positioned so that the line of maximum tension would be just above the deep gouge. In damage such as this, it is usually better not to apply tension directly over a long gouge. Tension lengthwise of a gouge will not have the proper lifting effect on the adjoining metal, because the stretched metal in the gouge creates a slack condition.

The close-up view in Fig. 322 shows the method used to prevent damage to the painted surface gripped by the clamp jaws. The arrow indicates a strip of light sheet metal, cut from an oil or food can, which was bent over the door edge before the clamp was attached. This will cushion the effect of the clamp jaws on the painted surface enough to prevent damage. These strips should not be used a second time, however, because the first use will leave an imprint of the rough jaws that will damage the paint.

Fig. 323 shows the key step in this tension application. The jack has been extended enough to place a strong lift effect on the surface but not enough to raise it all the way. Determining the exact amount of force to use was not difficult because it could be felt as an increase in the resistance of the jack handle; it also could be seen in the action of the panel as lifting stopped and the depressed area started to spread. This extra resistance is caused by the buckle above the molding. A few hammer blows spaced over the surface of the buckle, as shown in Fig. 323, caused the most of the depressed area to snap out without further extension of the jack. Note that the panel under the molding has snapped back all the way so that the fit is perfect.

There is a fine point in the procedure described here which should not be missed either by the beginner or the metal man seeking to improve his

Fig. 322 Close-up of the clamp attachment to the door flange. The arrow points to a piece of thin metal used to protect the paint.

Fig. 323 Relieving the buckle under the molding to permit the dent to snap out under tension.

technique. Telltale signs, such as the increased resistance and the spreading instead of lifting, indicate that the jack is pushing hard enough to lift the metal in the line of direct tension, but the resistance of the buckle above the molding prevents the lift. The solution is to relieve the resistance of the buckle; when this was done, the panel snapped into place. Pumping the jack further to attempt to pull the broad, hollow area up against this resistance will not accomplish the desired result. The buckle above the molding is too far from the direct line of tension to be affected directly by increased jack pressure.

The result of the tension application and the relief of the buckles is shown in Fig. 324. Before the tension was released, the hammer was used to relieve further the sharp bends on the front and lower edges. A small part of the buckle above the molding remains. The gouge and most of the buckles below it remain in the lower section.

The procedure to straighten the remaining part of the buckle above the molding is shown in Fig. 325. The pry rod being used is shown in Fig. 58. The curved end of this rod is longer than the distance from the inner to the outer panel of most doors. Thus, when the rod is twisted by turning the lever, the end of the rod will apply a lifting action to the panel. It is easy to maneuver the end of the rod to the underside of a low spot and turn the lever to raise it. The same care is required in using this tool as that taken with any other pry rod or a pick hammer.

This tool was inserted through one of the drain holes which was enlarged by driving a tapered punch through it. It is not good workmanship to leave this hole. It can be partly closed on most door panels, because it will be in a narrow offset between the weather strip and the outer panel. The edge of the metal can be driven back into place and sealer put in the hole. Most doors have three drain holes in each corner, so there should be no serious ill effects caused by sealing one of them.

In Fig. 326, the buckles below the gouge have been pried out, using a smaller pry rod, and the entire area gone over with the disc sander. In Fig. 327, the surface has been metal finished except in the gouged area. Note that above the molding it was not necessary to remove the paint close to the molding edge. In Fig. 328, the gouge has been solder filled. The gouge in the fender was filled at the same time. In Fig. 329, the solder has been metal finished and the area is ready for painting. In Fig. 330, the painting has been completed. The surface is perfectly smooth and the space between the door edge and the fender is uniform.

ROOF ALIGNMENT AND REPLACEMENT

The automobile shown in Fig. 331 has been damaged in the type of accident in which the driver loses control and rolls it over. It is quite probable that the cause of roll was either a sudden brake application or

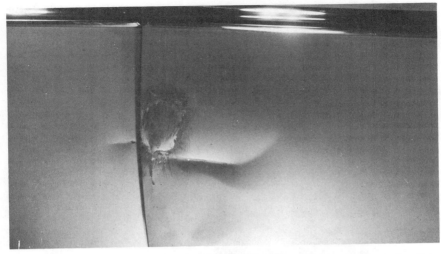

Fig. 324 All that remained of the dent after it popped out. Note the light buckle above the molding and the area surrounding the gouge.

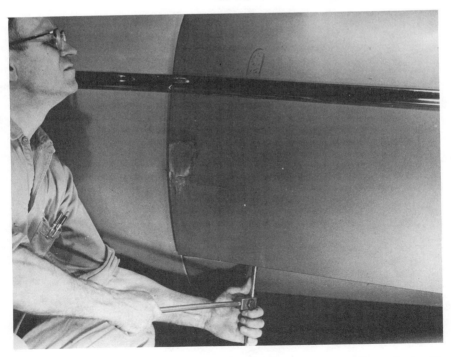

Fig. 325 Using the twist-type pry rod to raise the low metal above the molding. Crayon marks indicate the area being worked.

Fig. 326 The result of the first disc-sander operation.

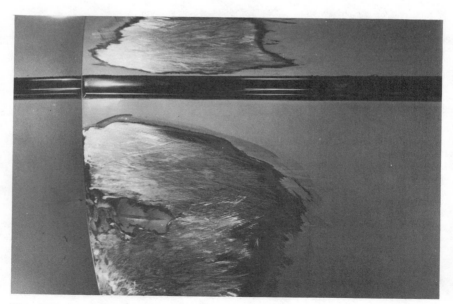

Fig. 327 Appearance of the dented area after it has been metal-finished except for the gouge.

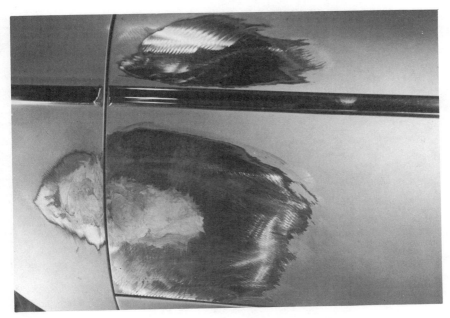

Fig. 328 Unfinished solder over the gouged area.

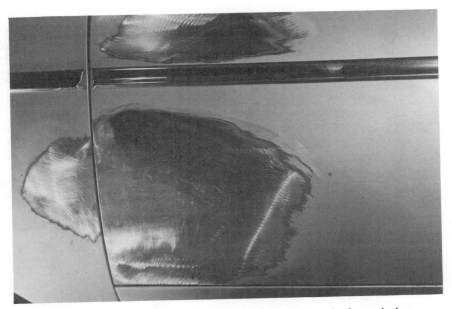

Fig. 329 The damaged area, metal-finished and ready for painting.

Fig. 330 The repainted panel.

Fig. 331 Roof and pillar damage caused by a roll-over type of accident.

a sharp turn. In either case, it was moving at a high speed; otherwise the force required to crush this roof and the pillars would not have been developed.

As with the door panel in the preceding section, this repair job has been retained from the original edition because the procedures would be essentially the same on current models having similar damage.

In selecting this damaged automobile for discussion, it was recognized that this is much more severe than the normal, day-to-day work of most body shops. This automobile had been judged a total loss and sold for salvage by the insurance company with which it was insured. It was rebuilt by a body shop operator who makes a practice of keeping such work in his shop to fill in during slack periods. This is one way that the small shop can level off the employment situation without losing hard-to-replace employees. It also provides a real test of skill, because such work naturally is much more difficult than lesser damage.

Because this is a severe damage, it offers many interesting problems to test the metal man's ingenuity. First, ways must be found to set up jacks to apply force where it is needed. As with all other jobs, it is the responsibility of the man who does the work to know what to do. This responsibility is much greater on a job such as this because mistakes can be more costly. Experience in doing work on very difficult jobs pays off, however, by increasing efficiency on the less severe damage.

A strong argument can be made for the replacement of all of the damaged pillars and roof rail assemblies instead of straightening them and only replacing the roof. Certainly, it could have been done. However, the cost of the parts would have been added to the total cost of the job; and, on a body which has been racked as badly as this one, there is no guarantee that new parts will solve all of the problems by falling into alignment without effort.

INSPECTION

An inspection of the damage on this automobile reveals the following facts which should be considered in planning the repair procedure:

1. At the time this automobile struck the ground it had turned almost over while traveling at relatively high speed. It continued in forward motion after striking the ground—note the straight, lengthwise scratches on the top of the roof. For some reason, which cannot be determined without knowing the history of the accident, the rolling action seems to have stopped when the roof struck.

2. Except for minor scratch damage below the side molding, the doors are in good condition. This scratch damage probably was caused by a glancing blow against some object after the driver lost control, but before the rolling action started.

3. The left side is not shown in any of the illustrations, but it was in a condition similar to the condition of the right. However, the damage also extended into the left front fender.

4. The angle of the impact caused the roof to turn to the left as the right pillars collapsed. The least movement was in the left rear pillar upper section. The upper section of the right pillar is lying almost flat. The upper section of the right front pillar is within 4 inches of the instrument panel and angled inward sharply by the side shift in the front end of the roof; the short radius curve in the upper end has been crushed flat. The upper section of the left upper pillar has been pushed to the left by the side shift, but otherwise seems to have held most of its shape. In effect, the two right pillars and the left front seem to have swung around the left rear as though it were a center point.

5. Of the roof members, headers, and roof rails, the windshield header has been damaged the worst. The center section has been driven down; the short radius bend in the right end has been mashed nearly flat, and the short radius bend in the left side has been pushed into a sharp peak.

6. The wide buckle in the center of the roof has pushed outward, making a sharp buckle in the right roof rail close to the dividing line between the front and rear door glasses.

7. Damage may be seen on the right, underside of the rear window header. This was caused by the roof crushing the rear window glass. It is probable that before the glass broke it carried enough force through to the lower edge to cause damage.

8. The alignment of the doors in the lower part of the openings is almost unaffected. Only minor adjustment on the hinges and lock strikers should be required to fit them after the strain on them from the upper section has been relieved.

REPAIR PLAN

Although this is a rather complicated job, it can be broken down into a series of steps which, when viewed separately, are not difficult. It is simply a matter of reversing the fold pattern so that the framework of pillars and roof rails will shift back into their original positions. When this has been accomplished, there should be no trouble in fitting a new roof panel to this framework.

The size of the job and, particularly, the number of sharp bends in the heavy metal of the pillars limits the amount that can be done in each step. The ideal situation would be to have some means of grasping the roof so that it could be lifted up and turned into position with one operation. Obviously, this would be impractical because of the equipment problem, but it can be done by taking it a little at a time.

The first step will be to start lifting the right side of the roof and reverse the twisting action. It was pointed out in the inspection that the left rear pillar has served as a pivot for the complete roof. To reverse the twisting action, the complete assembly must be pivoted back around the same point. At the right rear corner, the pillar will have to swing up and slightly outward, moving the roof to the right and rearward as it lifts. At the right front corner, the pillar will have to swing much more to the right as it swings rearward. At the left front pillar, most of the movement will be to the right, but it will have to be slightly rearward also. Although the roof is to be replaced, it will be much better to leave it in place while these operations are performed so that it can keep the various parts in the proper relationship.

All of the parts which make up the roof framework will have to be straightened individually after the general alignment has been restored as much as possible. Straightening the individual parts can be done better after the roof has been removed. This will permit access to all sides, making it much easier to do whatever is necessary to finish the job.

To remove the roof means breaking the spot welds which hold it. This is somewhat easy to do on the windshield and rear window headers, but rather difficult on both roof rails because on outward flange of the roof is spot welded electrically in the bottom of the narrow channel of the drip molding. The solution is to replace the drip moldings along with the roof panel.

It would be desirable to weld the new roof in place by electric resistance spot welding. However, such equipment was not available in the shop in which this work was done so welding was done by means of the oxyacetylene torch. In this case, braze welding will be used because it can be done with less heat distortion.

REPAIR OPERATIONS

The first jack setup is shown in Fig. 332. Note that the one on the front pillar is set at an angle so that it pushes the roof to the right as it lifts, and the one on the rear pillar is pushing to the rear and lifting. Heat has been used on the upper end of the front pillar because this area has been bent sharply. Both jacks in this view are under load; if released, the pillars would spring back a considerable distance from the positions they are now in.

A close-up view of the jack on the front pillar is shown in Fig. 333. A block of wood was used under the end of the jack to prevent crushing the inner surface of the windshield header; this is the better procedure here than to use a rubber flex head, because the block fits to the surface and spreads the load over a wider area. The torch flame is being used on the sharp kink at the base of the windshield opening to soften it so that it will straighten without breaking. The heat also reduces the load

Fig. 332 Two-jack setup used to raise the right pillars.

on the header, reducing the risk of collapsing the section which the jack is pushing against.

In the close-up view of the rear pillar (Fig. 334), the jack has been extended 2 or 3 inches from the position shown in Fig. 332. Heat is being applied to the base of this pillar section also. Note that the bending of the pillar has broken the welds between the flanges of the inner and outer panels. There is some torn metal in this area, and, unless heat is used, there will be more. Nothing is needed to protect the flange of the pillar where the jack bears against it, because the metal in this pillar is extra heavy to compensate for relatively small size.

The much more complicated setup shown in Fig. 335 was used to push the left side of the roof back, which meant tipping back the upper section of the left lock pillars. The upper horizontal jack, with the chain hook-up, is applying a bending force directly to the rear upper pillar. The lower horizontal jack is applying pressure against the lower end of the front upper pillar. In operation, as the upper jack is extended, it pulls the roof rail with it. As the roof rail moves, it strains the joints at the upper and lower ends of both the front and rear pillars; as these joints bend, the pillar assumes a more nearly vertical position.

The lower jack in this setup is needed to add rigidity to the front hinge pillar. Without it, rearward movement would tend to spring the entire cowl side and pillar back, instead of concentrating the bending action in the lower end of the upper pillar. Unless this pillar were reinforced in

Fig. 333 Heating the right front pillar to aid straightening.

Fig. 334 Heating the right rear pillar to aid straightening.

Fig. 335 Jack and chain sling hookup used to shift the left roof rail rearward. The rear end of the lower jack bears against the kickup section of the floor.

some manner, it would be practically impossible to bend it enough to permit the roof to stay back where it should be.

The light-duty jack standing upright under the end of the upper horizontal jack is serving as a prop. A stick of wood or any other object stiff enough to bear the load would serve as well. However, if available, a jack serves this purpose ideally because it is a prop which can be adjusted under load.

This hookup frequently is called a *chain sling*. Making a chain sling hookup requires a little time, but, where it is needed the time is well justified. The secret of using force properly to straighten a body is to apply exactly the right amount where it is needed. In this instance it was necessary to concentrate force on the upper and lower ends of both pillars. Without this hookup, the alternative would be to place jacks at an angle across the door openings. Where only a minor movement of the pillar is needed, the angle jack may be satisfactory. The downward thrust of the angle jack may push the door opening out of alignment without accomplishing the necessary effect in the upper section. In attempting to correct a condition in another area, there is nothing whatever to be gained by straining an undamaged area of the body enough to cause misalignment.

Two operations in the removal of the roof panel are shown in Figs. 336 and 337. In Fig. 336, a special spot weld cutter driven by a light-duty

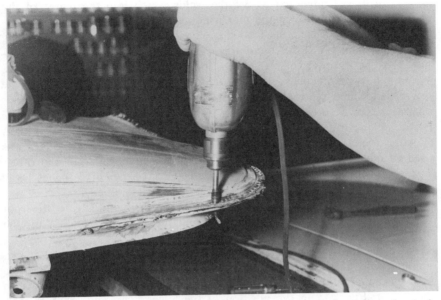

Fig. 336 Using a hole saw-type spot weld cutter to separate the roof panel from the rear header.

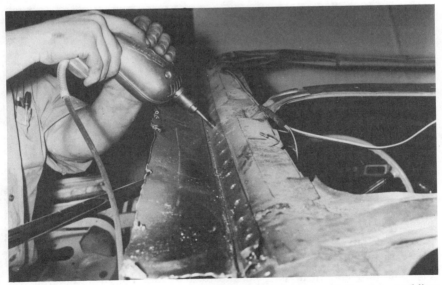

Fig. 337 Using a hole saw-type spot weld cutter to separate the drip molding and a section of the roof panel from the roof rail.

electric drill, is being used to cut the welds which join the flange of the roof panel to the flange of the rear window header. This tool is a miniature hole saw with a spring-loaded, pointed pilot. It operates by cutting a ⁵⁄₁₆-inch diameter slot around the weld; the depth of cut may be adjusted to go through one thickness only or through both thicknesses. When only one thickness is cut, the center of the weld is left on the lower panel in the form of a button about ³⁄₁₆ inch in diameter. In this operation, the weld buttons were left in place and ground off later because it was not desirable to weaken this narrow flange by cutting holes in it.

After the welds on both headers were cut, an air-driven chisel was used to cut along both sides of the roof from one header to the other. To avoid damage to the roof rail, this cut was kept about 5 inches away from the drip molding. The strip of roof panel left along the edges was then bent out to reveal the welds holding the drip molding to the roof rail. The inside of this strip of metal and the cutting operation on the drip molding welds are shown in Fig. 337.

After the roof was removed, the hookup shown in Fig. 338 was made. The purpose of this hookup was the same as that of the similar one used on the left side of the automobile, Fig. 335. This hookup differs from the one in Fig. 335 in the position of the lower jack, and the fact that, the roof having been removed, there is less resistance to movement offered by the rail and the pillars. Note that the lower jack is bearing di-

Fig. 338 Jack and chain sling hookup used to shift the right roof rail rearward. The lower jack bears against the clamp instead of the kickup section of the floor as in Fig. 335.

rectly on the clamp used to connect the chain to the inner quarter panel. This arrangement transfers part of the thrust of the upper jack to the lower one. The desirable feature of this is that the effect of both jacks is horizontal. Also, there is no tendency to strain the door openings and cause misalignment. Using a single jack diagonally across the upper part of this door opening could spoil the door fit by lifting pillars and still not accomplish the desired result in the upper section.

On a hookup such as this, careful operation of the jacks is necessary. The lower jack serves only as a prop, but the load on it increases as the upper jack is extended. As the load increases, the lower jack should be extended enough to make up for deflections in the rubber flex head and the metal parts which it is supporting. The movement of the roof is controlled by the upper jack. If both jacks are operated properly, it is possible to bend these pillars to hold the roof rail in any fore-and-aft position required. In this case, about a ¾-inch movement was needed. This was obtained by pushing the rail well past the point of alignment and applying heat at the upper and lower ends of both the front and the rear pillars. Without the use of heat, far more force would have been needed than desirable to gain that much movement. This could mean that the pillars would have to be pushed so far past the point of correction, to allow for spring back, that other damage would be done.

Until the windshield opening had been fitted, the exact amount to move the roof rail (Fig. 338) could not be determined. For that reason, the alignment was figured out as closely as possible by checking the door fit in the openings, the work on the roof rail was stopped, and work was started on the windshield opening. The tension plate on the roof rail and the tab brazed on the upper inner quarter panel were left in place so that if the roof rail needed to be moved further, the jack could be set up quickly.

The first operation on the windshield header is shown in Fig. 339. This hookup is quite similar to that in Fig. 338 in that the jack is anchored in a horizontal position by means of chain and a prop. It was not necessary here to brace the right lower pillar because it is quite rigid.

Careful selection of the point of attachment for the clamp is important. It was attached quite close to the right side to take advantage of the tendency to reshape the ends. Tension, which will follow the clamp from any point on the header, will help to reduce the high peak in the left end. Pressure, which will push ahead of the clamp, will increase the curvature in the flattened section at the right end. This hookup pushed the pillars back into position but it did not reshape the corners of the windshield completely. However, it has improved them so that they can be reshaped easily with simple hookups.

Heat is shown being used in the illustration. It was not applied, how-

Fig. 339 Using a jack and chain sling hookup to shift the windshield header to the right and partially reshape the outer end.

ever, until the assembly had been shifted as far to the right as it could without it. This assembly is naturally springy and is often difficult to force into a new position. The right pillar was not heated to full red temperature, and no heat at all was applied to the left pillar.

After the pillars had been set as nearly as could be to the right position, the setups shown in Figs. 340 and 341 were made. In Fig. 340, a variation of the chain sling is being used to finish raising the flattened right corner. By using the clamp and chain, the lifting effect is limited to the upper part of the pillar. This is a much better procedure than simply using the jack from the floor because it avoids lifting the upper part of the pillar away from the lower. The length of chain which extended to the left is hooked around the lower end of the left upper piller. There is no risk of damaging the left pillar, however, because the angle of the chain is such that most of the strain is on the right side.

The right side was done first because this lift tended to shorten the header as the corner was raised. Because of the flattened condition, the header was too long at the start. The logic of first reducing the excess length before straightening the left side, which would tend to increase it more, should be obvious.

Fig. 341 shows the operation of reducing the peak on the left end of the header by using tension across the inside of a bend to straighten it. The left end of the jack is bearing directly on the flanged inner edge of

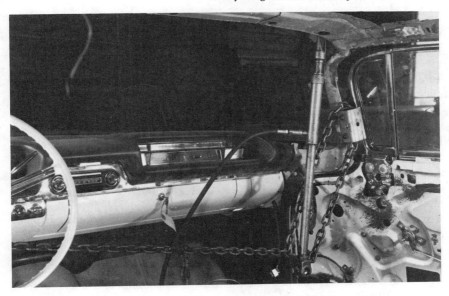

Fig. 340 Using a jack and chain sling hookup to finish reshaping the right end of the windshield header. The end of the chain extending to the left is hooked to the left pillar.

Fig. 341 A jack setup to pull a bend out of the left end of the windshield header.

the door opening; the metal in this flange is heavy and needs no reinforcement. Note that a chisel has been placed between the right end of the jack and the clamp on the header flange. The purpose is to fill the angular space between the clamp and the end of the jack so that the force application will be as close to the flange as possible. Otherwise, the clamp would tend to twist and damage the flange.

Heat was necessary in the inside of the bend because this metal is heavier than the metal in the header where the clamp is attached. Unless the heavy metal was weakened, it would have been difficult to release the buckle on the inside without causing severe damage to the header.

The three setups shown in Fig. 339-341 could have been used at the same time. If the damage had been more severe, it would have been worthwhile to do so. However, three jack setups in one windshield opening create a complicated problem because of interference. Always avoid such problems when you can.

The setup shown in Fig. 342 was used to straighten the buckle in the right roof rail. This was pointed out in the inspection and may be seen in Fig. 339. It is a short kink at the end of the center roof bow, caused by the outward thrust as the roof and bow were flattened on impact.

The procedure on this was first to extend the jack enough to start inward movement, apply heat to the buckles on the inner roof rail panel, and then use a hammer and block of wood to aid the final inward movement of the rail. A buckle such as this in a strong member is too stiff

Fig. 342 Jack and tension plate setup used to straighten the right roof rail.

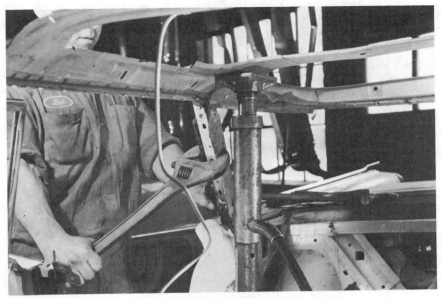

Fig. 343 Jack setup used to lift and twist the roof rail as the metal man twists the upper section of the pillar with the wrench.

to pull out cold, because it offers more resistance than the strength of the metal which pulls against it. If it is heated enough, it could be pulled out with tension alone. However, by heating just enough so that it can be helped into place by reasonable use of a heavy hammer, the same result can be accomplished without overheating to the point of losing strength.

The position of the tension plates should be noted in this setup. They were set quite widely apart because it was planned to use both heat and hammer blows to straighten the buckle. If for some reason it would not be feasible to use the hammer, it would be much better to set the plates much closer together to increase the leverage angle. In this case, however, they were set far enough apart to be on sections of the rail that would not move as it straightened. If they were close together on sections of the rail that would move inward as it straightened, the inertia of the jack would resist the hammer blows; there would be a tendency to flatten the box section of the rail, instead of straightening it.

Two operations are shown in Fig. 343. The action with the large adjustable wrench should be self-explanatory. Note that a flat spoon was used under the outer wrench jaw to avoid damage to the surface as the pillar was twisted. The metal in this pillar is quite heavy, however, and it is probable that the spoon did not need to be used.

The purpose of the jack in Fig. 343 is to lift the roof bow by twisting the roof rail. From the appearance of the roof in the original view, Fig. 331, it is quite obvious that this section has struck the ground quite hard; a flattened section such as this could not be seen in making the original inspection, but such damage should be expected.

There are two problems with this roof bow, both caused by the flattened roof rail. The inner edge of the roof rail is pushed down, carrying the bow away from contact with the roof panel, and is pushed inward, causing the bow to rise too high. To relieve both of these conditions completely would have required cutting the roof rail open so that force could be used to reshape it. However, the flattened condition was not severe enough to justify this procedure. Instead, the inner edge was raised as shown, the right end of the bow was cut loose from the top of the rail, shifted outward enough to allow the raised center to drop into position, then tack welded. The final welding was postponed until the roof panel had been tried in position so that the fit of the bow to it could be checked.

Fig. 344 may be difficult to understand at a glance because the view is looking up under the rear window header. This shows the crushed lower surface, caused by the impact on the roof which drove the header against the upper edge of the rear window. Before the glass broke, it carried the impact force through to the lower edge of the opening, causing the damage shown being corrected in Fig. 346.

Fig. 344 View, looking upward, of the underside of the rear window header on the right side.

Fig. 345 Section cut out of the rear window header.

Fig. 346 Jack, length of jack tubing, and clamp setup used to lift rear window flange.

The method used to straighten the rear header is shown in Fig. 345. Cutting this piece out of the upper side of the header permitted a caulking iron to be used on the inside of the sharp ridge. Careful use of the caulking iron was all that was needed to drive this ridge back into shape so that no metal finishing was required except to solder fill over the re-welded joint. The piece cut out of the upper side was replaced by straightening the edges and rewelding. The top of this header is completely hidden, and the only requirement is that its full strength be restored.

The setup used to lift the crushed lower side of the opening is shown in Fig. 346. This is an awkward spot to lift because the roof structure above does not provide a rigid point from which to pull. However, the jack and lever setup shown here worked very satisfactorily. The lever is made up of two 30-inch lengths and one 10-inch length of body jack tubes. Note that it was held on the left side of the body (the right side of the illustration) by inserting it through a hole in the inner quarter panel. The position of the jack on the right side provides sufficient leverage to lift the flanged section of the opening without the risk of damage to the left quarter inner panel.

Note in this view that the metal tab which was brazed to the inner quarter panel has been left in place. If it is found necessary to shift the roof further when fitting the windshield and back window glass, this tab may be needed.

The final check on the accuracy of the preceding alignment operations is in the fit of the windshield and rear window openings to the glasses. Both are important, but the windshield is the more critical because the least misalignment will cause the glass to crack. The tempered glass used in back windows will withstand strain better than the laminated glass used in windshields; however, it also will break if not fitted properly.

If possible, the final checking should be done with the new glass which is to be installed in the opening after the job is completed. To save handling and reduce the risk of breaking a high-priced glass, it is good practice to do the checking between operations with a glass which has been cracked or stone pitted. Thus, the new glass will be used only when the opening is close to the proper shape. Using the new glass itself for this final check will eliminate the possibility of fitting the opening to a glass slightly different in shape from the one to be installed.

The opening should be checked by setting the glass on "L" shaped spacer blocks, as shown in Figs. 347 and 348. These particular blocks are short lengths of bar solder which have been hammered to the proper thickness, found in manufacturer's shop manual, and bent to shape. The arrows indicate the position of two blocks on the lower edge and

Fig. 347 Windshield glass set in opening on spacer blocks to check alignment. The three arrows indicate the position of the blocks made of bent solder.

Fig. 348 Homemade spacer blocks.

Fig. 349 Using a pull jack to pull down the rear window header.

Fig. 350 Replacing the left drip molding.

one on the header. Three more blocks were placed in similar positions on the opposite side of the opening.

A close-up view of four of these blocks used to support the glass is shown in Fig. 348. These blocks support the windshield to allow for the thickness of the rubber weather strip when checking an opening. When the opening is aligned properly, the space between the flange of the opening and the side of the glass should be uniform, and the space between the edge of the glass and the base of the opening should be at least the thickness of the spacer. Extra space between the edge of the glass anr the base of the opening can be tolerated better than either too little or too much space between the flange and the side of the glass. The checking procedure for the rear window opening is similar to that for the windshield.

A setup used to lower the rear end of the header is shown in Fig. 349. This was found to be too high when the opening was checked with the glass in place; note that one spacer block is still in place in the lower front corner of the opening. The distance between the edge of the header and the shelf panel was measured, then the pull jack was used to pull it down the required amount. Heat was used in the upper, inner corners of the opening to soften the metal and prevent some of the spring back.

Roof Panel Replacement

The first step in replacing this roof panel was to replace the drip moldings, the original ones having been removed with the damaged roof panel. They must be placed in the proper alignment and welded to the roof rail. The alignment should be checked closely, because, even through the roof rail has been straightened, it can vary slightly from its original shape.

Fig. 350 shows some of the spots which were welded with steel filler rod. Earlier, light tack welds were made in the center of the molding and at both ends, then the roof panel was set in place to check fit. The same was done on the opposite side. The panel then was pushed back into the position shown to permit the welding operations to be finished.

The moldings were prepared for welding by drilling ¼-inch holes about 3 inches apart, as can be seen in the illustration. The purpose of the hole is to permit the flame to reach through to the metal below and start a puddle quickly; filler rod added to the puddle will fill the hole and make a weld spot joining the drip molding to the roof rail.

It would have been desirable to have made twice as many welds of this type, except for the problem of heat distortion. At 3 inches apart, there will be some overlap of the drawing effect of adjoining welds; at 1½ inches, this overlap would be much greater. The additional draw could pull the rail out of alignment enough to cause trouble. As an alternative, short tack welds are made along the inner edge of the drip molding halfway between each spot. These welds caused some heat distortion also, but it was less than if all of them had been placed in a straight line. The finished welding job is shown in Fig. 351.

The skip method of placing these welds was followed (see Fig. 350). By allowing the last weld made to cool while another is made at some distance away on cool metal, it is possible to prevent excessive heating of the roof rail. To have started at one end and worked progressively down the line to the other probably would have caused serious misalignment.

Use of the electric arc-spot welding gun, shown in Chapter 5, Fig. 147, would have simplified this job considerably. Only a fraction of the time would have been required, and the problem of heat distortion would have been almost completely absent. However, as this operation shows, this job can be done with the torch if the proper procedure is followed.

The replacement of the roof panel was done by braze welding spots in "V" notches along the edges of the flanges (Fig. 352). When done properly, brazing provides a strong joint and causes less heat distortion than fusion welding with a steel filler rod. The secret of the strength of the weld lies in making the brazing material flow along the joint by capillary action.

Before clamping the roof in place to be welded, the "V" notches were cut and the contacting surfaces of the roof flange and the inside of the drip molding were cleaned to remove any material which might prevent the flow of brazing metal. Powdered brazing flux also was sprinkled in the

Fig. 351 The drip molding after welding. Note the spacing of the welds.

Fig. 352 Roof flanges notched to simplify braze welding.

molding. These two operations ensured that the melted brazing metal would flow as far as the surfaces were heated sufficiently to keep it melted.

The brazing operations are shown in Fig. 353 and 354. In Fig. 353, the torch flame is being used to heat the lower side of the drip molding. In this operation, the flame should be played back and forth as far as the jaws of the welding clamp permit. The purpose is to preheat the molding so that it will not chill and set up the melted bronze. Note that the filler rod is being held in readiness for use. In Fig. 354, the torch has been shifted to the inside of the drip molding, at one of the "V" notches, and filler rod is being added. When these two operations are performed correctly, the filler rod will flow into the joint as it is added; the flow stops when the preheated drip molding cools enough to set up the bronze.

A low melting point, flux-coated brazing rod was used in this operation because it will cause less heat distortion than the higher temperature material. Other precautions taken to reduce heat distortion were skip welding and the use of the wet shop towel. On a joint as long as this, it is possible to skip back and forth enough to avoid making any weld close to another one still hot. The shop towel serves as an excellent protector for the roof panel. It should be quite wet, but not so that water will run out of it onto the weld.

Asbestos, either sheet or powdered, may be used in place of the shop towel, but neither will do any better job of protecting the metal. As the

Fig. 353 Preheating the underside of the drip molding.

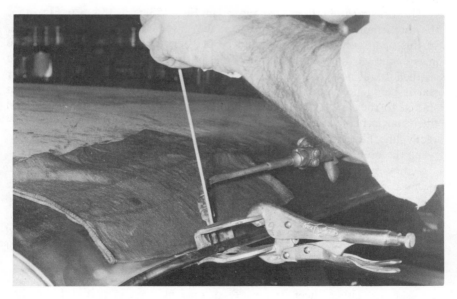

Fig. 354 Braze welding the roof to the drip molding at one of the notches in the flange. The wet shop towel reduces heat distortion.

water is driven out of the shop towel by the heat, additional water will run down into the heated area, because the coarse weave of the fabric permits it. As the water is driven out of the asbestos, however, it stays dry because the closely packed fibers do not permit nearly as much free flow.

The welding operation shown here was performed with a single torch. A better joint with even less heat distortion can be made if two torches and two operators are available. With two operators, one preheats the underside, and the other stands ready to make the brazed joint when the temperature is right. The preheating torch can be kept on the molding as the filler metal is added. This will help in spreading the molten metal farther from the "V."

Welding this seam with an electric resistance spot welder would be simple. With tongs and welding tips shaped to fit into the molding properly, one side could be welded in the same time required to make a few of the welds in the manner shown. However, when only the torch is available, the job can be done without too great difficulty.

It was necessary to metal-finish the area of the roof adjoining the roof rail because of slight heat distortion, particularly in the drip molding. The start of this operation is shown in Fig. 355. The bent spoon lying on the roof was used to pry out low places in the roof panel. The special drip molding pliers, lying under the end of the spoon, were used to work heat buckles out of the drip molding. About a half hour was required to metal-finish this side.

Fig. 355 Metal-finishing the edge of the roof and the drip molding.

Fig. 356 Final check of the windshield glass in the opening.

Fig. 356 shows the windshield glass resting on the spacer blocks in the opening after the automobile has been repainted. The position of the glass was adjusted so that it was exactly centered, and then it was marked with the strips of tape shown on the upper edge of the glass and the front end of the roof. To obtain proper alignment, a single piece of tape was stretched across the edge of the roof and the glass, and a piece torn out of its across the opening. The use of tape strips in this manner simplifies the task of centering the glass in the opening after the rubber weather strip has been installed. Now only the glasses, trim parts, and the moldings need to be replaced and the job is complete.

FRAME REPAIR

An automobile having front end frame damage is shown in Fig. 357. Although partially disassembled, it is obvious that this automobile has suffered severe collision damage on the right front corner. A photograph taken before any disassembly had been started would have shown how the impact object had driven back the end of the bumper and applied considerable force against the front wheel. This view is actually a reconstruction, made by setting the front end assembly back on the frame after it had been straightened. The bumper could not be put back on because the brackets were bent too badly. Even though it is only a reconstruction, the photograph does provide considerable information about the na-

Fig. 357 Reconstructed view of automobile having front end frame damage. Front end sheet metal was replaced after frame was straightened.

ture of the accident in which the automobile was damaged. After seeing this view, it is not surprising to find the frame damage shown in the following photographs.

This frame straightening job has been included in this chapter because it is the type of damage which any experienced metal repair man should be able to handle with portable equipment. The repair man may feel that such jobs are too difficult to attempt. As he gains experience with them, he will find them no more difficult than severe body damage. The body repair man starting to do frame straightening should gain some experience on smaller jobs before attempting one as severe as this one.

This is typical front end damage on a perimeter type frame. This is the type of frame in which the side rails under the passenger compartment are set out to the full width of the rocker panels. This construction permits the floor pans of the body to be dropped between the frame rails and a consequent lowering of the overall height requirements of the body. It has the disadvantage of requiring sharp outward bends in the side rails just forward of the cowl. These bends are required to accommodate the narrow width of the frame, between the front wheels, to the wider section under the body. They must be fairly sharp because clearance must be provided for the front wheels to turn. These bends can be expected to collapse under a hard front end impact in the manner shown in Figs. 358, 359 and 360. The repair problems which result will be quite similar to the ones explained and discussed on this job.

INSPECTION

Inspection of this damage reveals the following information which is essential to planning the repair procedure:

1. The impact object has approached the front of the automobile from an angle to the left. Or, it may have been that the automobile approached the impact object. In either case, the impact has been with a relatively small and rigid object. It has driven the bumper end back, torn the front end of the fender outward, and caught the front wheel, blowing the tire. (The tire and wheel were not available to photograph.) Thus, the front end of the frame horn has been subjected to direct impact. This primary impact was followed by a twisting action on the frame cross member, transmitted from the wheel through the control arms. Most of the force would be transmitted through the lower control arm because the impact was low and the spindle is much closer to the lower arm than the upper.

2. The position of the three major frame buckles is indicated by arrows on the photograph in Fig. 358.

Fig. 358 View of front of right side rail. Arrows indicate sharp buckles.

Fig. 359 Front view of damage. Lines parallel to side rails at cross member show the extent of the misalignment.

Fig. 360 Close-up view of buckle back of cross member and the buckled flange under the cowl hinge pillar.

On the right, arrows at the upper and lower edge indicate a sharp buckle at the base of the horn. In the center, two more arrows indicate a much more severe buckle just to the rear of the front cross member. On the left, another arrow indicates a buckle in the center side rail under the body hinge pillar.

3. Lines parallel to the side members have been placed on the photograph in Fig. 359. These lines extend back far enough to show the alignment of the front section of the frame to the body. Similar lines placed on a photograph of an undamaged automobile should interesect the cowl at points which are the same distance inboard from the outside edge on the right and left sides. These lines fall far to the left of where they should be, indicating that this section of the frame twisted to the right as it was driven back.

4. The severity of the buckle in back of the front cross member can be seen in more detail in Fig. 360. Before being damaged, this surface was smooth above and below the oblong hole. Now it has a sharp crease where the side of the rail has collapsed under the backward movement of the front section. The buckle under the cowl section is the result of the swinging movement of the section of the frame between it and the front cross member.

5. There are no obvious bends in the front cross member, but it has been twisted severely as the side rail collapsed. Another condition not shown clearly in any of the photographs is that the left side rail has been pulled to the right. A small buckle in the left side rail under the cowl bears out this conclusion. This side shift can be also seen in Fig. 359.

6. It should be obvious that a measurement taken from a reference point under the body to the front cross member would be much shorter on the right than on the left.

7. The center section may be diamonded, meaning that the right side rail has been driven back in relation to the left. But, it is difficult to determine this accurately because the reference points under the cowl have been shifted sideways as the right rail collapsed. This will have to be determined after the general shape has been restored, so that accurate measurements can be made.

REPAIR PLAN

The question of a probable diamonded condition in the center section complicates the repair plan slightly. A hookup could be made which would tend to relieve this condition, while relieving the main buckle back of the cross member. The problem would be in determining exactly when the diamonded condition was relieved. It was felt that in this case it would be better procedure to straighten the side rail first, then make an accurate check for diamonding, and make a hookup to correct it if it was bad enough to make it necessary.

The first hookup will be to pull the right side rail back to length and relieve as much twist in the front cross member as possible. The first pull will be made on the outer end of the lower control arm. This will have the most effect on the buckle back of the cross member and have a strong lever effect on the twist in the front cross member. There is considerable extra mechanical advantage in pulling on the control arms as compared to a pull on the end of the frame horn.

A second pull on the end of the frame horn will be needed if only to relieve the buckle at its base. It may be needed also to restore final length, depending on the results obtained from the first pull.

Heat will be needed on the buckle in back of the cross member and at the base of the horn. No heat will be needed on the buckle under the cowl. It is a simple flange which can be driven back into place with a few hammer blows as the side rail moves back to shape.

The off-center and twisted condition of the front end of this frame is too severe to expect to restore alignment with a single lengthwise hookup. Two additional hooks, and possibly a third, may be needed. The first two would take the twist out of the cross member and restore center-line alignment. The third would remove the diamonded condition which will probably be found in the final checking.

It is quite probable that some of these hookups will have to be repeated because the results obtained with one will affect the other. The time lost in repeating an operation may be far less than the time and damage involved in undoing the effect of carrying a hookup too far.

A job of this nature must be recognized as having many variables. After the most careful planning of procedure, progress must be watched carefully to be sure that the results obtained are those desired. If not, the procedure must be changed before serious damage is done. This is simply a matter of sighting and measuring the frame as the work progresses and making the changes dictated by good judgment.

Repair Procedure

A view of the first hookup is shown in Fig. 361. Two light chains have been used to anchor the machine at the rear end. One light chain has been wrapped twice around the box frame member and hooked to form as tight a double loop as possible. Then, another light chain has been double looped through the first and the clevis on the upright anchor bar on the frame machine. At the point chosen for this hookup, the frame member increases in size so that the chain can hold without slipping. This makes a satisfactory hookup, but a special clamp, made for the purpose, could have been used. The clamp would have been attached

Fig. 361 The first hookup. The machine is pulling on the end of the lower control arm and anchored to a chain double wrapped around the frame at the rear end of the center section.

to the lower flange of the side rail, just forward of the position of the chain.

The front end of the machine has been hooked to the outer end of the lower control arm by means of a long chain. This control arm will later be replaced because it has been damaged. It is serving as an ideal lever for this operation, however. (There are many cases in which a control arm has been torn off where it will pay to bolt an old one to the cross member to make an important pull and then take it off again.)

A closeup of the application of heat to the buckle in back of the cross member is shown in Fig. 362. This picture was taken when the pull was about one half completed. Note that some of the top of the buckle has started to roll out. A cluster type torch tip is being used for this operation. Instead of a single orifice, this tip has ten arranged in a cluster. This type of tip is very effective for any heavy heating job, much more so than an extra large tip having a single orifice.

No heat was applied to the buckle under the hinge pillar. This being

Fig. 362 Heating the buckle back of the cross member while tension is applied to pull the frame back to shape.

a simple flange buckle, it will only require a few hammer blows after the frame has been pulled into shape.

In Fig. 363, the connection has been changed to the end of the frame horn and the pull continued. Checking to determine the exact length was done as shown in Fig. 366. The centerline gauges were used also as shown in Fig. 371. The in-between checking steps are not shown, for they would be essentially the same, except that the front centerline gauge would not be in alignment.

After the overall length was established, the right side rail still angled downward when compared to the left. This indicated that considerable twist still remained in the cross member. A close-up of part of the hookup used to relieve the twist is shown in Fig. 364. A chain, partly hidden by the hub and drum assembly, has been passed over the side rail and through the eye bolt to tie the frame to the beam. The jack, just forward of the drum assembly, is lifting against the side member to twist the cross member. The rest of the hookup, not showing, is simply a block between the frame and the beam to stop downward motion.

Fig. 363 The hook-up to the end of the frame horm. The rear anchor connection is unchanged.

Fig. 364 Twist setup on the front cross member. Tie down chain, partially hidden by brake drum, is wrapped over frame and through eye bolt. The jack is lifting just forward of the cross member. A block between the frame and the beam is too far back to show in the picture.

Heat was applied to the underside of the cross member as it was twisted. The area shown being heated in Fig. 364 is roughly rectangular in shape. Some heat was applied to each of the four corners. The result was checked with the centerline gauges, as shown in Fig. 371.

Extreme care is essential in an operation such as this. The problem stems from the need to allow for spring-back after the jack has been released. Forcing the cross member far enough to remove all of the twist, without using excessive heat, would have damaged the already straightened right side rail. Using more heat would eliminate the spring-back, but the question is where to apply it. Unlike the side rail, which was buckled sharply, the cross member is twisted. The effect of the twist extended over its full length and, probably, into the left side rail. It was felt that safer procedure would be to reduce the twisted condition about only one half and change to the hookup to restore final centerline alignment.

The side shift hookup, to restore centerline, is shown in Fig. 365. This is frequently referred to as a "bow and arrow" because of the similarity to a drawn bow. As shown here, pressure is being applied to the left side

Fig. 365 Bow-and-arrow hook used to shift front end to left.

rail just to the rear of the cross member. This position was selected because the off-center condition of the rear lower control arm pivot bolts
was much less serious than that of the front ones. This was determined
by hanging the front centerline gauge on each pair of pivot bolts and
sighting the alignment with the other two gauges installed in the frame
center section.

This hookup is a no-heat operation. There are two reasons for not
using heat. One is that the problem is a slight bend condition which extends over a long section instead of a collapse in a small section, as was
the case on the right rail. Heating will concentrate the yield in a relatively small section because it is neither practical nor desirable to heat
long sections.

The other reason for not using heat on this hookup has to do with the
angle of the chain. This angle subjects the frame to a compressive force
between the two points to which the chain is attached. Heat applied at
any point could cause a collapse in the side rail.

This would not be true if it was possible to set up the machine so that
the force would be applied from separate points so that the chains would
be parallel. This is one of the disadvantages of the portable frame ma-

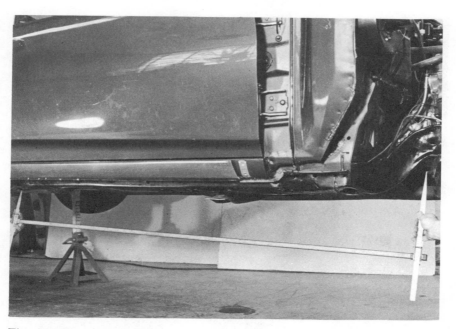

Fig. 366 Use of the tram to measure the distance from pivot bolt on lower
control arm to pivot bolt on rear axle trailing link. This was compared to length
on opposite side. Similar tram checks were made to other points.

chine, as compared to the conventional, drive-on type. The portable machine works at a mechanical disadvantage for this type of hookup. Only a part of the force exerted by the machine acts to pull the frame sideways. The rest of the force resolves into the lengthwise compressive force which can cause damage, sometimes even when heat is not used. Whenever this type of hookup is used, the machine should be extended as far as possible from the frame so that the chain angle is as small as possible.

The result of the bow and arrow hookup was checked with both the tram and the centerline gauges. A tram check for length between the pivot bolts on the front control arm and the rear axle trailing link is shown in Fig. 366. The final centerline check is shown in Fig. 371; several centerline checks were needed as the frame approached its proper shape. The side-to-side comparison for length between the pivot points was within tolerance, but the "X" check between the same points was not, indicating a diamonded condition.

Two views of the hookup to correct the diamonded condition are shown in Figs. 367 and 368. Referring to Fig. 367, the machine was

Fig. 367 Right side view of hookup to correct diamonded condition. Machine is anchored by chain running diagonally to front corner of center section of frame. The pull chain is wrapped around the frame at the right front corner of the center section.

Fig. 368 Left side view, under center section, of the anchor hookup. Light jack, placed diagonally at rear end, is to prevent machine from tipping under the automobile.

placed on the right side of the automobile. The pull chain was passed through the front suspension and double wrapped around the frame close to the front body bolt. The heavy construction and in-swinging shape of the frame at this point make this a logical place from which to pull.

The machine was anchored by a chain running diagonally across to the opposite front body bolt area. The upright bar on the anchor end of the machine bears against the outside of the side rail but is free to move fore and aft. Some of the details of the anchor hookup are shown better in Fig. 368. The anchor chain was hooked to a toggle type chain tightener which, in turn, was connected to the corner of the frame by a double wrapped light chain. Use of the chain tightener made it possible to take the slack out of the hookup before starting to extend the jack.

The light-duty jack, extending from the rear end of the machine to the left side rail, was to prevent the machine from tipping under the automobile as force was applied. The tipping action is caused by the necessity of attaching the anchor chain to the machine below the level of the right side rail. The light jack is simply an adjustable prop to prevent the lower end of the anchor from moving to the left.

Extending the machine with this hookup will tend to move the right rail forward in relation to the left rail, relieving the diamonded condition. There will also be a tendency to cause the left rail to move inward at the point of attachment of the anchor chain. This condition was relieved by the hookup shown in Fig. 369. For this hookup, the pullchain was double wrapped around the right side rail at the front cross member. Unfortunately, this view does not show the details of the connection to the anchor end of the machine. The chain and a clevis can be seen in this view. The clevis is connected to the homemade bracket shown in Fig. 370. This bracket, which is actually a hook with a large bearing surface, was hooked into a large hole in the lower surface of the frame corner. A chain could have been used instead by tying it around the frame.

This last hookup restored all but the frame horns to usable tolerances of length, diagonals, and centerline. A jack set up to restore proper width between frame horns is shown in Fig. 372. Note that heat is being applied at the base of the left horn. To check this, the front centerline gauge was moved from the position shown in Fig. 372 to the end of the horns. The horns were jacked apart until the distance between them

Fig. 369 Diagonal hook-up across front section.

Fig. 370 Homemade hook, used for anchor hookup in Fig. 369. This consists of a piece of flat steel with a hole in one end for the clevis and a piece of round stock welded to the other. The round stock—pipe could be used—is cut on a bevel so that it slants toward the hole. The tab welded on top prevents the hook from dropping out when the chain is slack.

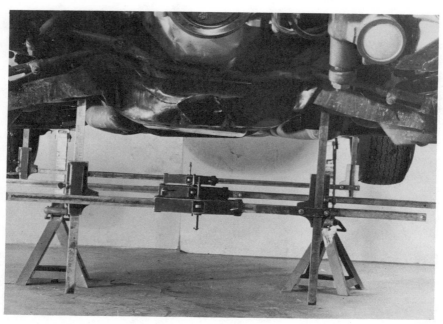

Fig. 371 Final centerline check. The front gauge is hanging on the control arm front pivot bolts. This is one of several centerline checks made during the repair operations.

agreed with shop manual specifications and they were in alignment with the centerline.

Final checking with the centerline gauges was done with the front gauge in three positions, only one of which is shown in Fig. 370. In this view, the front gauge is shown hanging from the front control arm pivot bolts. It was used also on the rear pivot bolts; this is an "A" frame type control arm having separate front and rear pivot bolts. When both the front and rear pivot bolts are level and centered with the rest of the frame, the most critical points in the front suspension have been restored to dependable condition.

The third position of the front centerline gauge, on the front end of the frame horns, has been discussed previously. It should be pointed out that in all three of these checks it has been assumed that the height of the left side of the front cross member was correct. There was no evidence that this side had been subjected to any force which would tend to either raise or lower it to an appreciable extent. The twisting action of the cross member, as the damaging impact was absorbed, probably tended to turn down the front end of the left side rail and horn. However, the reverse twist applied in the repair operation, Fig. 364, would restore the left side to position, within reasonable tolerances. If there had been evidence that the height of the left side had been either raised or lowered, a datum line check would have been made. The procedure for making a datum line check is explained in Chapter 7 and restated briefly here.

Each of the three gauges should be adjusted to hang in its position so that the horizontal bars hang below the frame in the same relationship to the datum line. Thus, if the datum line was specified as the bottom of metal in the center section, the two gauges in the center section might be adjusted to hang four inches below the bottom of the rail. Four inches would be added also to the adjustment of the front gauge when setting it to specifications. When the three gauges were hung in the frame, the horizontal bars should hang at the same level. This can be sighted or, if exact checking is thought necessary, a light string can be stretched across them. A reasonable tolerance would be to have one of the three gauges ⅛ inch away from the string when it contacted the other two.

The finished frame, ready for the front end to be rebuilt, is shown in Fig. 373. The right lower control arm will be replaced. The right upper and both of the left control arms should be usable. No pictures were available of the finished automobile after the front end sheet metal was reassembled. However, this frame is in condition for the front end to be rebuilt.

Fig. 372 Final straightening operation on the frame horns. Heat was used at the base of the left horn to make it move more than the right horn.

Fig. 373 Final view of straightened frame. It is ready to rebuild the right front suspension and the front end sheet metal.

9

Basic Skill Development for The Beginner

The exercises suggested in this chapter are intended to serve as a guide for the beginner in learning to use his tools well enough to attempt simple repair work. After that point is reached, they will have no further purpose, because skill must be developed on the job. The only reason for using an exercise instead of an actual repair job is to prevent serious damage to valuable automobiles by inexperienced beginners.

These exercises are limited to the use of the hammer and dolly block, the body file, the disc sander, and solder filler. Welding has been omitted because normally it is taught in a class by itself. However, the student should be studying welding at the same time he is studying sheet metal repair.

The student should spend enough time on each exercise to develop enough skill to control his tools. Beginners naturally seem to want to try something new before the project at hand is mastered. Whether the work is being done under the supervision of a competent instructor or as a do-it-yourself project, best results will be obtained by practicing until one operation becomes automatic before proceeding to the next.

These practice operations can be performed on scrap panels obtained from a local body shop or automobile salvage yard. Considerable space can be saved if the practice fixture, shown in use in Fig. 372, is used for as many operations as possible. These include the hammer and dolly block, some of the uses of the file, solder filling, and some of the metal shrinking procedures. It should not be used for practice with the disc sander.

Exact specifications for building this practice fixture are not given, because each instructor will have his own ideas. However, it is suggested that it be made to hold a piece of sheet metal approximately 16 inches long by 10 inches wide. The fixture shown consists of an angle iron base which can be clamped or bolted to a bench top, two upright bars 5 inches long, and a pair of clamps. The complete unit was assembled by arc welding. Note that the clamps are welded to the upright bars at a slight

385

Fig. 374 Student using fixture for practice with the hammer and dolly block.

angle so that the sheet will be bowed upward in the middle about ¾ inch. All of the stock is ¼ inch thick. If curved stock is not available to make the clamp bars, a spacer can be welded to the lower clamp bar to provide proper clamping action.

TOOLS AND EQUIPMENT

The items listed here as tools are those which normally would be a part of the metal man's personal hand tools. The items listed as equipment are those which would be a part of shop equipment or are necessary to operate a training program.

Tools required for the beginner are:
1. Bumping hammer, similar to the one shown in Fig. 39, Chapter 3.
2. Pick hammer, similar to the one shown in Fig. 40, Chapter 3.
3. General-purpose dolly block, similar to the one shown in Fig. 41, Chapter 3.
4. Body file, either wood or steel.
5. Plastic face shield.
6. Solder paddle.

This is far from being a complete tool kit, but the list does include the items essential for the beginner. As more experience is gained and additional tools are needed, the student will be in a better position to determine for himself what they should be.

The selection of equipment must be governed by the size of the class group and the time to be devoted to the subject. If the program is to be limited, probably only the equipment listed above will be needed. If the program is to be more extensive, however, there will be a need for all of the equipment commonly used in a body shop. No detailed list of such equipment is given here, because there is too wide a variation in what different persons in the business feel to be essential. With the rapid growth in the number of automobiles of unit body and frame construction, it is quite probable that one of the first items to be added to this list is one of the portable frame machines which are almost a necessity for straightening any damage which extends into the structural members of the body.

SUPPLIES

Supplies may be considered as anything used up in the course of the work. Essential supplies are listed below.

1. Sheet metal panels, 10 x 16 x .037 inches.
2. Scrap panels with areas of undamaged surface.
3. Fourteen-inch body files.
4. Sanding discs, 24-, 36-, and 50-grit.
5. Body solder.
6. Solder flux, or tinning compound.
7. Flux brushes, or steel wool if tinning compound is used.
8. Solder paddle lubricant.
9. Oxygen.
10. Acetylene.
11. Welding rod.
12. Brazing rod.
13. Eighty-grit production sandpaper or abrasive cloth.
14. Shop towels or rags.
15. Hydraulic jack fluid.

PRACTICE EXERCISES

The following exercises are suggested for practice:

1. Hammer-on-dolly.
2. Hammer-off-dolly.
3. Use of body file and pick hammer.
4. Use of disc sander.
5. Metal shrinking.
6. Solder filling.
7. Straightening simple dents in scrap panels.

It is desirable that the first two and the last of these be practiced in the sequence they are listed. The others may be changed in sequence to suit the need.

The directions for each of these exercises are limited to the steps to be taken and the skill levels to be achieved. Detailed instructions on procedure and the illustrations are not repeated here because they were given in the preceding chapters. The student should refer to this material as necessary.

In practicing these exercises and in later work, the student should learn to think for himself. Study and practice will enable him to acquire information and develop manual skill, but he also must develop the ability to apply them in an intelligent manner.

HAMMER-ON-DOLLY

This exercise involves the following steps or skill levels:

1. Developing the muscular co-ordination required to place the dolly block under a spot of metal and strike it with the hammer.

2. Developing an accurate hammer blow so that the surface of the metal is not chopped up by marks made by the edge of the hammer face.

3. Developing a "feeling" for the effect of the hammer and dolly on the metal being worked.

This operation should be started by instructing the student to use his hammer and dolly block frequently enough to get accustomed to them. The work should be done on a sheet of metal mounted in the practice fixture. Hammer blows should be placed in lines running back and forth over an assigned area. Every effort should be made to keep the metal surface smooth.

Best results will be obtained by starting with light hammer blows, then gradually increasing both the speed and the force. When this has been practiced enough to move on to the next operation, the student should be able to cover an assigned area with hammer-on-dolly marks that are either light or heavy. With light hammer blows, there should be little or no rise in the area worked. With heavy hammer blows, there should be a smooth raised crown on the area worked. In neither case should there be edge marks left by the hammer.

HAMMER-OFF-DOLLY

This operation involves these steps or skill levels:

1. Developing the muscular co-ordination necessary to place the dolly where required, away from the hammer blow.

2. Learning to judge visually where to place the hammer blow and the dolly block.

3. Developing the reflex action necessary to increase the dolly rebound.

This operation should be started by making a small dent in a panel mounted in the practice fixture. The dolly should be held firmly under the lowest part of the dent and the hammer used around it to raise the surface.

The key to success in this operation is in the pressure on the dolly block and the accuracy of the hammer blows. When the procedure is mastered, the student will have learned to press hard enough on the dolly to raise the depressed area and to drive the raised area back. If the panel is mounted in the fixture properly, so that it has a slight crown, the beginner will find that more hammer blows are needed above and below the dent than on each side of it. Above and below in this case means in the direction of the highest crown.

This should be practiced until such dents can be smoothed out with a few hammer blows. Smoothness should be judged by feeling the surface with the finger tips. The hand should be laid flat on the panel and drawn backward. The feel will be much more sensitive if a cotton glove is worn, because it eliminates the friction of the skin on the metal.

USE OF BODY FILE AND PICK HAMMER

These operations involve the following steps or skill levels:

1. Learning to stroke the file properly.
2. Learning to select the desired spot.
3. Learning to judge, visually and by feeling, where to pick up low spots.
4. Learning to judge when a surface has been filed enough.

In practicing, the beginner should learn to stroke the file on smooth metal. A panel in the practice fixture may be used, but the work should be shifted to scrap panels as soon as possible.

After the proper stroke is acquired, the use of the pick hammer should be practiced by filing and picking a surface which has slight low spots in it. As soon as enough skill has been developed to risk work on an automobile, the student should get some practice on actual repair work. If advanced students are working in the area, it is desirable to assign him as helper on metal finishing operations.

The student who has mastered this skill will be able to file a surface so that it looks smooth instead of scratchy, and he should be able to "hit where he is looking."

USE OF DISC SANDER

This operation involves these steps or skill levels:

1. Learning to manipulate the sander in the black-and-forth stroke used as a metal finishing operation.
2. Learning to manipulate the sander in an up-and-down stroke used as a buffing operation.
3. Learning safety as it applies to the use of the disc sander.

The student should begin his practice with the disc sander by using it on an undamaged section of a scrap panel. He should spend enough time on each operation to become accustomed to the feel of the machine as he manipulates it in either the metal finishing or the buffing stroke.

Before the student is assigned to use a sander on an automobile, he should be able to control the pattern of the disc swirl marks on the metal by the proper tilt of the spindle and the angle of the pad. He should practice until these manipulations become automatic.

The beginner never should be allowed to use the sander without adequate eye protection, and every effort should be made to impress upon him its importance whether he is under the supervision of an instructor or working alone.

He should not use star discs until he has learned to control the machine. Because of the extra hazards involved in using the star disc along an edge where the points can catch and tear, any student using one should be at some distance from other persons.

METAL SHRINKING

This operation involves the following steps or skill levels:

1. Learning to recognize the conditions where shrinking is required.

2. Learning to estimate the size and temperature of the spot to be heated by observing the conditions of the area to be shrunk.

3. Developing the skill with the hammer and dolly block to work hot metal.

4. Learning to recognize, by quick visual inspection, whether a spot should be quenched or not, and if so, how much.

Before starting to shrink metal, the student should have developed enough skill with his hammer to place a hammer blow on the metal without marking the surface. He should begin on small raised areas which have been made by hammering on-dolly on a small spot until it rises in a sharp bump. These spots should be shrunk and metal finished smooth.

Practice shrinking should be done on relatively flat areas which can be reached with the dolly block easily. It is quite probable that in his early practice with the hammer and dolly block, the student will have made several rough areas which should be shrunk if the surface is to be smoothed properly. Some of his practice shrinking can be done on these. As soon as he can produce reasonable results, he should be allowed to shrink minor stretched conditions on scrap panels.

Provision must be made for safe handling of the torch when it is laid aside to use the hammer after heating. A hook on which it can be hung securely will be satisfactory; otherwise a helper should be assigned with instructions to shut off the torch immediately after it is handed to him.

SOLDER FILLING

This exercise involves these steps and skill levels:

1. Learning to recognize the conditions on which solder filling will make an acceptable repair.

2. Learning to tin without overheating or wiping the surface too much.

3. Developing the co-ordination necessary to maintain temperature while solder is being applied to the surface and smoothed with the paddle.

4. Learning to metal finish the solder fill.

A horizontal surface should be used for the first practice with solder filling, but as soon as some skill has been developed, the operation should be done on vertical surfaces. The horizontal work can be done on the practice fixture, but scrap panels are more desirable for work on vertical surfaces.

Every solder fill should be metal finished if it is possible to do so. However, in cases where the solder has been worked so long that it has become grainy, it is best to melt it off and start over.

STRAIGHTENING SIMPLE DENTS IN SCRAP PANELS

If the student has completed the preceding exercises in a satisfactory manner, he should have progressed far enough to work without close supervision. Before starting to straighten any dent, he should be required to examine it closely and plan the repair procedure. This should be discussed with the instructor before the job is started.

Instruction after the job has been started must be varied to suit the situation. Advice and assistance should be offered where necessary, but it should not be overdone. From this point on, no detailed procedures can be supplied; each instructor must work them out with each student to the best of his abilities.

Index

About the Author

Robert L. Sargent has been connected with General Motors Institute for many years. As a Specialist in automobile sheet metal repair for the Institute's Mechanical Engineering Laboratories, he has had many an opportunity to use his knowledge of the subject and his practical skill in making repairs in lectures and demonstrations for groups of students, repair men and insurance adjusters in the United States and Canada. For thirteen years, he participated in the Institute's Teacher Training Program for vocational high school personnel, his specialty being auto body construction and the repair of sheet metal. He has also handled special assignments at GM Training Centers.